Lecture Notes in Computer Science 12584

More information about this subseries at http://www.springer.com/series/7408

Georg Grossmann · Sudha Ram (Eds.)

Advances in Conceptual Modeling

ER 2020 Workshops CMAI, CMLS,
CMOMM4FAIR, CoMoNoS, EmpER
Vienna, Austria, November 3–6, 2020
Proceedings

 Springer

Editors
Georg Grossmann (iD)
University of South Australia
Adelaide, SA, Australia

Sudha Ram (iD)
University of Arizona
Tucson, AZ, USA

ISSN 0302-9743   ISSN 1611-3349   (electronic)
Lecture Notes in Computer Science
ISBN 978-3-030-65846-5   ISBN 978-3-030-65847-2   (eBook)
https://doi.org/10.1007/978-3-030-65847-2

LNCS Sublibrary: SL2 – Programming and Software Engineering

This Springer imprint is published by the registered company Springer Nature Switzerland AG
The registered company address is: Gewerbestrasse 11, 6330 Cham, Switzerland

Preface

Nobody would have expected at the beginning of 2020 what kind of impact COVID-19 would have on academic events like conferences and workshops. Especially on international events like the Conference on Conceptual Modeling (ER) which every year attracts researchers from all over the world to come together and discuss emerging and exciting topics in modeling concepts. Like many other international conferences, the ER conference became an online event so that it could still take place in a safe environment. A number of satellite events were also held online for the first time in its 39-year history. The local organizers at the Vienna University of Technology (TU Wien), Austria, and the Business Informatics Group chaired by Prof. Gerti Kappel quickly responded to the challenges of showcasing an online conference. While the attendees did not have a chance to experience the Vienna flair in person, the organizers prepared an excellent online event that allowed everyone to experience the state of the art in conceptual modelling and exchange ideas for future development of ER-related topics.

This volume contains the proceedings of a number of satellite events held in conjunction with the 39th International Conference on Conceptual Modeling (ER 2020). Given the long tradition and broad scope of ER as a key conference in the area of conceptual modeling, the workshops organized therein play an important role, such as being a forum for: very interactive debates about emerging ideas; broadening the scope of what conceptual modeling is about; bridging conceptual modeling and other complementary communities; and reflecting on the scope and nature of the area itself. In that respect, this volume contains papers that were accepted for publication and presentation in the following five workshops: First Workshop on Conceptual Modeling Meets Artificial Intelligence and Data-Driven Decision Making (CMAI 2020), First Workshop on Conceptual Modeling for Life Sciences (CMLS 2020), Second Workshop on Conceptual Modeling, Ontologies and (Meta)data Management for Findable, Accessible, Interoperable and Reusable (FAIR) Data (CMOMM4FAIR 2020), First Workshop on Conceptual Modeling for NoSQL Data Stores (CoMoNoS 2020), and Third Workshop on Empirical Methods in Conceptual Modeling (EmpER 2020).

A sixth satellite event was the Workshop on Conceptual Modeling for Digital Twins (CoMoDiTy 2020). This workshop invited a number of interesting speakers to discuss various topics around the digitalization of industry and was organized by Markus Stumptner (University of South Australia, Australia), Manuel Wimmer (Johannes Kepler University Linz, Austria), and Andreas Wortmann (RWTH Aachen University, Germany).

The CMAI 2020 workshop combined the interesting topics AI and data-driven decision making in the context of conceptual modeling. This workshop was founded by

Dominik Bork (TU Wien, Austria), Peter Fettke (German Research Center for Artificial Intelligence, Germany), Wolfgang Maass (German Research Center for Artificial Intelligence, Germany), Ulrich Reimer (University of Applied Sciences St. Gallen, Switzerland), Christoph G. Schütz (Johannes Kepler University Linz, Austria), Marina Tropmann-Frick (University of Applied Sciences Hamburg, Germany), and Eric S. K. Yu (University of Toronto, Canada). Four papers were accepted for presentation in the workshop.

CMLS 2020 was organized by Anna Bernasconi (Politecnico di Milano, Italy), Arif Canakoglu (Politecnico di Milano, Italy), Ana León Palacio (Universitat Politècnica de València, Spain), and José Fabián Reyes Román (Universitat Politècnica de València, Spain). The proceedings of CMLS included six interesting papers and organizers also secured a special issue to publish extended versions of the best papers.

The FAIR data movement has been gaining a lot of attention in the past years, with awareness and endorsement ranging from research institutions and funding agencies to international organizations such as the G7 and G20. The second edition of CMOMM4FAIR was organized by Luiz Olavo Bonino (GO FAIR, University of Twente, The Netherlands), Barbara Magagna (Environment Agency Austria and University of Twente, The Netherlands), João Moreira (University of Twente, The Netherlands), Maria Luiza Machado Campos (Federal University of Rio de Janeiro and GO FAIR, Brazil), Peter Mutschke (GESIS - Leibniz Institute for the Social Sciences, Germany), and Robert Pergl (Technical University of Prague, Czech Republic). In this edition, three full papers were accepted for publication and presentation.

CoMoNoS 2020 explored opportunities for conceptual modeling to address real-world problems that arise with NoSQL data stores. The workshop was organized by Meike Klettke (University of Rostock, Germany), Stefanie Scherzinger (University of Passau, Germany), and Uta Störl (Darmstadt University of Applied Sciences, Germany) and accepted three papers for publication and presentation. Further, the workshop included an invited industry talk by Pascal Desmarets, founder and CEO of Hackolade, on "NoSQL Data Modelling in Practice."

EmpER 2020 was organized by Dominik Bork (TU Wien, Austria) and Miguel Goulao (Universidade Nova de Lisboa, Portugal). It included five papers with topics ranging from schema evolution in embedded databases to measuring the comprehensibility of modeling constructs.

We would like to thank all the workshop chairs for the organization of the aforementioned high-quality and inspiring events. These events significantly increased the value of ER 2020. We are also indebted to the authors and numerous reviewers for their time and expertise ensuring the quality of the workshops. Additionally, we express our gratitude to the general chairs of the conference Gerti Kappel and Heinrich C. Mayr as well as Manuel Wimmer and Dominik Bork for their continuous support.

October 2020   Georg Grossmann
                                                                 Sudha Ram

ER 2020 Conference Organization

General Chairs

Gerti Kappel   TU Wien, Austria
Heinrich C. Mayr   Alpen-Adria University Klagenfurt, Austria

Program Committee Chairs

Gillian Dobbie   The University of Auckland, New Zealand
Ulrich Frank   University of Duisburg-Essen, Germany
Stephen W. Liddle   Brigham Young University, USA

Workshop Chairs

Georg Grossmann   University of South Australia, Australia
Sudha Ram   University of Arizona, USA

Tutorial Chairs

João Paulo A. Almeida   Federal University of Espírito Santo, Brazil
Michael Schrefl   Johannes Kepler University Linz, Austria

Panel Chairs

Micahel Grossniklaus   University of Konstanz, Germany
Maurizio Lenzerini   Università di Roma La Sapienza, Italy

Forum/Demo/Poster Chairs

Judith Michael   RWTH Aachen University, Germany
Victoria Torres Bosch   Polytechnic University of Valencia, Spain

Sponsoring and Industry Chairs

Reinhold Plösch   Johannes Kepler University Linz, Austria
Manuel Wimmer   Johannes Kepler University Linz, Austria

Publicity and Social Media Chair

Dominik Bork   TU Wien, Austria

Web Chairs

Bernhard Wally   Austrian Council for Research and Technology
                                   Development, Austria
Micahel Vierhauser   Johannes Kepler University Linz, Austria

ERSC Liaison

Matthias Jarke   RWTH Aachen University, Germany

Organization Chair

Claudia Habersack   TU Wien, Austria

Steering Committee

Silvana Castano   KU Leuven, Belgium
Peter P. Chen   McMaster University, Canada
Isabelle Comyn-Wattiau   Harvard University, USA
Valeria De Antonellis   Ritsumeikan University, Japan
Karen Davis   University of Porto, Portugal
Lois Delcambre   University of the Aegean, Greece
Giancarlo Guizzardi   Free University of Bozen-Bolzano, Italy
Matthias Jarke   RWTH Aachen University, Germany
Paul Johannesson   Stockholm University, Sweden
Alberto Laender   Federal University of Minas Gerais, Brazil
Stephen Liddle   Brigham Young University, USA
Tok Wang Ling   National University of Singapore, Singapore
Hui Ma   Victoria University of Wellington, New Zealand
Heinrich Mayr   Alpen-Adria University Klagenfurt, Austria
Antoni Olivé   Universitat Politécnica de Catalunya, Spain
José Palazzo Moreira de   Federal University of Rio Grande do Sul, Brazil
   Oliveira
Jeffrey Parsons   Memorial University of Newfoundland, Canada
Oscar Pastor   Universidad Politécnica de Valencia, Spain
Sudha Ram   University of Arizona, USA
Motoshi Saeki   Tokyo Institute of Technology, Japan
Peretz Shoval   Ben-Gurion University, Israel
Il-Yeol Song   Drexel University, USA
Veda Storey   Georgia State University, USA
Juan Carlos Trujillo   University of Alicante, Spain
Yair Wand   University of British Columbia, Canada
Carson Woo   University of British Columbia, Canada
Eric Yu   University of Toronto, Canada

ER 2020 Workshop Organization

Conceptual Modeling Meets Artificial Intelligence and Data-Driven Decision Making (CMAI) 2020 Co-chairs

Dominik Bork	TU Wien, Austria
Peter Fettke	German Research Center for Artificial Intelligence (DFKI), Germany
Wolfgang Maass	German Research Center for Artificial Intelligence (DFKI), Germany
Ulrich Reimer	University of Applied Sciences St. Gallen, Switzerland
Christoph G. Schuetz	Johannes Kepler University Linz, Austria
Marina Tropmann-Frick	University of Applied Sciences Hamburg, Germany
Eric S. K. Yu	University of Toronto, Canada

Conceptual Modeling for Life Sciences (CMLS) 2020 Co-chairs

Anna Bernasconi	Politecnico di Milano, Italy
Arif Canakoglu	Politecnico di Milano, Italy
Ana León Palacio	Universitat Politécnica de Valéencia, Spain
José Fabiáan Reyes Rom	Universitat Politécnica de Valéncia, Spain

Conceptual Modeling, Ontologies and (Meta)Data Management for Findable, Accessible, Interoperable and Reusable (FAIR) Data (CMOMM4FAIR) 2020 Co-chairs

João Moreira	University of Twente, The Netherlands
Luiz Olavo Bonino da Silva Santos	University of Twente, The Netherlands
Maria Luiza Machado Campos	Federal University of Rio de Janeiro, Brazil
Barbara Magagna	Environment Agency, Austria
Peter Mutschke	Leibniz Institute for the Social Sciences, Germany
Robert Pergl	Czech Technical University in Prague, Czech Republic

Conceptual Modeling for Digital Twins (CoMoDiTy) 2020 Co-chairs

Markus Stumptner	University of South Australia, Australia
Manuel Wimmer	Johannes-Kepler University Linz, Austria
Andreas Wortmann	RWTH Aachen University, Germany

Conceptual Modeling for NoSQL Data Stores (CoMoNoS) 2020 Co-chairs

Meike Klettke   University of Rostock, Germany
Stefanie Scherzinger   University of Passau, Germany
Uta Störl   Darmstadt University of Applied Sciences, Germany

Empirical Methods in Conceptual Modeling (EmpER) 2020 Co-chairs

Dominik Bork   TU Wien, Austria
Miguel Goulao   Universidade NOVA de Lisboa, Portugal

ER 2020 Workshop Program Committees

CMAI 2020 Program Committee

Klaus-Dieter Althoff	University of Hildesheim, Germany
Kerstin Bach	Norwegian University of Science and Technology, Norway
Ralph Bergmann	University of Trier, Germany
Loris Bozzato	Fondazione Bruno Kessler, Italy
I. Comyn-Wattiau	ESSEC and CNAM, France
Ernesto Damiani	University of Milan, Italy
Tatiana Endrjukaite	NTT, Latvia
Michael Fellmann	University of Rostock, Germany
Hans-Georg Fill	University of Fribourg, Switzerland
Aditya Ghosh	University of Wollongong, Australia
Knut Hinkelmann	FHNW University of Applied Sciences and Arts Northwestern Switzerland, Switzerland
Kamalakar Karlapalem	IIIT Hyderabad, India
Josef Küng	Johannes Kepler University Linz, Austria
Julio Cesar Leite	PUC-Rio, Brazil
Bernd Neumayr	Johannes Kepler University Linz, Austria
Jeffrey Parsons	University of Newfoundland, Canada
Barbara Re	University of Camerino, Italy
Oscar Romero	Universitat Politècnica de Catalunya, Spain
Matt Selway	University of South Australia, Australia
Bernhard Thalheim	University of Kiel, Germany
Stefan Thalmann	University of Graz, Austria
Rosina Weber	Drexel University, USA
Tatjana Welzer	University of Maribor, Slovenia
Mathias Weske	University of Potsdam, Germany
N. Wickramasinghe	Swinburne University, Australia
Takahira Yamaguchi	Keio University, Japan

CMLS 2020 Program Committee

Raffaele Calogero	Università di Torino, Italy
Mario Cannataro	Università Magna Graecia di Catanzaro, Italy
Davide Chicco	Krembil Research Institute, Canada
Johann Eder	Alpen-Adria University Klagenfurt, Austria
Jose Luis Garrido	University of Granada, Spain
Giancarlo Guizzardi	Free University of Bozen-Bolzano, Italy

Sergio Lifschitz   Pontifícia Universidade Católica do Rio de Janeiro, Brazil
Paolo Missier   Newcastle University, UK
José Palazzo   Universidad Federal do Río Grande do Sul, Brazil
Ignacio Panach   University of Valencia, Spain
Pietro Pinoli   Politecnico di Milano, Italy
Rosario Michael Piro   Politecnico di Milano, Italy
Maria Rodriguez   IBM Zürich Research Laboratory, Switzerland
  Martinez

CMOMM4FAIR 2020 Program Committee

Luiz Olavo Bonino   University of Twente, The Netherlands
Barbara Magagna   University of Twente, The Netherlands
João Moreira   University of Twente, The Netherlands
Maria Luiza Machado Campos Federal University of Rio de Janeiro, Brazil
Peter Mutschke   Leibniz Institute for the Social Sciences, Germany
Robert Pergl   Technical University of Prague, Czech Republic
Yann Le Franc   eScience Factory, France
Tobias Kuhn   VU Amsterdam, The Netherlands
Giancarlo Guizzardi   Free University of Bozen-Bolzano, Italy
João Paulo Almeida   Federal University of Espirito Santo, Brazil
Tiago Prince Sales   Free University of Bozen-Bolzano, Italy

CoMoDiTy 2020 Program Committee

Loli Burgueño   Open University of Catalonia, Spain
Jordi Cabot   Internet Interdisciplinary Institute, Spain
Benoit Combemale   University of Toulouse and Inria, France
Manuela Dalibor   RWTH Aachen University, Germany
Romina Eramo   University of L'Aquila, Italy
A. Mazak-Huemer   Johannes Kepler University Linz, Austria
Bran Selic   Malina Software Corp., Canada
Michael Weyrich   University of Stuttgart, Germany
Mark van den Brand   Eindhoven University of Technology, The Netherlands

CoMoNoS 2020 Program Committee

Md.-A. Baazizi   Sorbonne University Paris, France
Angela Bonifati   University of Lyon, France
Dario Colazzo   Paris Dauphine University, France
I. Comyn-Wattiau   ESSEC Business School, France
E. C. de Almeida   UFPR, Brazil
Jesús García Molina   University of Murcia, Spain
Sven Hartmann   University of Clausthal, Germany
Irena Holubova   Charles University, Czech Republic
Jiaheng Lu   University of Helsinki, Finland

Michael Mior	Rochester Institute of Technology, USA
Norbert Ritter	University of Hamburg, Germany
Diego Sevilla Ruiz	University of Murcia, Spain
Carlo Sartiani	University of Pisa, Italy
Johannes Schildgen	OTH Regensburg, Germany
Heiko Schuldt	University of Basel, Switzerland
Lena Wiese	Fraunhofer Institute ITEM Hannover, Germany
Wolfram Wingerath	Baqend, Germany

EmpER 2020 Program Committee

João Araújo	Universidade NOVA de Lisboa, Portugal
Robert Buchmann	Babeş-Bolyai University, Romania
Javier Cánovas	Universitat Oberta de Catalunya, Spain
Michel Chaudron	University of Gothenburg, Sweden
N. Condori-Fernandez	VU Amsterdam, The Netherlands
Marian Daun	Universität Duisburg-Essen, Germany
Sepideh Ghanavati	University of Maine, USA
Catarina Gralha	Universidade NOVA de Lisboa, Portugal
Jens Gulden	Utrecht University, The Netherlands
Irit Hadar	University of Haifa, Israel
Jennifer Horkoff	University of Gothenburg, Sweden
Katsiaryna Labunets	TU Delft, The Netherlands
Sotirios Liaskos	York University, Canada
Judith Michael	RWTH Aachen University, Germany
Geert Poels	Ghent University, Belgium
Iris Reinhartz-Berger	University of Haifa, Israel
Ben Roelens	Open University of the Netherlands, The Netherlands
Zahra Shakeri	University of Calgary, Canada
Manuel Wimmer	Johannes Kepler University Linz, Austria

Contents

Conceptual Modeling Meets Artificial Intelligence and Data-Driven Decision Making (CMAI) 2020

Preface

Dominik Bork[1] ⓘ, Peter Fettke[2,3] ⓘ, Wolfgang Maass[2],
Ulrich Reimer[4], Christoph G. Schuetz[5] ⓘ, Marina Tropmann-Frick[6],
and Eric S. K. Yu[7]

[1] Business Informatics Group, TU Wien, Vienna, Austria
dominik.bork@tuwien.ac.at
[2] German Research Center for Artificial Intelligence (DFKI),
Saarbrücken, Germany
peter.fettke@dfki.de,
wolfgang.maass@iss.uni-saarland.de
[3] Saarland University, Saarbrücken, Germany
[4] University of Applied Sciences St. Gallen, St. Gallen, Switzerland
ulrich.reimer@acm.org
[5] Johannes Kepler University Linz, Linz, Austria
schuetz@dke.uni-linz.ac.at
[6] University of Applied Sciences Hamburg, Hamburg, Germany
marina.tropmann-frick@haw-hamburg.de
[7] University of Toronto, Toronto, Canada
eric.yu@utoronto.ca

Artificial Intelligence (AI) is front and center in the data-driven revolution that has been taking place in the last couple of years with the increasing availability of large amounts of data (big data) in virtually every domain. The now dominant paradigm of data-driven AI, powered by sophisticated machine learning algorithms, employs big data to build intelligent applications and support fact-based decision making. The focus of data-driven AI is on learning (domain) models and keeping those models up-to-date by using statistical methods and machine learning over big data, in contrast to the manual modeling approach prevalent in traditional, knowledge-based AI.

While data-driven AI has led to significant breakthroughs, it also comes with a number of disadvantages. First, models generated by machine learning algorithms often cannot be inspected and comprehended by a human being, thus lacking explainability. Furthermore, integration of preexisting domain knowledge into learned models – prior to or after learning – is difficult. Finally, appropriate application of data-driven AI depends on the domain, problem, and organizational context. Conceptual modeling can be the key to applying data-driven AI in a meaningful and time-efficient way. Conceptual modeling can also improve maintainability, usability, and explainability of AI systems.

The Workshop on Conceptual Modeling Meets AI and Data Driven Decision Making (CMAI) provides a forum for researchers and practitioners working at the intersection of AI and data-driven decision making on the one hand and conceptual modeling on the other hand. For this first edition of the workshop we accepted four high-quality papers. The first paper describes an approach to increase trust in medical AI systems. The second paper investigates methods for explaining the results of machine learning. The third paper aims to provide support for automated diagnosis and repair of conceptual models. Finally, the fourth paper describes how machine-learning outputs can be augmented with conceptual models in striving for explainable AI.

We thank all authors who submitted papers for consideration and members of the Program Committee, whose effort and dedication in the review process made this workshop possible. We also thank the ER workshop chairs and the other members of the Organizing Committee for their trust and support.

How to Induce Trust in Medical AI Systems

Ulrich Reimer[✉][ID], Beat Tödtli[ID], and Edith Maier[ID]

Institute for Information and Process Management,
Eastern Switzerland University of Applied Sciences, St. Gallen, Switzerland
{ulrich.reimer,beat.toedtli,edith.maier}@ost.ch

Abstract. Trust is an important prerequisite for the acceptance of an Artificial Intelligence (AI) system, in particular in the medical domain. Explainability is currently discussed as the key approach to induce trust. Since a medical AI system is considered a medical device, it also has to be formally certified by an officially recognised agency. The paper argues that neither explainability nor certification suffice to tackle the trust problem. Instead, we propose an alternative approach aimed at showing the physician how well a patient is represented in the original training data set. We operationalize this approach by developing formal indicators and illustrate their usefulness with a real-world medical data set.

Keywords: Trust · Machine learning · AI · Medical device · Explainability · Certification · Sampling bias

1 Medical AI Systems

Artificial Intelligence (AI) systems are beginning to have an impact in the medical domain [8,15]. Current systems tend to focus on quite specific aspects, for example on image interpretation [7,13], or the analysis of huge numbers of textual sources as is the case with IBM Watson Health. Its cancer algorithm, for instance, is used in hospitals to find the most appropriate treatment for a patient [18]. Other approaches based on text analysis help diagnose rare diseases by suggesting differential diagnoses [2,12]. AI systems with a broader focus will eventually find their way into practical use, raising the question what will make physicians and patients trust such a system. Since trust between patient and physician does not usually depend on the tools the physician is using, we are primarily concerned with how a physician comes to trust an AI. An analysis of trust-influencing features of automated systems in general is given by Chien et al. [1]. Among the categories suggested by the authors are understandability, reliability, perceived usefulness and certification. According to [5], even if these features are present human intelligence will still be required for effective medical decision-making.

Understandability of AI systems in general is currently widely discussed under the heading of *explainability* [3,4,9,11]. It might seem reasonable to consider explainability as an essential feature of a medical AI system. Otherwise,

© Springer Nature Switzerland AG 2020
G. Grossmann and S. Ram (Eds.): ER 2020 Workshops, LNCS 12584, pp. 5–14, 2020.
https://doi.org/10.1007/978-3-030-65847-2_1

a physician either just has to trust the conclusions of the system or has to go through a subsequent verification process, which may well be costly and time-consuming and thus nullify any potential efficiency benefits of the AI system. At the same time, he or she may not be willing to go through a lengthy explanation to understand the decision offered by the system. Neither approach is desirable or practicable (see the detailed discussion in [10]).

Since medical AI systems are considered medical devices they need to be *certified* by an officially recognised agency or regulatory body such as the Food and Drug Administration (FDA). By assuming responsibility for the adequacy of the medical AI system, regulatory bodies provide an established source of trust, freeing the physicians to establish trust themselves. Depending on its complexity, the certification of an AI system can require a huge effort. Furthermore, certification amounts to *model testing*, meaning that the absence of errors (wrong diagnoses, wrong therapies) cannot be shown. Even worse, when the certification process uses a sample with a similar bias as the sample used for developing the AI system, existing fundamental flaws might not be uncovered during certification.

Sampling bias refers to the bias incurred due to the data set chosen to train an AI system. The resulting system extrapolates from the training data to the general case. If the training set is skewed the system does not generalize well. For example, if a medical AI system is trained on data from Asian people it might not work well for Africans or Europeans. While the bias concerning gender and ethnic group can be controlled relatively easily [17] other, less obvious biases may exist that neither the developer nor the certification agency are aware of. The problem is that we usually do not know the effect of a feature on the generated model and how its values should be distributed to provide a representative sample.

We can conclude that even after a medical AI has successfully passed certification there might still be cases when it gives inadequate advice. As a consequence the physician and possibly the patient as well might hesitate to fully trust the system. Since we have also ruled out an explanation component to be of practical benefit in the medical domain, the question remains what can be done to enhance trust.

In the following section we will propose an approach to help a physician better estimate the reliability of an AI system's advice and provide indicators for its trustworthiness on a case-by-case basis.

2 Formal Measures for Estimating How Well a Patient Is Covered by an AI System

When using medical AI systems a patient may rightfully ask how well she or he is represented in the training data. In the following we introduce an approach to inspire *trust* in the decision of an AI system, which we consider more useful than the focus on explainability. The basic idea can be described as follows: When a medical AI system comes up with a diagnosis or treatment suggestion for a specific patient, a critical question is how well that patient is covered by the input data from which the AI system was generated – is the patient typical for

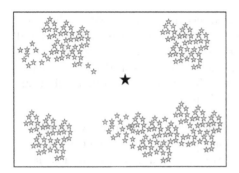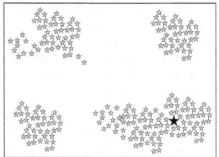

Fig. 1. Two example cases (left and right) of how a patient (black star) is embedded in the original input data.

that data set, i.e. similar to most patients, or is the patient an outlier? In the former case the physician can assume that the system's suggestion is appropriate while in the latter case the physician would be reluctant to accept it.

While there exist approaches that audit the reliability of a classifier after training, e.g. by detecting inaccurate predictions [14], our approach aims at giving a physician a tool to estimate reliability for a specific patient. In the following, we formalize our ideas.

Let p_0 be a patient who was classified by the AI system as belonging to one of two classes – usually being ill or healthy with respect to a particular disease but, of course, any other labels such as "receive a specific therapy" vs. "therapy not appropriate" are possible. To estimate how well p_0 is covered by the original input data used for training the AI system, we introduce a distance metric on the space of patients, $distance(p_0, p)$, indicating the distance between two patients p_0 and p. Given such a metric we can state several criteria for estimating a patient's coverage by the input data:

a) Is p_0 in the midst of a cluster of similar patients?
b) How dense is that cluster, i.e. how close are those patients to p_0?
c) Does that cluster comprise a significant number of patients?
d) How many of them belong to the same class as p_0?
e) How close does the class boundary run to p_0?

For example, in the situation in the right half of Fig. 1 the patient identified by the black star is much better covered than in the situation shown in the left half according to the criteria a) to c) (cf. the density criterion in [6]). Criteria d) and e) are not yet considered in Fig. 1.

We now operationalize these criteria and derive three indicators that help a physician to estimate how well an AI system's decision for a given patient is supported by the data used to train the AI system. The *first indicator* operationalizes criteria a) to c) by estimating how big the radius r_0 of a sphere around

p_0 needs to be so that it includes a sufficient fraction x of all patients in the input data. The smaller the size of r_0 the more tightly packed the space around p_0 and the better p_0 is represented in the input data. The *second indicator* adds criterion d) by considering only patients in the vicinity of p_0 with the same label as p_0. The *third indicator* focuses on criterion e). To prepare the formal definitions of the indicators we introduce several definitions.

1. Let $P = P_h \cup P_s$ be the set of all healthy and sick patients from which the AI system was trained. We define a function for giving the number of patients inside an n-dimensional hypersphere of radius r around a given patient p:

$$N(p, r) \doteq |\{p' \in P : distance(p', p) \leq r\}| \qquad (1)$$

   Similarly, we define the number $N^h(p, r)$ of healthy and $N^s(p, r)$ of sick patients within a distance r. We have $N(p, r) = N^h(p, r) + N^s(p, r)$.
2. Let p_0 be a patient for which the AI system has generated a suggestion to the physician. We then determine the minimal radius r_0 of a hypersphere around p_0 such that a given fraction x of all patients is inside the hypersphere. The function R gives us that radius:

$$r_0 = R(p_0, x, P) \doteq min(\{r : N(p_0, r) \geq x \cdot |P|\}), \qquad (2)$$

   where $|P|$ is the number of patients in the set P. We set the radii $r_0^h = R(p_0, x, P_h)$ and $r_0^s = R(p_0, x, P_s)$.
3. The medians of the correspondingly determined radii (for the same fraction x) over all patients in the sample data serve as a reference to how well a given patient is covered by the sample:

$$\bar{r} = median(\{R(p, x, P) : p \in P\})$$
$$\bar{r}^h = median(\{R(p, x, P_h) : p \in P_h\})$$
$$\bar{r}^s = median(\{R(p, x, P_s) : p \in P_s\})$$

We use medians instead of averages because the latter are not robust against outlier patients, which may distort the reference values significantly.

Based on these definitions we can now define two coverage indicators.

Definition of Coverage Indicator 1
If $r_0 = R(p_0, x, P)$ is smaller than $\bar{r}$ then patient p_0 is better covered than the average patient in the input data. A good value for x could e.g. be 3% (see Sect. 3).

Definition of Coverage Indicator 2
Let p_0 be a healthy patient. If $r_0^h = R(p_0, x, P_h)$ is smaller than $\bar{r}^h$ then patient p_0 is better covered than the average patient with the same label in the input data. Accordingly, if p_0 is sick.

At present, the indicators are binary and can be used to give a physician a *green or red light for trusting the AI's advice* for the patient p_0.

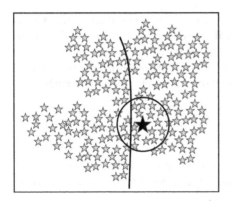 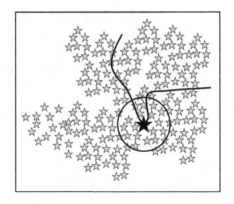

Fig. 2. Two situations of how differently close to a given patient (black star) the class boundary might run while giving the same results for Indicators 1 and 2.

A third indicator is based on the idea that even if Indicators 1 and 2 give good results it might still be the case that the class boundary runs close to p_0. For example, in the situation shown in the left half of Fig. 2 about 20% of the data points in the radius around p_0 (indicated by a black star) belong to the other class. The same holds for the right half of Fig. 2, giving the same results for Indicators 1 and 2, but being clearly worse than the situation in the left because p_0 is much closer to the class boundary and might actually belong to the other class. We introduce Indicator 3 to take into account how close the class boundary is to p_0. For that purpose we introduce a few auxiliary functions.

1. Let us assume patient p_0 is healthy. Take $r_0^h = R(p_0, x, P_h)$ as determined by Indicator 2 and set the radius $r_c \leq r_0^h$ such that at least the fraction y of the data points within it belong to the same class as p_0. We define

$$\widetilde{R}(p, r, y) \doteq \begin{cases} max(\{r' : r' \leq r \wedge \frac{N^h(p,r')+1}{N(p,r')+1} \geq y\}), & \text{if } class(p) = \text{h} \\ max(\{r' : r' \leq r \wedge \frac{N^s(p,r')+1}{N(p,r')+1} \geq y\}), & \text{if } class(p) = \text{s} \end{cases} \tag{3}$$

We can then set

$$r_c = \widetilde{R}(p_0, r_0^h, y)$$

We then calculate the quotient r_c/r_0^h (since p_0 was assumed to be healthy), or more exactly:

$$q(p_0, y) = \begin{cases} \widetilde{R}(p_0, R(p_0, x, P_h), y)/R(p_0, x, P_h), & \text{if } class(p_0) = \text{h} \\ \widetilde{R}(p_0, R(p_0, x, P_s), y)/R(p_0, x, P_s), & \text{if } class(p_0) = \text{s} \end{cases} \tag{4}$$

We proceed in the same way if p_0 is sick.

The quotient $q(p_0, y)$ indicates how much the sphere around a patient p_0 has to shrink in order to include a sufficient fraction y of data points of the same class as p_0. It is thus an indicator for how close the class boundary runs to p_0. If it is too close $q(p_0, y)$ can become 0; if there is no patient from the other class already within r_0^h (resp. r_0^s) then $q(p_0, y)$ is 1.

2. Calculate $q(p, y)$ for each object p in the input data with the same label as p_0. Determine the median over all these values, e.g. in case p_0 is healthy:

$$\bar{q} = median(\{q(p, y) : p \in P_h\})$$

Definition of Coverage Indicator 3
If $q(p_0, y)$ is greater than $\bar{q}$ then p_0 is better embedded in the class it is associated with than the average patient in the input data. A good value for y could e.g. be 80% (see Sect. 3).

Please note that the definitions of all indicators avoid any reference to absolute values because physicians would not be able to make sense of them. Instead we compare the calculated values with the median of the corresponding values over all the other patients in the input data. This gives physicians an idea of how typical a patient is with respect to the original input data of the AI system.

To estimate the feasibility of our approach and what would be appropriate values for x (Indicators 1 and 2) and y (Indicator 3) we have conducted some experiments on a real data set that are presented in the following section.

3   Experiments

We next illustrate the indicators introduced above on a publicly available data set for cardiovascular disease [16]. The data set consists of 70,000 patients with 12 attributes, of which five are ratio-scaled, five are binary (including the target variable) and two are ordinal. The target feature indicates the presence or absence of a cardiovascular disease. 1,239 patients were eliminated from the data set because their systolic and diastolic blood pressures were outside the ranges 30 to 150 and 50 to 250, respectively. A training subset of 32,993 patients was then selected, with an ill-to-healthy patient ratio of 49.5%. Feature engineering consisted of adding the body-mass-index feature. By training a random forest, a support vector classifier and even a k-nearest-Neighbour classifier, accuracy values of 70 to 73% were achieved.

Due to the mixed nature of the features, defining an appropriate distance measure for the function N (formula (1)) is somewhat challenging. The numerical features are approximately normally distributed, such that a euclidean distance measure after standardisation is quite natural. The binary and ordinal features have been mapped to integer numerical coordinates in $\{0, 1\}$ and $\{1, 2, 3\}$, respectively. This we considered the most natural choice but will have to be analyzed in more detail.

Figure 3 shows the number of ill patients $N^s(p, r)$, inside a sphere as a function of its radius r. The dashed and dashed-dotted lines show $N^s(p, r)$ for two ill patients. They should be compared to the median (thin solid line) and the 90%-confidence bound (shaded area around the median line), both taken over a

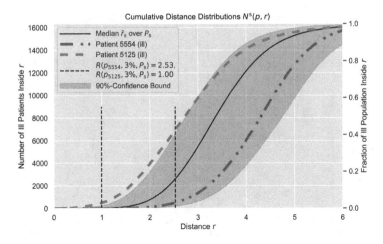

Fig. 3. Indicator 2: number of patients within a given radius (Eq. (1)).

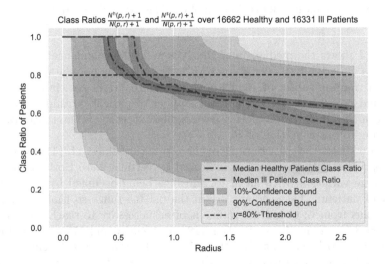

Fig. 4. Indicator 3: class ratios underlying the definition of $\widetilde{R}$ (Eq. (3)).

population of 16,331 ill patients. The vertical dashed lines intersect these curves at 3% of the total number of patients and indicate $R(p, 3\%, P)$ on the abscissa for the two highlighted ill patients 5554 and 5125. The left ordinate axis gives the absolute number of ill patients inside r, the right ordinate axis gives the fraction of ill patients (between 0 and 1). Note that patient 5125 (dashed line) is rather close to the 90%-confidence border, indicating that this patient is among the top 5% of ill patients with respect to his coverage in the training data. In contrast, patient 5554 has a much larger value of $r_0 = R(5554, 3\%, P)$ which indicates that an AI trained on this data set might be less accurate for her.

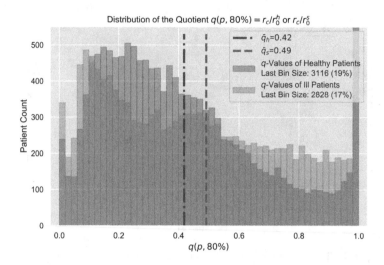

Fig. 5. Indicator 3: distribution of q values for $y = 0.8$ (Eq. (4)).

Figure 4 shows the medians and the 10% and 90%-confidence bands of the class ratios underlying the definition of $\tilde{R}$ in Eq. (3). The population consists of a random training subset of 16,662 healthy and 16,331 ill patients. The sharp rise around $r \sim 0.5$ is due to the total number of patients within r becoming small, such that more patients with few neighbours receive a class ratio value of 1 according to our definition of $\tilde{R}$.

Figure 5 shows the distributions of the $q(p, 80\%)$ values (cf. (4)) for healthy and ill patients, with the medians indicated by vertical lines. Both populations have a large variation, with all histogram bins being occupied by a significant number of patients. The medians are in the 0.4–0.5-range so that a reduction of the radius from r_0 to half its radius is often necessary to reach a class ratio above $y = 80\%$. A significant fraction (19% of healthy and 17% of ill patients) is in the $q = 1.0$ bins, indicating that for $x = 3\%$, the $y = 80\%$ class ratio is often already present so that there is no need to shrink r_0 to avoid a near-by class boundary.

The experiments show that, at least for the selected data set, the distributions of the values underlying our indicators tend to be distributed around their median. We conclude that the indicators have a discriminating effect as intended.

4   Discussion and Outlook

The indicators we have introduced in this paper compare an individual patient with various subpopulations of the training set of patients, in particular the same-class patients and the fraction x of nearest patients (see formula (2)). The indicators are *independent of the internal workings of an AI system*, but take into account the feature engineering performed to build the AI. Moreover, the indicators avoid any reference to absolute values because they would not make sense for a physician. Instead we compare the calculated values with the median of the corresponding values across all the other patients in the input data.

Our experiments in Sect. 3 are predicated on an approximately normal distribution of the numerical features. This has allowed us to standardize all features and use them as coordinates in a multi-dimensional euclidean space. If outliers are present, they must be handled with care as they might significantly distort standardization. Furthermore, the choice of an appropriate distance metric requires further investigation in the case of categorical and ordinal features. For the sake of simplicity, we have treated all features as equally important. In future work we intend to assign different weights to features in the distance metric to reflect their domain-specific importance.

The results will have to be visualised in a way that makes it easy to understand if a person is well represented in the training data or not, e.g. by translating them into a traffic light system. A red colour would signal that he/she is not well represented in the data set, in which case a doctor might want to reassess the relevance of an AI's prediction. How to present indicator results to a physician as well as the *evaluation* of the proposed indicators are issues for future work.

The indicators rely on the *hyperparameters* x and y and a binary class label. The hyperparameter values chosen have proven meaningful and useful for this data set, but this might not be true of other data sets. We expect experiments with further data sets to give us insights on how to properly set these parameters, how to extend our approach to multi-class settings, and how to deal with the currently high computational complexity.

An interesting aspect raised by one of the reviewers refers to cases where only one or two features are responsible for the weak coverage of a patient by the input data. In such cases a physician might want to double-check if those features have been properly measured (e.g. high blood pressure) or are influenced by interacting factors such as medication.

We see our contribution as complementary to inducing trust via explainability and certification. We expect our approach to facilitate a physician-AI partnership, where the doctor can assess the AI's advice and decide if to follow it or back it up with additional evidence or tests. In this way, human intelligence remains in the loop, as requested by Korot et al. [5].

Acknowledgement. We would like to thank the reviewers for their helpful comments to an earlier version of the paper.

References

1. Chien, S.-Y., Lewis, M., Semnani-Azad, Z., Sycara, K.: An empirical model of cultural factors on trust in automation. In: Proceedings of the Human Factors and Ergonomics Society Annual Meeting, vol. 58, pp. 859–863, October 2014
2. Choi, E., Bahadori, M.T., Schuetz, A., Stewart, W.F., Sun, J.: Doctor AI: predicting clinical events via recurrent neural networks. In: Machine Learning for Healthcare Conference, pp. 301–318 (2016)

3. Došilović, F.K., Brčić, M., Hlupić, N.: Explainable artificial intelligence: a survey. In: 2018 41st International Convention on Information and Communication Technology, Electronics and Microelectronics (MIPRO), pp. 0210–0215. IEEE (2018)
4. Gilpin, L.H., Bau, D., Yuan, B.Z., Bajwa, A., Specter, M., Kagal, L.: Explaining explanations: an overview of interpretability of machine learning. In: Proceedings of 2018 IEEE 5th International Conference on Data Science and Advanced Analytics, pp. 80–89, October 2018
5. Korot, E., et al.: Will AI replace ophthalmologists? Transl. Vis. Sci. Technol. **9**(2), 1–5 (2020)
6. Leonard, J.A., Kramer, M.A., Ungar, L.H.: A neural network architecture that computes its own reliability. Comput. Chem. Eng. **16**(9), 819–835 (1992)
7. Mandal, S., Greenblatt, A.B., An, J.: Imaging intelligence: AI is transforming medical imaging across the imaging spectrum. IEEE Pulse **9**(5), 16–24 (2018)
8. Matheny, M., Israni, S.T., Ahmed, M., Whicher, D.: Artificial intelligence in health care: the hope, the hype, the promise, the peril. Natl. Acad. Med. 94–97 (2020)
9. Miller, T.: Explanation in artificial intelligence: insights from the social sciences. Artif. Intell. **267**, 1–38 (2019)
10. Reimer, U., Maier, E., Tödtli, B.: Going beyond explainability in medical AI systems. In: Proceedings of Modellierung 2020 Short Papers, Workshop Papers, and Tools & Demo Papers, vol. 2542, pp. 185–191. CEUR-WS.org (2020)
11. Ribeiro, M.T., Singh, S., Guestrin, C.: why should i trust you?: explaining the predictions of any classifier. In: Proceedings of the 22nd ACM SIGKDD International Conference on Knowledge Discovery and Data Mining, pp. 1135–1144. ACM (2016)
12. Ronicke, S., Hirsch, M.C., Türk, E., Larionov, K., Tientcheu, D., Wagner, A.D.: Thu0564 could a probabilistic reasoning AI accelerate rare disease diagnosis? Evaluating the potential impact of a diagnostic decision support system in a retrospective study. Ann. Rheum. Dis. **78**(Suppl 2), 572–574 (2019)
13. Savadjiev, P., et al.: Demystification of AI-driven medical image interpretation: past, present and future. Eur. Radiol. **29**(3), 1616–1624 (2019)
14. Schulam, P., Saria, S.: Can you trust this prediction? Auditing pointwise reliability after learning. In: Proceedings of 22nd International Conference on Artificial Intelligence and Statistics, pp. 1022–1031 (2019)
15. Topol, E.J.: High-performance medicine: the convergence of human and artificial intelligence. Nat. Med. **25**(1), 44–56 (2019)
16. Ulianova, S.: Cardiovascular disease dataset. https://www.kaggle.com/sulianova/cardiovascular-disease-dataset. Accessed 17 Oct 2019
17. Zafar, M.B., Valera, I., Gomez-Rodriguez, M., Gummadi, K.P.: Fairness constraints: a flexible approach for fair classification. J. Mach. Learn. Res. **20**(75), 1–42 (2019)
18. Zhou, N., et al.: Concordance study between IBM watson for oncology and clinical practice for patients with cancer in China. Oncologist **24**(6), 812 (2019)

Towards Automated Support
for Conceptual Model Diagnosis
and Repair

Mattia Fumagalli$^{(\boxtimes)}$, Tiago Prince Sales$^{(\boxtimes)}$, and Giancarlo Guizzardi$^{(\boxtimes)}$

Conceptual and Cognitive Modeling Research Group (CORE),
Free University of Bozen-Bolzano, Bolzano, Italy
{mattia.fumagalli,tiago.princesales,giancarlo.guizzardi}@unibz.it

Abstract. Validating and debugging conceptual models is a very time-consuming task. Though separate software tools for *model validation* and *machine learning* are available, their integration for an automated support of the debugging-validation process still needs to be explored. The synergy between model validation for finding intended/unintended conceptual models instances and machine learning for suggesting repairs promises to be a fruitful relationship. This paper provides a preliminary description of a framework for an adequate automatic support to engineers and domain experts in the proper design of a conceptual model. By means of a running example, the analysis will focus on two main aspects: *i)* the process by which formal, tool-supported methods can be effectively used to generate negative and positive examples, given an input conceptual model; *ii)* the key role of a learning system in uncovering error-prone structures and suggesting conceptual modeling repairs.

Keywords: Conceptual models · Model simulation · Inductive learning

1 Introduction

The complexity of building conceptual models is a widely recognized research issue. Works like [9] and [7] underline the limitations of human cognitive capabilities in managing the huge and difficult activities involved in conceptual modeling. This is the main reason why, over the years, multiple solutions aimed at supporting conceptual model design have been provided by different communities. Most of these solutions can be categorized as *complexity management engineering tools*, and they offer semi-automated or fully-automated support facilities for model design, validation, or verification [8].

To adequately support the engineering of complex conceptual models, besides these tools, we have seen, in the last decade, an increasing interest in the use of *ontology-driven conceptual modeling languages* [16]. These languages mainly seek to offer a reference layer for conceptual modeling construction, validation,

G. Grossmann and S. Ram (Eds.): ER 2020 Workshops, LNCS 12584, pp. 15–25, 2020.
https://doi.org/10.1007/978-3-030-65847-2_2

and code generation. In this spirit, the recent work presented in [14] describes a novel validation strategy using visual *model finding* [10], that can be used for eliciting *anti-patterns* in conceptual models. The empirically-elicited research output in [14] offers a concrete example of how *error-prone modeling decisions* can be uncovered and made explicit, thus offering a methodology to diagnosis and repair of conceptual models.

In approaches such as [14], however, anti-pattern detection as well as the construction of rectification plans is done manually, i.e., the authors have manually validated dozens of models, manually detected these emerging error-prone structures, and have manually proposed effective rectification plans. As shown therein, with this process, they have managed to propose a catalog containing dozens of anti-patterns. Manually conducting this process, however, is a difficult and time-consuming task, which, as consequence, limits the number of models that can be analyzed and, hence, the number of structures that can be discovered. To address this limitation, we are interested in identifying how, by using *model finding* and *machine learning* (ML), the design activities of this approach can be supported. In other words, we want to reduce the effort to uncover error-prone structures in conceptual models and identify repairs suggestion, by automating these tasks as much as possible.

Though separate software tools for model finding and machine learning are available, their integration for automating the debugging-validation process still needs to be explored. Inspired by the work of Alrajeh and colleagues [2, 3], who proposed an approach to automatically diagnose and repair temporal logic software specifications based on the integration of *model checking* and *machine learning*, we seek to develop an approach for conceptual modeling, which in turn, leverages on *model finding*[1] and *machine learning* techniques.

The contributions of this paper are three-fold. Firstly, we propose a framework to implement the aforementioned synergy between model finding and machine learning for conceptual modeling diagnosis and repair. Secondly, we contribute to the identification of how formal, tool-supported methods can be effectively used to generate a data set of negative and positive examples of instances for a given conceptual model. We do this by carrying out an empirical simulation over a simple example conceptual model. In particular, we adopt the *Alloy Analyzer* [10] to generate multiple simulations of the input conceptual model and we propose a series of steps to encode information about intended/unintended models. Thirdly, once the data set of negative and positive examples has been elicited, we show how this data can be given as input to a *learning system*, which can be used to automatically uncover error-prone structures and suggest repairs to the modeler.

The remainder of this paper is organized as follows. In Sect. 2, we briefly introduce our running example. Section 3 introduces the framework, by describing the main steps, agents, and components involved. Section 4 shows how to go from model finding, through annotation, to example set generation. Section 5 describes the role of a learning system in identifying error-prone structures and suggesting

---

[1] For a detailed analysis of model checking and model finding see [10].

repairs. Finally, Sect. 6 presents some final considerations and describes future work.

2   Conceptual Modeling: Learning by Feedback

We take here the general methodological practice employed in natural sciences [5] of starting with simple models to explore a fuller extent of the ideas at hand before making progress to complex ones. In that spirit, although the ultimate goal of this research program is to develop a framework target at ontology-driven conceptual modeling languages (in particular, OntoUML [7]), we start here with standard UML and with the toy model depicted in Fig. 1 below.

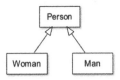

Fig. 1. A toy example in UML.

Now suppose that we can run simulations (or configurations) of the given example model with at most 2 instances per configuration[2]. The list of possible configurations of this model is depicted in Fig. 2, in which solid arrows mean direct instantiation and dashed arrows indirect instantiation.

By looking at these possible outputs, the modeler may identify some *unintended* configurations, namely instances that she does not want her model to allow. Now suppose that by looking at these outputs, the modeler can annotate what are the intended/unintended configurations. From these annotated configurations, what can we learn as the most general rules? Looking at the super-simple model above the modeler may want to avoid all the cases in which 'Person' has direct instances (e.g., 'c' and 'e' in Fig. 2) and where an instance is both a 'Man' and a 'Woman' (e.g, 'i' and 'm' in Fig. 2). If this is the case, the simple rule to be inferred can be informally expressed as *"Every person is either a man or a woman and no person is both a man and a woman"*. To repair the input conceptual model, a knowledge engineer would simply have to add a constraint that forbids these two generic configurations represented in Fig. 3. In UML, this could be achieved with a generalization set that is complete (isCovering = true) and disjoint (isDisjoint = true).

---

[2] From now on we use the terms "simulation run" and "configuration" interchangeably, where a simulation run is the result of *an interpretation function satisfying the conceptual model*. In other words: if we take the UML diagram as a M1-model (in the MDA-sense), a configuration is a M0-model that could instantiate that M1-model; if we take the UML diagram as a logical specification, then a configuration is a logical model of that specification. Finding these valid configurations given a specification is the classical task performed by a *model finder*.

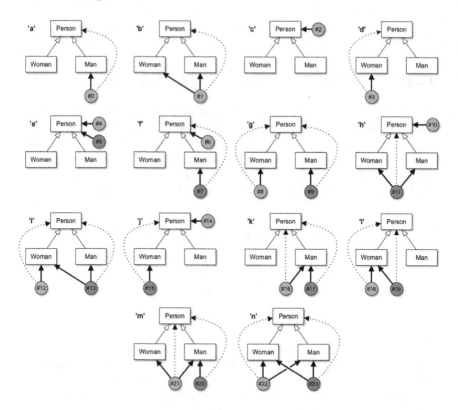

Fig. 2. List of simulations for the model of Fig. 1.

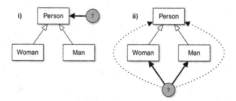

Fig. 3. Simulations of the model in Fig. 1 allowing for unintended instances.

From this example, we make two main observations. Firstly, consider a much more complex model than the one in Fig. 1. The activity of debugging the model by checking all the intended/unintended configurations is very time consuming and it may not be easy for the modeler to understand *where* the errors come from, *how* to repair the model, and *what* rules need to be added (if any). Secondly, consider a scenario where several people simulate the same model and people diverge on what they assign as intended and unintended configurations. We can then offer to the modelers possible options giving them an indication of how often people chose each of the options. This is about repairing a particular model by learning from a *collective judgment* (in this case, a type of *meaning negotiation* activity).

In summary, from the marriage between model validation, for finding faults, and machine learning, for suggesting repairs, a fruitful synergy emerges, which can support knowledge engineers in understanding how to design and refine rigorous models.

3   From Model Validation to Repairs Suggestion

The framework we envision should be able to produce, from a given conceptual model, a set of rules that forbid the occurrence of configurations marked as unintended by knowledge engineers. The key idea here is to combine and exploit model validation and learning technologies in order to: *i)* automatically generate a set of configurations of the input conceptual model and identify unexpected outputs; *ii)* carry out diagnosis and repair tasks by learning from the identified errors and suggesting rules to adjust the model accordingly.

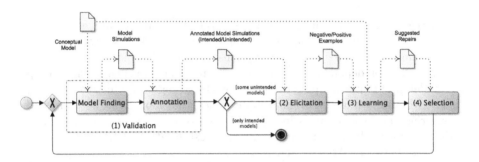

Fig. 4. Automated support for conceptual modeling diagnosis and repair: the proposed framework.

This framework comprises four steps explained in the sequel (see Fig. 4), which can be executed iteratively:

Step 1. Validation. This step consists in automatically generating possible configurations from an input conceptual model and asserting whether these should indeed be allowed by it. If no unintended configurations are identified, the process terminates, otherwise it proceeds to step 2. The generational part of this step requires feeding the input model to a *model finder.*[3] The assertional part requires one or more knowledge engineers to decide on its validity. Considering the example in Fig. 2, an unintended configuration could be represented by 'i', where an instance is both 'Man' and 'Woman'). If unintended models are found, the process continues to the next step.

---

[3] This step may require a previous conversion step, from the language used to design the conceptual model (e.g. UML, OntoUML) to the model finder specifications as in, e.g., [4].

Step 2. Elicitation. At this point, the model configurations generated by the model finder and annotated by knowledge engineers do not specify *why* they are intended or unintended. In an unintended configuration, indeed, we may have both allowed and forbidden instances (i.e. particular individuals that instantiate a class in the model). For example, in Fig. 2, configuration 'f', the instance '6' is forbidden, while '7' is allowed. Step 2 allows the modelers to mark which instances represent negative or positive examples. Once negative and positive examples are produced, they are ready to be given as input, along with the structure of the original conceptual model, to the learning system.

Step 3. Learning. Having identified the negative and positive examples that make the configurations unintended or intended, a learning system software carries out the diagnosis process automatically. The goal of this step is to identify the structures of the model that are "error-prone" [14]. The output of the learning process, considering the super-simple model introduced above, can be exactly the negation of the two configurations represented in Fig. 3. This, of course, depends on the information collected with the modeler annotation.

Step 4. Selection. The learning system may produce multiple examples of "error-prone" structures for the same model. For the repair task, a selection step for deciding among the possible repairs options is required. This selection step is always application dependent (i.e., it depends on the final purpose of the conceptual model) and requires inputs from the knowledge engineer. Once the selection is made, the update of the original input conceptual model can be addressed. Considering the two examples in Fig. 3, if both of them are selected, the suggested repairs would be a negation of direct instantiation of 'Person' and the disjointness between 'Woman' and 'Man'.

The presented combination of model finding and (logic-based) learning is intended to support an iterative process for evolving and repairing conceptual models by adding constraints that prevent unintended configurations. The iterative aspect of the process is relevant because there is no guarantee that a single application of the four steps will ensure the correctness of the model. Thus, it should be repeated until no unintended configurations can be found.

4   Highlighting Possibly Erroneous Decisions

Let us now consider model validation more formally. In the proposed framework, following the strategy in [14], the input conceptual model is translated into Alloy [10], a logic language based on set theory, which offers a powerful model analysis service that, given a context, generates possible instances for a given specification (it can also allow model checking and counterexamples generation). For example, once the conceptual model of Fig. 1 is converted into an Alloy specification, multiple configurations of the model (for two instances) can be produced. Figure 5 below presents the full list of possible configurations, covering also the example diagrams provided in Fig. 2.[4] Notice that "`this/...`" refers to a class, and the values within curly brackets refer to its generated instances. So if `this/Person` contains `Person3` and `this/Woman` contains `Person3`, it means the individual `Person3` is a 'Person' and a 'Woman' at the same time.

```
#   'Toy' model Alloy configurations
'a' this/Person={Person0}, this/Man={Person0}, this/Woman={}
'b' this/Person={Person1}, this/Man={Person1}, this/Woman={Person1}
'c' this/Person={Person2}, this/Man={}, this/Woman={}
'd' this/Person={Person3}, this/Man={}, this/Woman={Person3}
'e' this/Person={Person4, Person5}, this/Man={}, this/Woman={}
'f' this/Person={Person6, Person7}, this/Man={Person7}, this/Woman={}
'g' this/Person={Person8, Person9}, this/Man={Person9}, this/Woman={Person8}
'h' this/Person={Person10, Person11}, this/Man={Person11}, this/Woman={Person11}
'i' this/Person={Person12, Person13}, this/Man={Person13}, this/Woman={Person12, Person13}
'j' this/Person={Person14, Person15}, this/Man={}, this/Woman={Person15}
'k' this/Person={Person16, Person17}, this/Man={Person16, Person17}, this/Woman={}
'l' this/Person={Person18, Person19}, this/Man={}, this/Woman={Person18, Person19}
'm' this/Person={Person20, Person21}, this/Man={Person20, Person21}, this/Woman={Person21}
'n' this/Person={Person22, Person23}, this/Man={Person22, Person23}, this/Woman={Person22,
↪   Person23}
```

Fig. 5. Configurations generated by Alloy (empty model excluded). Each individual, e.g., *Person0*, maps into the corresponding instance in Fig. 2, e.g., *#0*.

At this point, as a first task, the modeler should annotate those configurations that are intended or unintended. Following the super-simple model example the annotation can be represented as from Fig. 6 below, where the red cross marks the unintended simulation.

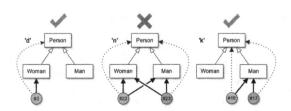

Fig. 6. Examples of simulations annotated as intended/unintended.

The further step here is to convert the above annotation into an example set collecting information about the input conceptual model and the annotation provided by the modeler. This will involve an additional input from the modeler, namely the annotation of what instance in the simulation makes the configuration intended or unintended. For instance, looking at Fig. 6 the two instances to be marked as "negative" are '#22' and '#23'.

---

[4] Notice that Alloy produces '0' and '1' instances only, we numbered the instances considering the full list of possible configurations.

Notice that, the plan is to use an *ad hoc* editor to support the annotation process and the example set generation step. In particular, we will employ the capabilities embedded in the OntoUML editor [6], which will play a key role along the process, with some additional features (some of them already implemented), such as: a) exploration of Alloy simulations; b) simulations annotation; c) negative/positive example set generation.

The overall phase from the input conceptual model, through the generation of multiple simulations, to the annotation and the generation of the negative/positive examples set, can be formalized as a composed function f_a, where:

$$f_a : f_b \circ f_c \tag{1}$$

$$f_b : M \to (A_M \times \mathcal{S}_{A_M}^{+/-}) \tag{2}$$

$$f_c : (A_M \times \mathcal{S}_{A_M}^{+/-}) \to E^{+/-} \tag{3}$$

With M being the conceptual model. A_M being the conceptual model converted into Alloy specifications. $\mathcal{S}_{A_M}^{+/-}$ being a set of simulations generated through Alloy, annotated as intended/unintended, given A_M. $E^{+/-}$ being a data set collecting negative and positive examples. The output of f_b is an Alloy model associated to a list of intended/unintended simulations. The output of f_a is an example set that can be given as input to the learning system.

As a final remark, f_a can be seen as a semi-automatic process. If the conversion steps (e.g., from the conceptual model to the Alloy specifications, or the generation of $E^{+/-}$) can be easily automatized, some manual work from the modelers, which need to provide feedback within the loop, is still required.

Table 1. Embedding knowledge engineers input into neg/pos examples matrix.

	#Person0	#Person1	#Person2	#Person3	#Person4	#Person5	#Person6	#Person7	#Person8	#Person9	#Person10	#Person11	#Person12	#Person13	#Person14	#Person15	#Person16	#Person17	#Person18	#Person19	#Person20	#Person21	#Person22	#Person23
label	1	0	0	1	0	0	0	1	1	1	0	0	1	1	0	1	1	1	1	1	1	0	0	0
{ ?x <#type> <#Person> }	1	1	1	1	1	1	1	1	1	1	1	1	1	1	1	1	1	1	1	1	1	1	1	1
{ ?x <#type> <#Man> }	1	1	0	0	0	0	0	1	0	1	0	1	0	1	0	1	0	0	1	1	0	0	1	1
{ ?x <#type> <#Woman> }	0	1	0	1	0	0	0	0	1	0	0	1	1	0	0	1	0	0	1	1	0	1	1	1

5   Uncovering Error-Prone Structures

The output of the phase described in previous sections should be as represented by Table 1. In order to generate the above matrix we adopted a standard propositionalization process [12], where: *i*) we converted the conceptual model and the related instances (e.g., '#1', '#2', '#3', etc.) into a logical knowledge base specification (KB) (i.e., the combination of the so-called TBOX and ABOX); *ii*) we gave the reference KB as input of a script to generate a matrix of patterns; *iii*) we extended the matrix with the information about positive and negative examples (see the 'label' attribute). From this input, there may be multiple ways to set-up the learning step and automatically extract repairs suggestions. For instances, the learning system can be used to implement an *Association Rule Mining* (ARM) [1] approach, or to implement relational learning based on *Inductive Logic Programming* (ILP) [13].

```
//Rule1
if { ?x <#type> <#Man> } = false and { ?x <#type> <#Woman> } = false then false
//Rule2
if { ?x <#type> <#Man> } = false and { ?x <#type> <#Woman> } = true then true
//Rule3
if { ?x <#type> <#Man> } = true and { ?x <#type> <#Woman> } = false then true
//Rule4
if { ?x <#type> <#Man> } = true and { ?x <#type> <#Woman> } = true then false
```

Fig. 7. Rules extracted from the annotation of the output presented in Fig. 5.

In this paper, we adopted a standard approach. We derived the rules by using a simple *Decision Tree* model, where the attributes for splitting are selected according to the *gain ratio* criterion [11], and we run *subgroups discovery* to induce an exhaustive rule set plus a list of insights to better explain the results. Notice that the role of ML statistical techniques to extract rules and insights from the modelers' feedback becomes more useful as the complexity of the model increases and the number of feedback increases. For instance, having multiple (and possibly inconsistent) feedback for the same simulation, the labels for each instance may have multiple values encoding *weights*, instead of binary values, such as '0' and '1', like in the example of Fig. 1.

'Rule 1' and 'Rule 4', in Fig. 7, represent the rules accounting for the unintended configurations, namely: *i)* when instances of 'Person' are neither instances of 'Man' nor 'Woman' ('1'); *ii)* when instances of 'Person' are both 'Woman' and 'Man' ('4'). The following formulas represent a *First Order Logic* (FOL) formalization of the derived 'negative' rules.

$$\exists x \, Person(x) \wedge \neg(Woman(x) \vee Man(x)) \tag{4}$$

$$\exists x \, Person(x) \wedge (Woman(x) \wedge Man(x)) \tag{5}$$

A further analysis can be run by checking the results provided by the subgroup discovery implementation, as from Table 2 below, where we grouped the most 'precise' rules.

Table 2. Extracted rules: some additional insights.

Rule	Conclusion	Pos	Neg	Size	Coverage	Precision	Lift	Length
//Rule1	false	0	6	6	0,250	1,000	2,182	3
//Rule2	true	6	0	6	0,250	1,000	1,846	3
//Rule3	true	7	0	7	0,292	1,000	1,846	3
//Rule4	false	0	5	5	0,208	1,000	2,182	3

Besides collecting information about the *Size* (i.e., how many instances are involved), the *Length* (i.e., how many predicates are involved) and the *Coverage* (i.e., how many instances covered over the total instances), a ranking of the rules can be provided in terms of, for instance, *Precision* and *Lift*. The *Precision* value explains the ratio of different values ('Pos' and 'Neg', for a certain rule) for the same instance (in the example we have precision '1', meaning that values are only 'Pos' or 'Neg'). The *Lift* value measures the value of a certain rule considering the ratio of premises and consequences in the given data set (see [15] for further details). Given the above derived 'negative' rules, the repairs that can be selected by the modelers would be quite straightforward. The input conceptual model (assuming here a FOL formalization of that model) can be then constrained as follows:

$$M = \{\forall x\, Woman(x) \rightarrow Person(x), \forall x\, Man(x) \rightarrow Person(x)\} \tag{6}$$

$$M^R = \{M, \forall x\, Person(x) \rightarrow (Woman(x) \vee Man(x)), \forall x\, Man(x) \rightarrow \neg Woman(x)\} \tag{7}$$

Where M represents the original conceptual model and M^R represents the new repaired (i.e., constrained) version of the conceptual model.

6   Conclusion and Perspectives

This paper presents preliminary results towards a framework for diagnosing and repairing faulty structures in conceptual models. In particular, our objective is to combine, on one hand, the *model finding* techniques for generating positive (intended) and negative (unintended) model configurations and, on the other hand, use this curated base of positive/negative examples for feeding a *learning process*. Our overall research program, aims at addressing the full ontological semantics of the OntoUML. In that sense, it will leverage on the existing OntoUML support for model validation via visual simulation in Alloy [4,14]. A further objective is learning from the configurations *structures that are recurrent* in several OntoUML models (i.e., anti-patterns) as well as reusable cross-model rules that could rectify them. Addressing these objectives for a particular model with a subset of the semantics of that language is a first step in that direction.

References

1. Agrawal, R., Imieliński, T., Swami, A.: Mining association rules between sets of items in large databases. In: 1993 ACM SIGMOD, pp. 207–216 (1993)
2. Alrajeh, D., Kramer, J., Russo, A., Uchitel, S.: Elaborating requirements using model checking and inductive learning. IEEE TSE **39**(3), 361–383 (2013)
3. Alrajeh, D., Kramer, J., Russo, A., Uchitel, S.: Automated support for diagnosis and repair. Commun. ACM **58**(2), 65–72 (2015)
4. Braga, B.F., Almeida, J.P.A., Guizzardi, G., Benevides, A.B.: Transforming OntoUML into Alloy: towards conceptual model validation using a lightweight formal method. Innovat. Syst. Softw. Eng. **6**(1–2), 55–63 (2010)

5. Cairns-Smith, A.G.: The Life Puzzle: On Crystals and Organisms and on the Possibility of a Crystal as an Ancestor. University of Toronto Press, Toronto (1971)
6. Guerson, J., Sales, T.P., Guizzardi, G., Almeida, J.P.A.: Ontouml lightweight editor: a model-based environment to build, evaluate and implement reference ontologies. In: 19th IEEE EDOC (2015)
7. Guizzardi, G.: Ontological foundations for structural conceptual models. Telematica Instituut/CTIT (2005)
8. Guizzardi, G.: Theoretical foundations and engineering tools for building ontologies as reference conceptual models. Semant. Web 1(1, 2), 3–10 (2010)
9. Guizzardi, G., Sales, T.P.: Detection, simulation and elimination of semantic anti-patterns in ontology-driven conceptual models. In: Yu, E., Dobbie, G., Jarke, M., Purao, S. (eds.) ER 2014. LNCS, vol. 8824, pp. 363–376. Springer, Cham (2014). https://doi.org/10.1007/978-3-319-12206-9_30
10. Jackson, D.: Software Abstractions: Logic, Language, and Analysis. MIT Press, Cambridge (2012)
11. Karegowda, A.G., Manjunath, A., Jayaram, M.: Comparative study of attribute selection using gain ratio and correlation based feature selection. Int. J. Inf. Technol. Knowl. Manage. 2(2), 271–277 (2010)
12. Kramer, S., Lavrač, N., Flach, P.: Propositionalization approaches to relational data mining. In: Džeroski, S., Lavrač, N. (eds.) Relational Data Mining, pp. 262–291. Springer, Heidelberg (2001). https://doi.org/10.1007/978-3-662-04599-2_11
13. Muggleton, S., De Raedt, L.: Inductive logic programming: theory and methods. J. Log. Program. 19, 629–679 (1994)
14. Sales, T.P., Guizzardi, G.: Ontological anti-patterns: empirically uncovered error-prone structures in ontology-driven conceptual models. Data Knowl. Eng. 99, 72–104 (2015)
15. Tufféry, S.: Data Mining and Statistics for Decision Making. Wiley, Hoboken (2011)
16. Verdonck, M., Gailly, F.: Insights on the use and application of ontology and conceptual modeling languages in ontology-driven conceptual modeling. In: Comyn-Wattiau, I., Tanaka, K., Song, I.-Y., Yamamoto, S., Saeki, M. (eds.) ER 2016. LNCS, vol. 9974, pp. 83–97. Springer, Cham (2016). https://doi.org/10.1007/978-3-319-46397-1_7

Superimposition: Augmenting Machine Learning Outputs with Conceptual Models for Explainable AI

Roman Lukyanenko[1]([✉]), Arturo Castellanos[2], Veda C. Storey[3], Alfred Castillo[4], Monica Chiarini Tremblay[5], and Jeffrey Parsons[6]

[1] HEC Montreal, Montreal, QC, Canada
`roman.lukyanenko@hec.ca`
[2] Baruch College, CUNY, New York, NY, USA
`arturo.castellanos@baruch.cuny.edu`
[3] Georgia State University, Altanta, GA, USA
`vstorey@gsu.edu`
[4] CalPoly, San Luis Obispo, CA, USA
`acasti63@calpoly.edu`
[5] William and Mary, Williamsburg, VA, USA
`monica.tremblay@mason.wm.edu`
[6] Memorial University of Newfoundland, St. John's, NL, Canada
`jeffreyp@mun.ca`

Abstract. Machine learning has become almost synonymous with Artificial Intelligence (AI). However, it has many challenges with one of the most important being explainable AI; that is, providing human-understandable accounts of why a machine learning model produces specific outputs. To address this challenge, we propose *superimposition* as a concept which uses conceptual models to improve explainability by mapping the features that are important to a machine learning model's decision outcomes to a conceptual model of an application domain. Superimposition is a design method for supplementing machine learning models with structural elements that are used by humans to reason about reality and generate explanations. To illustrate the potential of superimposition, we present the method and apply it to a churn prediction problem.

Keywords: Artificial intelligence · Machine learning · Superimposition · Conceptual modeling · Explainable AI · Human categorization

1 Introduction

Machine learning (ML), which is now almost synonymous with Artificial intelligence (AI), has become a key driver of innovation and change in organizational and daily life [1]. Machine learning consists of methods that use data and algorithms to build models that make inferences on new data and perform specific tasks without being explicitly programmed [2–4]. Growing numbers of organizations are turning to machine learning

© Springer Nature Switzerland AG 2020
G. Grossmann and S. Ram (Eds.): ER 2020 Workshops, LNCS 12584, pp. 26–34, 2020.
https://doi.org/10.1007/978-3-030-65847-2_3

as part of their drive to make data-driven decisions and seek new efficiencies [5–7]. However, decision makers and the public remain skeptical of relying on ML for their decisions and actions [8–12]. Given its focus on data and algorithms, an important challenge in using ML is being able to understand how and why models make their decisions – a challenge known as Explainable AI (XAI) [13, 14].

Explainable AI refers to "systems that can explain their rationale to a human user, characterize their strengths and weaknesses, and convey an understanding of how they will behave in the future" [15]. The problem of machine learning explainability is urgent as societal reliance on machine learning grows. At the same time, the tendency in machine learning practice is to employ more powerful and sophisticated algorithms that are increasingly opaque and difficult to explain. Many are considered "black box" models, such as deep learning networks, that are difficult to understand. The inability to understand why machine learning models make certain decisions makes it difficult to detect and mitigate biases, and prevent discriminatory practices embedded inside machine learning models, thus limiting adoption by organizations, especially in highly regulated fields. The rush to open the black box of AI is further fueled by calls from the public and policy makers to treat the "right to explanation" as a new basic human right [16].

There are many approaches to XAI. Most rely on calculating importance weights to reflect the contributions of features to the decision made by a ML model. None appear to consider using domain knowledge to contextualize the importance of features with respect to the entities or objects they describe.

Conceptual models (CM) are (semi-)formal diagrammatic representations of domain knowledge developed to support information systems development [17–20]. The conceptual modeling community has a rich research tradition of using conceptual modeling to improve various aspects of information systems development. Typical uses include database design, process reengineering, and software development. However, conceptual modeling has only recently been considered within the context of machine learning [21, 22], and has not been applied to the problem of explainable AI. We propose using conceptual models to improve explainability by superimposing the features used in the development of machine learning models to the conceptual models of the domain. We illustrate the use of this *superimposition* method by applying it to predicting customer churn and discuss the implications of doing so.

2   Background: The Problem of Explainable AI

Historically, artificial intelligence focused on symbolic representation using logical formalisms [23]. For example, some approaches developed an AI application by first engineering requisite rules in the domain (e.g., by using ontologies or semantic networks typically created manually). The resulting models were, thus, relatively easy to understand.

With the increased availability of data and advances in computing and hardware, the AI field shifted its focus from developing rule-based domain models to computationally intensive data-driven (machine learning) approaches [3, 24]. The power of modern machine learning rests on its ability to make thousands, if not millions, of iterations over the training data to detect complex relationships among the input variables (i.e., feature engineering) and the target variable. These approaches are generally not easily understood by humans, leading to the need for work on XAI.

XAI research includes methods that weight the importance of input features in contributing to a model's decision. Such techniques include local interpretable model-agnostic explanations (LIME) [25], game theoretic approaches to compute explanations of model predictions (SHAP) [26] and use of counterfactuals to understand how removing features changes a decision [27]. These approaches focus on specific features and fail to abstract to higher-level concepts.

In this research, we propose a new approach to explainable AI based on concepts from conceptual modeling. We focus on ML-model agnostic approaches that contribute to explainability of any ML model. Popular techniques include explanations by simplification (e.g., creating a decision tree in addition to a neural network) [28]. Others seek to reduce model complexity by grouping features, making it easier to follow the logic of the model [29]. Work also considers making the marginal contribution of each feature more explicit [26]. However, there does not appear to be research that considers superimposing the features onto domain models. Such an approach can complement existing approaches by combining the logic derived from a machine learning model with knowledge about the application domain. It can provide cognitive benefits that facilitate explanation and understanding.

3 Superimposition Method

Superimposition compensates for the absence of structural semantic information about the real-world domain in a dataset used for machine learning, which, we argue, impedes explainability. Although this information is absent in current ML practice, it is routinely employed by humans to understand their day-to-day experiences. The design idea of superimposition has theoretical roots in cognitive psychology, which argues that humans are continuously subjected to diverse sensory experience. To cope with the sensory input, humans actively employ conceptual structures to filter, interpret, and assimilate the information they receive [30–32]. Such structures are category-based and relational in nature, as we discuss below.

First, a fundamental tenet of modern psychology is that much of sensory and mental experience of humans are organized into categories or concepts. The categories group related (typically similar) individual objects or events, such as trees and birds. Grouping sensory and mental experiences into categories provide many benefits (e.g., cognitive economy, ability to draw inferences, communicative efficiency), leading to nearly automatic imposition of categories onto sensory input [30]. Categories are fundamental units of attention, perception and thought. Human understanding and explanation of phenomena invariably utilizes categories. A set of categories and relationships among them can be viewed as a theory of a domain [33].

Second, human knowledge organization and the mechanisms used to understand and interpret phenomena are also relational. To cope with the large number of acquired categories, humans organize them into higher order structures, such as hierarchies, taxonomies, or networks [34, 35]. These structures are based on some type of *relationships* among the categories (e.g., type of, part of, similar to).

Taken together, categories and relationships provide the fundamental structuring that facilitates reasoning, understanding and explanation. However, these elements are either absent from the typical output of machine learning models or inaccessible to the naked eye. For example, a model built using a deep learning algorithm is comprised of features, path coefficients, bias, and activation functions [2]. The categories and higher order categorical structures (e.g., hierarchies) are absent, whereas the relational elements, such as path coefficients between features are opaque and difficult to understand, especially in large models. Even a relatively simple decision tree, while containing interpretable relationships among features, lacks categories. Considering the preponderance of categories and relationships for human interpretation and explanation, we assume the lack of such mechanisms undermines explainability in machine learning models.

We propose *superimposition* as a design method for supplementing existing machine learning models with conceptual models. Specifically, we observe that any machine learning model is a model of some domain (e.g., credit card fraud, image classification, online auctions). The model itself is a set of rules for estimating a value of interest or discriminating among the cases of interest based on previously provided domain examples. Most commonly, these rules, through a series of mathematical transformations, describe patterns of relationships among variables of the domain and a target.

Based on the arguments above, we reason that, to support the understanding of a machine learning model in a domain, we can leverage the knowledge about the categories and the relationships within that domain. Such knowledge can be obtained from conceptual data models [36].

Major conceptual modeling grammars, such as the Entity-Relationship Diagrams or Class Diagrams in UML, rely on entity types or classes (i.e., categories) to represent domains. Classes distill essential features of objects for storage and use in an information system [37, 38]. Identifying classes has traditionally been viewed as one of the most important steps in systems development [39]. Likewise, relationships are also seen as fundamental to modeling, because they capture structural connections among the classes [40]. Research on conceptual modeling, has focused on facilitating accurate (and complete from the point of view of a predefined purpose) representation of domains using classes and relationships [20].

Superimposition maps the output of machine learning models (i.e., the features, rules and transformation functions) onto a conceptual model of the domain. First, the method assumes a conceptual model of the domain needs to be available or prepared in the form of an Extended Entity Relationship (EER) diagram. We assume the availability of a typical EER diagram containing entity types and their corresponding sets of attributes, which are the fields for the variables used in the machine learning. The entity types are connected through the relationship types.

Second, once a machine learning model from the same domain is developed, its output needs to be mapped to the related constructs of the conceptual model. The execution of this step depends on the type of the machine learning model. In all cases, a machine learning model includes features that are related to attributes in a conceptual model. These variables can be mapped to attributes in the conceptual model. However, as it is common to conduct feature engineering and transform variables (e.g., by merging them, or engineering new variables from the existing ones), this step may not be straightforward in all applications. The method is intended to provide traceability between the final variables used and the original source attributes in the conceptual model. This can be done, for example, by using graphical elements and comments inside the conceptual model to show transformations from the original features to their final form [25].

Third, the method suggests indicating inside the conceptual model information about the rules of the machine learning models. This step depends on the type of machine learning model. For example, if a regression model is used, these rules can be represented as feature weights or feature coefficients. These coefficients can be appended to the attributes in the conceptual model, or the attributes can be highlighted differently to indicate the different relative importance of each attribute.

The final step of the superimposition method involves analyzing the resulting conceptual model to gain a clearer understanding of the underlying rules machine learning models use to makes its decisions, and to identify opportunities to improve the machine learning model further.

4   Illustration: Superimposition Using EERD

We illustrate superimposition using a churn model on a publicly available dataset[1], Telco Customer Churn. The dataset includes information about customers who left (churned) within the last month. Each row represents a different customer. A customer may have signed up for different services such as a phone, multiple lines, internet, online security, online backup, device protection, tech support, or streaming service. In addition, the data contains demographic information (e.g., sex, age, gender) and information about the customer's account (e.g., tenure, contracts, payment method, monthly charges, and total charges).

For simplicity, we assume that the conceptual model already exists and is available to the analyst (see Fig. 1). Entity types represent the categories of interest in a domain, such as CUSTOMER, CONTRACT, PHONE, INTERNET, or SENIORCITIZEN. Relationships (e.g., isBilled, subscribes) in a conceptual model represent associations among entity types. Relationships also capture some constraints on the interactions among entities of different types. For example, a CUSTOMER isBilled through *multiple* CONTRACTS. In a typical ML process, information about relationships among entities is not explicit, and must be learned, requiring sufficient training data.

In this illustration the machine learning task is a classification task (i.e., the target variable is the binary variable *Churn*). The goal is to develop a predictive model that maps the input features to this target variable. Each customer can subscribe to many services such as phone, internet, online security, online backup, device protection, tech support, and streaming through different contracts. The contracts have information such as payment method, paperless billing, monthly charges, and total charges. Finally, there is information about customers, such as gender and age.

We construct a machine learning model using a general-purpose CPU compute Amazon AWS cloud instance with an Intel Xeon E5-2676 v3 (Haswell) processor, 16 Gb

---

[1] https://www.kaggle.com/blastchar/telco-customer-churn.

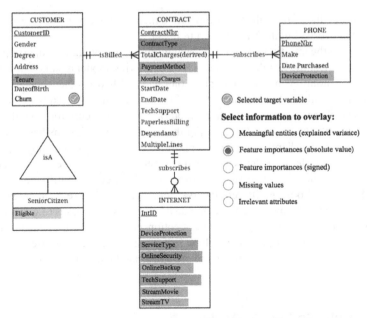

Fig. 1. Superimposed EER model for the telecom. Churn Dataset

Feature Importance	Weight
Contract	0.41
Tenure	0.352
OnlineSecurity	0.347
TechSupport	0.343
InternetService	0.322
PaymentMethod	0.303
OnlineBackup	0.292
DeviceProtection	0.282
StreamingMovies	0.231
StreamingTV	0.231
TotalCharges	0.199
MonthlyCharges	0.193
PaperlessBilling	0.192
Dependents	0.164
SeniorCitizen	0.151
Partner	0.15
MultipleLines	0.04
Gender	0.009

Fig. 2. Feature importance random forest (surrogate model)

RAM, and h2oai-driverless-ai-1.8.5 AMI (Amazon Linux). To build a machine learning model, we used random forest – a popular machine learning model. In Fig. 2, we retrieve the feature importance from the random forest model by weight in descending order.

We then followed the steps of the superimposition method. We color-code these weights which are then overlaid in the ER diagram in Fig. 1.

Compared to the traditional features shown in Fig. 2, following the superimposition (in Fig. 1) provide some insightful patterns for interpreting model results. For instance, Customers with month-to-month contracts (ContractType) had a higher chance of churning or, after 18 months of having the service (CustomerTenure), the likelihood of churn decreases. The sharp increase in the likelihood of churning occurs for customers who pay more than $65.86 a month. Considering that internet subscriptions has all features detected as important, there also may be opportunity for strategic bundling of internet service features in order to better serve existing customer needs. Note that we focus on the feature importance (absolute value). However, we can generate different representations in Fig. 1 by choosing different layers: Meaningful entities (e.g., aggregating the explained variance of all the features within an entity), missing values (e.g., potentially identify any structural issues in the data collection process), and irrelevant attributes (i.e., not relevant for our purpose) can help in feature selection. In each case, we provide more information to the decision makers to explain what the machine learning model is doing.

5 Discussion and Future Work

Our work contributes a method called *superimposition* to improve explainability of AI by using conceptual modeling. Although this is work-in-progress, it has potential to contribute to both conceptual modeling and machine leaning research and practice. The ML context expands the scope of conceptual modeling beyond traditional information systems development, process modeling, and database design [41]. The application of conceptual modeling to ML can create a bridge between the conceptual modeling and ML communities, foster interdisciplinary connections, and underscore the continued importance and value of conceptual modeling research [41].

The superimposition method can help increase ML explainability. The method makes it possible to indicate which entities contribute to an ML model's predictions and how these entities are related. It also allows the expression of the relationships between predictors and the target as the relationship between entities and the target. Such information is helpful for humans to make sense of phenomena; its absence from current XAI approaches inhibits their effectiveness. While the method cannot provide an explanation or justification why the model makes a certain prediction, it might aid humans in reasoning about the logic behind an ML model.

To better support our method, grammar extensions or new modeling grammars might be needed. For example, as complex ML models require translation of decision rules and path coefficients into conceptual modeling grammars, new conceptual modeling constructs may be needed to accommodate this. As we illustrate, grammars could allow color-coding of attributes included in the ML process as inputs and, perhaps, use one color to indicate a target attribute and a different color for attributes that cannot be used in a predictive model due to compliance to regulations (e.g., gender or race). Furthermore, the method can be applied to other representational artifacts (not just EER, as we showed here), and, for example, it could superimpose onto domain ontologies or semantic networks. We thus call on research to extend the method in response to the need to improve XAI.

We plan to experimentally evaluate the superimposition method by comparing it with current approaches to XAI based on feature weights as well as other approaches to explainability. We will expand the method by superimposing the outputs of more opaque models such as neural networks. Future work should study how to interpret abstract and complex engineered features using conceptual modeling, particularly when the underlying features are not from related or adjacent entities. Moreover, future work should extend the concept of superimposition beyond EER to more general ontologies.

References

1. Marr, B.: The top 10 AI and machine learning use cases everyone should know about. Forbes (2016)
2. Goodfellow, I., Bengio, Y., Courville, A.: Deep Learning. MIT Press, Cambridge (2016)
3. LeCun, Y., Bengio, Y., Hinton, G.: Deep learning. Nature **521**, 436–444 (2015)
4. Maass, W., Parsons, J., Purao, S., Storey, V.C., Woo, C.: Data-driven meets theory-driven research in the era of big data: opportunities and challenges for information systems research. J. Assoc. Inf. Syst. **19**, 1253–1273 (2018)
5. Chen, H., Chiang, R.H., Storey, V.C.: Business intelligence and analytics: from big data to big impact. MIS Q. **36**, 1165–1188 (2012)
6. Davenport, T., Harris, J.: Competing on Analytics: Updated, with a New Introduction: The New Science of Winning. Harvard Business Press, Cambridge (2017)
7. Khatri, V., Samuel, B.: Analytics for managerial work. Commun. ACM **62**, 100–108 (2019)
8. Akbilgic, O., Davis, R.L.: The promise of machine learning: when will it be delivered? J. Cardiac Fail. **25**, 484–485 (2019)
9. Bailetti, T., Gad, M., Shah, A.: Intrusion learning: an overview of an emergent discipline. Technol. Innov. Manage. Rev. **6** (2016)
10. Holzinger, A., Kieseberg, P., Weippl, E., Tjoa, A.M.: Current advances, trends and challenges of machine learning and knowledge extraction: from machine learning to explainable AI. In: Holzinger, A., Kieseberg, P., Tjoa, A.M., Weippl, E. (eds.) CD-MAKE 2018. LNCS, vol. 11015, pp. 1–8. Springer, Cham (2018). https://doi.org/10.1007/978-3-319-99740-7_1
11. Ransbotham, S., Kiron, D., Prentice, P.K.: Beyond the hype: the hard work behind analytics success. MIT Sloan Manage. Rev. **57**, 3–15 (2016)
12. Sun, T.Q., Medaglia, R.: Mapping the challenges of artificial intelligence in the public sector: evidence from public healthcare. Govern. Inf. Q. **36**, 368–383 (2019)
13. Castelvecchi, D.: Can we open the black box of AI? Nat. News **538**, 20 (2016)
14. Gunning, D.: Explainable artificial intelligence (XAI). Defense Advanced Research Projects agency. Defense Advanced Research Projects Agency (DARPA), nd Web, 2 (2016)
15. Gunning, D., Aha, D.W.: DARPA's explainable artificial intelligence program. AI Mag. **40**, 44–58 (2019)
16. Wachter, S., Mittelstadt, B., Floridi, L.: Why a right to explanation of automated decision-making does not exist in the general data protection regulation. Int. Data Priv. Law **7**, 76–99 (2017)
17. Bubenko, J.A.: On the role of 'understanding models' in conceptual schema design. In: Presented at the Fifth International Conference on Very Large Data Bases 1979 (1979)
18. Mylopoulos, J.: Information modeling in the time of the revolution. Inf. Syst. **23**, 127–155 (1998)

19. Pastor, O.: Conceptual modeling of life: beyond the homo sapiens. In: Comyn-Wattiau, I., Tanaka, K., Song, I.-Y., Yamamoto, S., Saeki, M. (eds.) ER 2016. LNCS, vol. 9974, pp. 18–31. Springer, Cham (2016). https://doi.org/10.1007/978-3-319-46397-1_2
20. Wand, Y., Weber, R.: Research commentary: information systems and conceptual modeling - a research agenda. Inf. Syst. Res. **13**, 363–376 (2002)
21. Lukyanenko, R., Castellanos, A., Parsons, J., Chiarini Tremblay, M., Storey, V.C.: Using conceptual modeling to support machine learning. In: Cappiello, C., Ruiz, M. (eds.) Information Systems Engineering in Responsible Information Systems, pp. 170–181. Springer International Publishing, Cham (2019). https://doi.org/10.1007/978-3-030-21297-1_15
22. Nalchigar, S., Yu, E.: Conceptual modeling for business analytics: a framework and potential benefits. Presented at the 2017 IEEE 19th Conference on Business Informatics (CBI) (2017)
23. Crevier, D.: AI: The Tumultuous History of the Search for Artificial Intelligence. Basic Books, New York (1993)
24. Cerf, V.G.: AI is not an excuse! Commun. ACM **62**, 7–9 (2019)
25. Ribeiro, M.T., Singh, S., Guestrin, C.: Why should i trust you?: explaining the predictions of any classifier. Presented at the Proceedings of the 22nd ACM SIGKDD International Conference on Knowledge Discovery and Data Mining (2016)
26. Lundberg, S.M., Lee, S.-I.: A unified approach to interpreting model predictions. In: Advances in Neural Information Processing Systems, pp. 4765–4774 (2017)
27. Martens, D., Provost, F.: Explaining data-driven document classifications. Mis Q. **38**, 73–100 (2014)
28. Rai, A.: Explainable AI: from black box to glass box. J. Acad. Mark. Sci. **48**, 137–141 (2020)
29. Henelius, A., Puolamäki, K., Boström, H., Asker, L., Papapetrou, P.: A peek into the black box: exploring classifiers by randomization. Data Min. Knowl. Discov. **28**, 1503–1529 (2014). https://doi.org/10.1007/s10618-014-0368-8
30. Harnad, S.: To cognize is to categorize: cognition is categorization. Presented at the, Amsterdam (2005)
31. Murphy, G.: The Big Book of Concepts. MIT Press, Cambridge (2004)
32. Palmeri, T.J., Blalock, C.: The role of background knowledge in speeded perceptual categorization. Cognition **77**, B45–B57 (2000)
33. Parsons, J., Wand, Y.: Extending classification principles from information modeling to other disciplines. J. Assoc. Inf. Syst. **14**, 2 (2012)
34. Collins, A.M., Quillian, M.R.: Retrieval time from semantic memory. J. Verbal Learn. Verbal Behav. **8**, 240–247 (1969)
35. Hutchinson, J., Lockhead, G.: Similarity as distance: a structural principle for semantic memory. J. Exp. Psychol. Hum. Learn. Mem. **3**, 660 (1977)
36. Burton-Jones, A., Weber, R.: Building conceptual modeling on the foundation of ontology. In: Computing handbook: information systems and information technology, Boca Raton, FL, USA, pp. 15.1–15.24 (2014)
37. Borgida, A.: Features of languages for the development of information systems at the conceptual level. IEEE Softw. **2**, 63 (1985)
38. Parsons, J., Wand, Y.: Choosing classes in conceptual modeling. Commun. ACM **40**, 63–69 (1997)
39. Sowa, J.F.: Top-level ontological categories. Int. J. Hum Comput Stud. **43**, 669–685 (1995)
40. Chen, P.: The entity-relationship model - toward a unified view of data. ACM Trans. Database Syst. **1**, 9–36 (1976)
41. Recker, J., Lukyanenko, R., Jabbari, M.A., Samuel, B.M., Castellanos, A.: From representation to mediation: a new agenda for conceptual modeling research in a digital world. MIS Q. (2021)

Evaluating Tree Explanation Methods for Anomaly Reasoning: A Case Study of SHAP TreeExplainer and TreeInterpreter

Pulkit Sharma[1(✉)], Shezan Rohinton Mirzan[1], Apurva Bhandari[1],
Anish Pimpley[2], Abhiram Eswaran[2], Soundar Srinivasan[2], and Liqun Shao[2(✉)]

[1] University of Massachusetts, Amherst, MA 01002, USA
{psharma,smirzan,apurvabhanda}@umass.edu
[2] Microsoft Corp., Cambridge, MA 02142, USA
{anpimple,abeswara,sosrini,lishao}@microsoft.com

Abstract. Understanding predictions made by Machine Learning models is critical in many applications. In this work, we investigate the performance of two methods for explaining tree-based models: 'Tree Interpreter (TI)' and 'SHapley Additive exPlanations TreeExplainer (SHAP-TE)'. Using a case study on detecting anomalies in job runtimes of applications that utilize cloud-computing platforms, we compare these approaches using a variety of metrics, including computation time, significance of attribution value, and explanation accuracy. We find that, although the SHAP-TE offers consistency guarantees over TI, at the cost of increased computation, consistency does not necessarily improve the explanation performance in our case study.

Keywords: Explanation · Feature attribution · Interventional evaluation · Tree interpreter · SHAP TreeExplainer

1 Introduction

Machine learning-based approaches have become popular in automatically detecting and predicting anomalies in a variety of applications. Anomaly Detection (AD) [2] has been applied to various domains, such as tracking anomalous events in traffic surveillance videos [18] and tracking irregular patterns in electrocardiographs of a patient [20]. AD has also become popular in the computing industry to detect system failures both in multi-server distributed systems [10] and in embedded systems [3]. A sister domain closely related to AD is Anomaly Reasoning (AR) that comprises delineating the causal factors associated with an anomaly. A robust system would not just predict the anomalous events, but also identify the root causes of a failure or an anomaly. In these applications, AR is crucial for an efficient analysis of faults, thereby reducing significantly, the time needed for manual investigation and the required computing resources.

© Springer Nature Switzerland AG 2020
G. Grossmann and S. Ram (Eds.): ER 2020 Workshops, LNCS 12584, pp. 35–45, 2020.
https://doi.org/10.1007/978-3-030-65847-2_4

Interpreting machine learning models correctly has been a challenging task. Although linear models are easy to interpret, they fail to generalize in real-world scenarios with predominantly non-linear behavior. This leads to the adoption of more accurate models at the cost of them being less interpretable. Hence, there has been a significant recent research emphasis on developing techniques that could add interpretability to these complex 'black-box models'.

The *LIME* [12] algorithm interprets the predictions of any given model by utilizing explainable analogues that are valid in "local" regions. Another popular apporach, *DeepLIFT* [15,16], is used for interpreting Neural Network-based models by assigning contribution scores to each neuron based on the difference in its activation to its "reference" activation. Other techniques [7,9,17] take a game-theoretic approach towards computing feature contributions to model explanations. Although, all three are primarily based on Shapley values [6], they calculate and further approximate the values differently to derive feature contributions.

In this paper, we compare the interpretation performance of two popular tree-explanation methods: the SHapley Additive exPlanation TreeExplainer (SHAP-TE) [8] for model-agnostic interpretations and the TreeInterpreter (TI) [13]. Specifically, we conduct a case study on the task of reasoning about anomalies in computing jobs that run in cloud platforms. An example of a recent effort in this domain is Griffon [14] - Microsoft's Reasoning infrastructure deployed on Azure clusters. SHAP-TE averages out contributions of each possible feature set to obtain the final feature attribution values. This helps in reducing the bias added to the computation of feature attribution values when only a specific ordering is considered. However, TI only considers one ordering of features depending on how the tree was formed. This makes TreeInterpreter as essentially an approximation of SHAP-TE. Hence, we examine the performance of SHAP-TE using Griffon's AD algorithm and investigate if the TreeInterpreter's approximation-based approach used in Griffon could be generalized to other datasets or scenarios.

We conduct experiments under a variety of conditions on the recently introduced PostgreSQL dataset [5] and compare the above methods across a variety of metrics. Our major contributions are summarized as follows:

- **Scale Comparison.** We compare, empirically, the scaling property of both methods, in terms of time-complexity, with respect to increasing data size and depth of trees.
- **Performance Comparison.** We analyze their trade-offs and provide a novel analysis of the two methods in ranking features according to their contributions and attribution accuracy, and also experimentally evaluate the variance among the contribution values generated by the two methods to measure the significance of produced ordering of FAs[1].

---

[1] *Feature Attribution* (FA) is defined as the contribution each independent variable or a "feature" made to the final prediction of a model.

– **Critique of TI and SHAP-TE.** We investigate whether the *consistency*[2] property of SHAP-TE is crucial to making it a preferred method over TI in this domain on publicly available data, which would facilitate replication by the research community.

2   Background Work

Unlike linear models, Decision Tree models cannot be represented as sum of linear contributions of each features for the whole model. Hence, they are difficult to interpret on the model level. However, individual predictions of a decision tree can be explained by decomposing the decision path into one component per feature. One can track a decision by traversing the tree and explain a prediction (y) by the additive contributions at each decision node as,

$$y = \text{bias} + \sum_{m=1}^{M} \text{feature\_contribution}\{m, x\} \tag{1}$$

where bias is the contribution of root node and feature_contribution$\{m, x\}$ is the contribution of feature m in predicting the outcome corresponding to an input x. Equation (1) forms the basis of TI Package [13], which is available for interpreting scikit-learn's decision tree and random forest predictions.

SHAP-TE [8] is another tree-based FAM[3] that uses Shapley values from game theory to make tree-based models interpretable. The feature values of an input data instance act as players in a coalition. These values essentially distribute the prediction result among different features. SHapley Additive exPlanation (SHAP) [9] value for a particular feature is the weighted average of all the marginal contributions to the prediction over all possible combinations of features. Using SHAP is inherently beneficial in terms of *consistency*. From [9], a FAM is consistent if a feature's attribution value does not decrease on increasing the true impact of that feature in the model.

Griffon [14], introduced in Sect. 1, uses the notion of **delta feature contribution** between two different instances of a job type to predict features that impacted the most to the difference in their runtimes. FA values for both the jobs are simply subtracted to compute how much each feature contributes to the deviation in the predictions for both jobs.

Work on the evaluation of Causal Models in [5] discusses the design of interventional and observational data to analyze the performance of model explanation paradigms. Motivated by their approach, we also adopt the postgreSQL data presented in their work in the experiments presented in this paper. This dataset is a collection of SQL queries submitted to stackoverflow server's database (large-scale software system) that enables the experimenter to run the same experiment

---

[2] *See Sect. 2 for the definition of consistency.*
[3] *Feature Attribution Method* (FAM), referred to as the explanation method that calculates FAs to interpret each prediction generated by a model.

multiple times under different, controlled conditions. The conditions are determined by setting few key configuration parameters, called **treatment** variables. The effect of change in one configuration is observed in the **output** variables such as Runtime. Using background, domain knowledge, the dependence between the runtime and the "treatment" variables is established. The features that describe a job are termed as **covariates**. Inspired by this work, we adopt the interventional data setting within the scope of Griffon; design of these experiments is discussed in Sect. 4.

3   Evaluation Approach

In order to group similar data points together, we split the entire data set into smaller subgroups termed as *templates*. A template is a group of data points in which the *covariate* input features are kept nearly constant[4] while the *treatment* feature variables are allowed to change for each data point. This approach allows us to easily establish a relationship between the prediction and the treatment feature variable for any two datapoints belonging to the same template. Hence, if we choose a pair of datapoints from a template such that both differ with respect to some m treatment feature variables, then the deviation in their predictions can be easily attributed to these m features.

For the case of anomaly detection, we consider pairs of data points from a particular template. FAM will calculate FA values for both these data points. These obtained FA values can then be used to reason about the output. In order to explain the difference in their predictions, we compute the difference in the computed FA values (See Fig. 1). This is motivated from the delta feature contribution technique used in Griffon. Using the obtained delta feature contributions, we create an ordered list that ranks all the features from the most important to the least important feature. From this list of ranked features, we compute a Rank Biased overlap (RBO) metric [19][5] to measure the similarity of ranked results produced by both the attribution methods. Motivated by the differences in RBO values observed Table 1, we further investigate the differences brought out by lower RBO values in terms of *attribution accuracy*. We define attribution accuracy as the fraction of times a FAM is able to correctly identify the cause of an anomaly. To assess the trade-off between using SHAP-TE and TI, we measure the attribution accuracy on interventional PostgreSQL data set using proposed Implicit and Explicit Interventional Measures.

3.1   Implicit Interventional Measure

We use the "Interventional Data" setup proposed by [5] to establish the attribution accuracy of a particular method of explanation. We refer to this approach as

---

[4] Some of the covariate variables in postgreSQL dataset are continuous, which when grouped reduces the number of data points per cluster.

[5] RBO implementation: https://github.com/changyaochen/rbo.

an "Implicit Interventional approach" due to the presence of pre-existing treatment variables in our evaluation data and contrast it with a manually manipulated "Explicit Interventional approach" that we will introduce in Sect. 3.2.

We first divide the data set into a set of templates and then choose a pair of data points from within each template. In this pair, one point acts as an anomaly, while the other as the base line. We obtain a ranked feature list after processing this pair of points through an explanation method. The attribution is deemed to be correct, if the top attributed feature matches the treatment variable (see Sect. 4). This gives us the Top-1 measure of attribution accuracy. Similarly by considering the first k elements of the ranked list, we obtain the Top-k attribution accuracy.

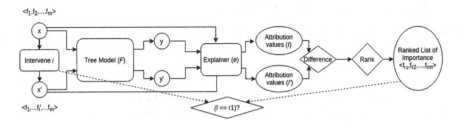

Fig. 1. Overview of the proposed evaluation approach. $(\mathbf{x}, \mathbf{y})$ and $(\mathbf{x}', \mathbf{y}')$ are the input, output pairs for original and intervened data points, respectively. Explainer ($\mathbf{e}$) refers to one of the explanation methods considered in our work and produces the FA values corresponding to a prediction. A ranked list is obtained based on their differences and then check whether the top attributed feature is the same as the intervened one.

3.2 Explicit Interventional Measure

This measure helps us in evaluating correctness of each explanation method irrespective of deployment. We design this experiment by manually intervening in the data set to change the value of a treatment variable. Let d be the dimension of feature space in data set and i represent the index of treatment variable that was intervened. When we change the ith index for a data point x, we obtain a new intervened point, x' (Shown in Fig. 1). Let $e(\cdot, F)$ represent the operator to produce FA values for a data point under a trained Random Forest model F. The most important feature is then considered to be the one with highest difference in attribution value between the original and manually-intervened data point. Here, our assumption is that this feature should be the same as the manually- or explicitly-intervened feature i.

$$i = \operatorname{argmax} |e(\boldsymbol{x}', F) - e(\boldsymbol{x}, F)| \tag{2}$$

Every data point that satisfies the above relation for a particular explanation method, contributes as a positive sample for that explanation method. For PostgreSQL data set used in our experiments described in Sect. 4, we apply the following two interventions on all the data points for all three treatment variables,

$$x_i \leftarrow (x_i \pm 1) \mod 3 \tag{3}$$

Since the range of each treatment variable is 0–2, the above operation covers the domain of each variable. As discussed earlier, change in the values of treatment variables would affect the run-time of the job as these variables correspond to system settings while running a query. Results for this experiment are discussed in Sect. 4.5.

4 Experiments and Results

4.1 Experiment and Data Settings

We perform our experiments on the PostgreSQL[6] data set that is a sample of the data from user generated queries on Stack Overflow[7]. It contains the execution information for $11,252$ queries run corresponding to $90,016$ different covariate-treatment combinations on Postgres. Treatment variables for this data set are three system parameters, namely (i) **MemoryLevel:** the amount of system memory available, (ii) **IndexLevel:** the type of indexing used for accessing a query in database and (iii) **PageCost:** the type of disk page access. Various outputs of each query are recorded. We choose query *Runtime* output to analyse our results.

The PostgreSQL dataset is a large dataset with nearly 1.5 million data points. Training a Random Forest model on the complete data generates a large model and this in turn increases the time for computing feature attributions, as explained in Sect. 4.2. To keep computation times tractable, we sample a subset from the entire data set ensuring that these samples preserve most of the unique samples in the original data set. After sampling, we have about $70,000$ data points, which are further sub-sampled into 60%–20%–20% *train-val-test* splits. We run our experiments on a cluster system with Xeon E5-2680 v4 @ 2.40 GHz processor and 128 GB of RAM.

SHAP-TE and TI can be compared using any tree-based models including Decision Trees, GBMs, and Random Forest. However, among these options, Random Forest models have empirically been shown to have higher accuracy, especially for high-dimensional data in most real world scenarios [1]. Apart from Griffon, other anomaly detection research [4,11] also use Random Forests as their base model. Hence, we choose to use Random Forest for comparing results.

4.2 Runtime Comparison

We train a Random Forest Regression model to predict job runtime in milliseconds with a hyper-parameter setting of 200 estimators and a maximum depth 20.

---

[6] Dataset can be found at https://groups.cs.umass.edu/kdl/causal-eval-data.

[7] This data is collected in the work by [5].

As running times are generally log-normally distributed, we use *logarithm* of Runtime as the output target.

With large number of jobs in a given computing cluster, the ability to detect and interpret anomalies in real time becomes crucial. SHAP-TE and TI both have an amortized computation-time complexity of $\mathcal{O}(TLD^2)$ where T is the number of individual estimators, L is the maximum number of leaves in any tree and D is the maximum depth of any tree. Although the amortized time complexity is the same for both, their practical running times differ significantly.

First, we compare the scaling of FAM computation time per data instance. We observe that TI scales at 0.058 s per data instance while SHAP-TE takes 3.44 s per data instance which is significantly higher. Second, red lines in Fig. 2 show the scaling of both methods with the depth of tree parameter of the Random Forest. We observe that both methods follow a square dependence, but SHAP-TE again scales worse that TI. The reason is that SHAP-TE averages out the contributions for each decision path while TI just considers the one decision path resulting in shorter computation time. This indicates that in a practical deployment scenario with large number of data cases and larger tree depth, TI can be more efficient compared to the SHAP-TE, in terms of computation times.

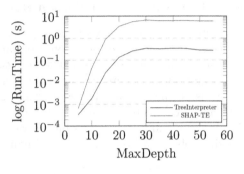

Fig. 2. Comparison of running time vs MaxDepth. SHAP-TE scales much faster than TreeInterpreter

4.3   Rank List Similarity

We now report results using the rank biased overlap (RBO) measure to bring out the difference in the feature rankings between the two methods. RBO measures the set overlap of top selected elements in two lists. We run SHAP-TE and TI on the entire test set and obtain a list of FAs corresponding to each test point. We then compute the RBO corresponding to the ranked feature list of each test data point. Since the top ranked features are more relevant in explaining the output, we report RBO by considering different number of top elements from each ranked list. Table 1 shows the median RBO values for different values of k. As observed, SHAP-TE and TI begin to differ significantly in rankings if we consider Top-3 and Top-5 ranked features. A median value of 0.61 implies that for more than 50% of the data points, only 1 feature out of top 3 is the same for these methods. This motivates us to investigate the differences in their behaviour in more detail, as described below.

Table 1. Median Rank biased Overlap values of SHAP-TE and TI.

k	RBO
All	0.77
Top-5	0.65
Top-3	0.61

Table 2. Median Variance of attribution values on test set.

k	SHAP-TE	TI
All	4.9×10^{-4}	6.8×10^{-4}
Top-5	5.4×10^{-4}	7.8×10^{-4}
Top-3	3.6×10^{-4}	5.6×10^{-4}

4.4 Significance of Attribution Ranking

Since we are using the FA values to generate an ordered ranking of features, it is necessary to note the the amount of variation in attribution values to interpret the significance of obtained orderings. Higher variance in attribution values would imply a more significant ordering of features.[8] For each data point, we measure the variance in the magnitude of Top k FA values and report the median for complete data set. From Table 2, we observe that TI captures nearly 50% more variance in the attribution values than SHAP-TE. This implies that rankings obtained from TI are more significant than from SHAP-TE.

4.5 Attribution Accuracy: How Correctly Are the Right Features Attributed

Figure 1 describes the outline of experiment to evaluate the correctness of feature attribution. To establish feature association, we apply SHAP-TE and TI to the trained Random Forest model to produce FA values of each feature for every test data point. These values represent the contribution of each feature in producing an output. If we have two data points which are almost same, except for changes across a few feature values, we expect to see change in the output to be attributed to these differing features. As proposed by Griffon [14], contribution of features for deviation in outputs can be computed by taking a difference of FA values.

Implicit Interventional Measure. In this scenario, we consider all the data points where only one of the treatment variable differs and all other variables including covariates remain the same. We believe this subset of data essentially emulates the real world scenario where one system parameter is controlled and remaining query variables are the same.

From the results in Table 3, we see that TI outperforms SHAP-TE for 2 out of 3 Treatment variables for both Top-1 and Top-3 measures. It is worth noting that the performance of SHAP-TE improves significantly from Top-1 to Top-3. This is because SHAP-TE always prefers *IndexLevel* over the other two treatment variables However, *PageCost* or *MemoryLevel* do appear in the attributions at Rank 2 or 3.

---

[8] For eg, consider 2 lists of attribution values $S_1 = [1, 1.1, 1.3]$ and $S_2 = [1, 3, 5]$. The ranking obtained from values in S_2 is more reliable than S_1.

Table 3. Implicit Interventional Attribution Accuracy (S-TE stands for SHAP-TE).

Treatment	Top-1		Top-3	
	S-TE	TI	S-TE	TI
IndexLevel	85%	68%	94%	91%
PageCost	46%	82%	84%	99%
MemoryLevel	62%	79%	86%	98%
Average	**64%**	**76%**	**88%**	**96%**

Table 4. Explicit Intervention Attribution Accuracy (S-TE stands for SHAP-TE).

Treatment	Top-1		Top-3	
	S-TE	TI	S-TE	TI
IndexLevel	81%	80%	92%	97%
PageCost	55%	82%	83%	96%
MemoryLevel	46%	83%	84%	97%
Average	**61%**	**82%**	**86%**	**97%**

Explicit Interventional Measure. This measure enables us to use the whole test set for evaluating performance for each treatment variable. We compute the explicit interventional attribution accuracy of both FAMs on the whole test set. Table 3 shows attribution accuracy measure when the true feature was among the top-1 or top-3 attributed features. We observe that average attribution accuracy of TI is better than that of SHAP-TE in both cases. Even for individual treatment variables, TI is significantly better in all cases except for Top-1 in *IndexLevel* (Table 4).

5   Conclusion

We evaluated two prominent feature attribution methods for explaining tree-based models. The results show that the two methods differ in various aspects of efficacy and efficiency. In our case study, we observe that the amount of time that SHAP-TE takes to compute attribution values is nearly **60×** higher than that of TI. This could be a potential constraint in certain large-scale computing applications.

We also compared the performance accuracy of these methods using two different interventional approaches and observe that, on average, TI outperforms SHAP-TE. Based on these results, we conclude that despite the consistency guarantees, SHAP-TE does not provide benefits, in terms of attribution accuracy, in our case study of explaining job anomalies in cloud-computing applications. In addition, we have found that using TI provides high quality results at a lower computational footprint.

We invite the research community to build on our findings. The code used for obtaining these results is available publicly[9].

Acknowledgements. We thank our mentors, Javier Burroni and Prof. Andrew McCallum, for their guidance. We also thank Minsoo Thigpen for organizational support, as well as Scott Lundberg for providing insightful suggestions on a earlier draft. Finally, we thank anonymous reviewers for their feedback.

---

[9] https://github.com/sharmapulkit/TreeInterpretability_AnomalyExplanation.

References

1. Caruana, R., Karampatziakis, N., Yessenalina, A.: An empirical evaluation of supervised learning in high dimensions. In: Proceedings of the 25th International Conference on Machine Learning, ICML 2008, pp. 96–103 (2008)
2. Chandola, V., Banerjee, A., Kumar, V.: Anomaly detection: a survey. ACM Comput. Surv. **41**, 1–58 (2009)
3. Cuzzocrea, A., Mumolo, E., Cecolin, R.: Runtime anomaly detection in embedded systems by binary tracing and hidden Markov models. In 2015 IEEE 39th Annual Computer Software and Applications Conference, vol. 2, pp. 15–22 (2015)
4. Duque Anton, S., Sinha, S., Schotten, H.: Anomaly-based intrusion detection in industrial data with SVM and random forests, pp. 1–6 (2019)
5. Gentzel, A., Garant, D., Jensen, D.: The case for evaluating causal models using interventional measures and empirical data. In: Wallach, H., Larochelle, H., Beygelzimer, A., d'Alché-Buc, F., Fox, E., Garnett, R. (eds.) Advances in Neural Information Processing Systems, vol. 32, pp. 11722–11732. Curran Associates Inc. (2019)
6. Kuhn, H.W., Tucker, A.W.: Contributions to the Theory of Games, vol. 2. Princeton University Press, Princeton (1953)
7. Lipovetsky, S., Conklin, M.: Analysis of regression in game theory approach. Appl. Stochast. Models Bus. Ind. **17**, 319–330 (2001)
8. Lundberg, S.M., et al.: From local explanations to global understanding with explainable AI for trees. Nat. Mach. Intell. **2**(1), 2522–5839 (2020)
9. Lundberg, S.M., Lee, S.-I.: A unified approach to interpreting model predictions. In: Advances in Neural Information Processing Systems, vol. 30 (2017)
10. Peiris, M., Hill, J.H., Thelin, J., Bykov, S., Kliot, G., Konig, C.: PAD: performance anomaly detection in multi-server distributed systems. In: 2014 IEEE 7th International Conference on Cloud Computing, pp. 769–776 (2014)
11. Primartha, R., Tama, B.A.: Anomaly detection using random forest: a performance revisited. In: 2017 International Conference on Data and Software Engineering (ICoDSE), pp. 1–6 (2017)
12. Ribeiro, M.T., Singh, S., Guestrin, C.: "why should I trust you?": explaining the predictions of any classifier. In: Proceedings of the 22nd ACM SIGKDD International Conference on Knowledge Discovery and Data Mining, San Francisco, CA, USA, 13–17 August 2016, pp. 1135–1144 (2016)
13. Saabas, A.: Treeinterpreter. https://github.com/andosa/treeinterpreter
14. Shao, L., et al.: Griffon. In: Proceedings of the ACM Symposium on Cloud Computing - SoCC 2019 (2019)
15. Shrikumar, A., Greenside, P., Kundaje, A.: Learning important features through propagating activation differences. CoRR abs/1704.02685 (2017)
16. Shrikumar, A., Greenside, P., Shcherbina, A., Kundaje, A.: Not just a black box: learning important features through propagating activation differences. CoRR abs/1605.01713 (2016)
17. Štrumbelj, E., Kononenko, I.: Explaining prediction models and individual predictions with feature contributions. Knowl. Inf. Syst. **41**, 647–665 (2013)
18. Sultani, W., Chen, C., Shah, M.: Real-world anomaly detection in surveillance videos. In: The IEEE Conference on Computer Vision and Pattern Recognition (2018)

19. Webber, W., Moffat, A., Zobel, J.: A similarity measure for indefinite rankings. ACM Trans. Inf. Syst. **28**, 4 (2010)
20. Wulsin, D., Blanco, J., Mani, R., Litt, B.: Semi-supervised anomaly detection for EEG waveforms using deep belief nets. In: 2010 Ninth International Conference on Machine Learning and Applications, pp. 436–441 (2010)

Conceptual Modeling for Life Sciences (CMLS) 2020

Preface

Anna Bernascon[1] ⓘ, Arif Canakoglu[1] ⓘ, Ana León Palacio[2] ⓘ,
and José Fabián Reyes Román[2] ⓘ

[1] Dipartimento di Elettronica, Informazione e Bioingegneria, Politecnico
di Milano, 20133 Milano, Italy
{anna.bernasconi,arif.canakoglu}@polimi.it
[2] PROS Research Center, Universitat Politécnica de Valéncia, Camino de
Vera s/n, 46022 Valencia, Spain
{aleon,jreyes}@pros.upv.es

The recent advances in unraveling the secrets of human conditions and diseases have encouraged new paradigms for their prevention, diagnosis, and treatment. As the information is increasing at an unprecedented rate, it directly impacts the design and future development of information and data management pipelines; thus, new ways of processing data, information, and knowledge in health care environments are strongly needed.

The International Workshop on Conceptual Modeling for Life Sciences (CMLS) was held in 2020 for the first time. Its objective is to be, both, a starting meeting point for Information Systems (IS), Conceptual Modeling (CM), and Data Management (DM) researchers working on health care and life science problems, and an opportunity to share, discuss, and find new approaches to improve promising fields, with a special focus on Genomic Data Management – how to use the information from the genome to better understand biological and clinical features – and Precision Medicine – giving each patient an individualized treatment by understanding the peculiar aspects of the disease. From the precise ontological characterization of the components involved in complex biological systems, to the modeling of the operational processes and decision support methods used in the diagnosis and prevention of disease, the joined research communities of IS, CM, and DM have an important role to play; they must help in providing feasible solutions for a high-quality and efficient health care.

This first edition of CMLS has attracted high quality submissions centered around the modeling of data, systems, and processes of the life sciences domain. Six papers were selected after a blind review process that involved at least two experts from the field for each submission. All of them provide significant insights related to the problem under investigation, and they confirm an interesting technical program to stimulate discussion, which is complemented with an invited keynote by Paolo Missier on workflow representation for genomic variants data. We expect a growing interest in this area in the coming years; this was one of the motivations for planning the workshop in conjunction with the ER 2020 conference.

Acknowledgements. We would like to express our gratitude to Stefano Ceri and Oscar Pastor who suggested the organization of this workshop and shared important insights along the way. We also thank the Program Committee members for their hard work in reviewing papers, the authors for submitting their works, and the ER 2020 Organizing

Committee for supporting our workshop. We also thank ER 2020 workshop chairs Georg Grossmann and Sudha Ram for their direction and guidance. CMLS 2020 was organized within the framework of the projects ERC Advanced Grant 693174 "data-driven Genomic Computing" and DataMe – Spanish State Research Agency (TIN2016-80811-P).

The Importance of the Temporal Dimension in Identifying Relevant Genomic Variants: A Case Study

Mireia Costa$^{(\boxtimes)}$, Ana León, and Óscar Pastor

Universitat Politècnica de València, 46022 Valencia, Spain
micossan@etsii.upv.es, {aleon,opastor}@pros.upv.es

Abstract. The identification of relevant genomic variants is key for providing a more reliable and precise diagnosis of diseases with a known genetic component. Nevertheless, this is a complex and time-consuming process that is affected by multiple factors such as the quality of the information and the heterogeneity of the data sources. Another characteristic of genomic knowledge is its evolution, which may cause the number of known relevant variants to change over time. This forces the experts to repeat the process multiple times to keep the information and the affected diagnosis correctly updated. For a particular disease, new relevant variants can be identified, while old ones may not be as significant as initially considered. The SILE method aims to systematize and facilitate the variant identification process, reducing the time required for the analysis and allowing the experts to repeat it as many times as needed in order to keep up to date with new knowledge. To highlight the importance of the temporal dimension and the need for such methods, SILE has been applied to a case study at two different time points to compare how the number of variants initially considered to be relevant has evolved during a short period of time. The results obtained demonstrate the need for considering the temporal dimension in the development of methods such as SILE in order to provide a more accurate and up-to-date genetic diagnosis.

Keywords: Information systems · SILE method · Case study

1 Introduction

The identification of relevant genomic variants is key for providing a more reliable and precise diagnosis of diseases with a known genetic component such as Early Onset Alzheimer's Disease (EOAD) [1], which was selected as a case study. Nevertheless, this is a complex and time-consuming process that is affected by multiple factors such as the quality of the information and the heterogeneity of the data sources.

The information related to the genomic variants and their role in the development of the disease is stored in specialized databases and repositories such as ClinVar [2], Ensembl [3], GWAS Catalog [4], and SNPedia [5]. In order to select the clinically actionable variants that are required to provide a genetic diagnosis from these data sources, the valuable information must be adequately identified, integrated, analyzed,

G. Grossmann and S. Ram (Eds.): ER 2020 Workshops, LNCS 12584, pp. 51–60, 2020.
https://doi.org/10.1007/978-3-030-65847-2_5

and interpreted. In clinical care and precision medicine, clinically actionable variants are changes in DNA that are clinically significant (commonly pathogenic, likely pathogenic, and risk factors) and that can be acted upon by health care providers (actionable) with their patients. However, this is a complex and time-consuming process for two main reasons. First, not all the information is valid to be applied in a clinical domain due to the following: the absence of information about its clinical relevance; the presence of discrepancies (conflicts) between experts when interpreting the clinical significance of the variants (e.g., one expert interprets the variant as pathogenic and other as benign); the absence of specification of the criteria (assertion criteria) used to make the interpretation (e.g., the thresholds used for allele frequencies or statistical measures; the type of studies considered, etc.); and the presence of outdated information in the genomic repositories. Second, the information associated with genomic variants is dynamic and in constant growth associated to the accumulated human genome knowledge that is under constant evolution which means that the number of known relevant genomic variants may change over time.

Because of these problems, it is necessary to define standardized processes for systematizing the relevant genomic variant selection. However, after doing a thorough review of the literature, we did not find any systematic approach for selecting the relevant variants from diverse, heterogenous databases and repositories. Some interesting works are oriented to evaluating the reliability of the variant interpretation [6–8], but none of them evaluates the quality of the information that can be obtained from the stored data. To meet these needs, the Research Center on Software Production Methods (PROS) from the Universitat Politècnica de València has developed the SILE method [9], which assists the experts in the identification process and allows the process to be repeated as many time as needed, thus reducing the effort required. The SILE method is explained in further detail in Sect. 2.

The SILE method provides a solution to the problem of identifying relevant genomic variants. However, even when using the same data sources, the application of SILE at different time points may produce different results, which is cumbersome when talking about information that is to be used in clinical, genome-based diagnosis. In this paper, we assess the impact of the temporal dimension of the genomic data, by applying the SILE method to a specific case study (EOAD) at two different time points. As is highlighted throughout the paper, confirming the fact that results change over time has two important implications: i) the importance of performing a continuous assessment of what is to be considered relevant information; and ii) the importance of tracking what information is changing over time in order to delimit how this can affect clinical reports that were done in the past.

The paper is structured as follows: after the introduction, Sect. 2 presents the SILE method as the methodological background. In Sect. 3, the workflow is applied to the EOAD case at two different time points. Finally, Sect. 4 discusses conclusions and future work.

2 Methodological Background: The SILE Method

The PROS R&D center has developed the SILE method [9] in order to define a strategy to systematize the process of identifying genomic variants with sufficient evidence and quality to be applied in the clinical field. The SILE method makes it possible to efficiently manage genomic data, which allows experts to easily identify a valuable and useful set of relevant genomic variants for diagnostic purposes. Thus, thanks to the SILE method, the experts can make a faster and more accurate genomic diagnosis, which also benefits the patients.

The name of the SILE method refers to the four stages that are necessary to achieve the proposed objective (see Fig. 1):

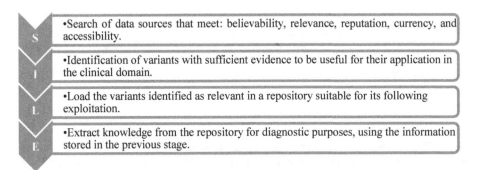

Fig. 1. Stages of SILE method

The goal of the identification stage of the SILE method is to obtain quality results for any disease by determining clinically significant variants. Figure 2 shows the different steps that make up the workflow used for the identification of those relevant variants.

This workflow is made up of 13 Steps (F1 to F13). Steps F1 and F2 evaluate the clinical significance of the variants. Specifically, Step F1 evaluates whether the clinical significance of the variant has been interpreted, and Step F2 evaluates if the significance is clinically relevant (pathogenic, likely pathogenic, or risk factor). These variants are known as "clinically actionable" because they can be used to suggest medical recommendations for health care.

Steps F3 and F7 are introduced to select the variants according to the relevance of the source where the interpretation comes from. First, Step F3 checks whether the source is a practice guideline or if the interpretation has been done by an expert panel (the most trustworthy type of sources); the variants with clinically actionable significance that come from these sources will be classified as Accepted with Strong Evidence. Second, to assess other levels of relevance or reputation, Step F7 checks the expertise of the experts that perform the interpretation, i.e., if the expert has at least 200 submissions in the database. Experts that have more experience in this task are considered to be more reliable.

Step F4 checks if the gene considered by the experts to be affected by the variant (e.g., located in a coding region or in a regulatory region) is a gene of interest for the disease (i.e., with a documented association to the development of the disease). It is important to remark that the consideration of a gene as being affected by a variant is information that is provided by the experts that perform the interpretation based on their expertise in the field.

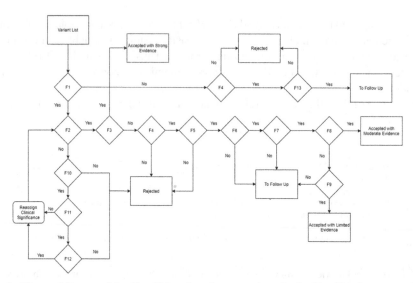

Fig. 2. The workflow used for identifying the relevant variants in the identification stage of the SILE method. Diamonds represent the steps where the quality of each variant is evaluated and have two different outputs (the variants that pass and those that do not). Rectangles indicate inputs and outputs from the workflow (list of variants). Rounded rectangles indicate actions to be taken.

The analysis continues with Step F5, which evaluates whether the method used to assess the association of the variant with the development of the disease is from clinical testing. This means that the variants have been found in studies that involve the analysis of samples coming from patients that are affected by the disease.

Steps F6 and F8 evaluate the assertion criteria (the criteria used by the expert to assign the variant its clinical significance). First, Step F6 checks if the assertion criteria are provided. Second, Step F8 checks if the American College of Medical Genomics/Association for Molecular Pathology (ACMG/AMP) guidelines are the assertion criteria used. As an internationally accepted, widely used criteria, the use of ACMG/AMP guidelines is a guarantee of the interpretation's quality. If Step F8 is fulfilled (along with Steps F2-F4-F5-F6-F7), the variant will be classified as Accepted with Moderate Evidence.

If Step F8 is not fulfilled, Step F9 evaluates if the last interpretation of the clinical significance was made in the last three years, ensuring that even when the criteria used are not the desirable ones, at least the information is updated. If this step fulfilled the variant will be classified as Accepted with Limited Evidence; otherwise, the variant will be classified as Rejected.

Steps F10 to F12 evaluate the presence of conflicts among experts regarding the clinical significance assigned to the variant. When there are conflicts, databases such as ClinVar assign the term "conflicting interpretation" as clinical significance. Nevertheless, a variant can be pathogenic for one disease and benign for another. This is not considered by ClinVar when assigning conflicts, which can lead to misclassifications. To ensure that no relevant variant is incorrectly rejected, Steps F10 to F12 verify whether there is a real conflict in a variant's clinical significance. First, Step F10 selects the variant with conflictive interpretations. Then, Step F11 evaluates whether the conflicts affect the same phenotype. If the conflict occurs in the same phenotype, Step F12 evaluates if there is agreement among at least 75% of the experts. If so, the interpretation of the variant will be reassigned.

Finally, there is an evaluation (Steps F4 and F13) of the variants that do not have an associated clinical significance because sometimes they could have information that supports their relationship with the disease. Step F13 analyzes the relevance of the related studies (in terms of their statistical relevance), and Step F4 analyzes whether the variants are located in a gene of interest, as explained above. If these steps are fulfilled, the variant will be classified as "To Follow Up", which is a classification given to the variants that do not have enough quality to be considered relevant right now but that could be relevant in the near future.

As mentioned above, depending on the criteria fulfilled by the variants, they can be classified into five different types: Rejected, To Follow Up, Accepted with Strong Evidence, Accepted with Moderate Evidence, and Accepted with Limited Evidence.

3   Case Study: Variant Identification in Early Onset Alzheimer's Disease

Alzheimer's disease (AD) is the most common type of dementia in the elderly [10], but a small percentage (2–10% of all cases of AD) appears in patients younger than 65 years old [11]. That form of the disease is known as Early Onset Alzheimer's Disease (EOAD).

Since the most significant factor for the development of this disease is the genetic component (92–100% of heritability) [1], determining relevant genomic variants is important to be able to achieve a more reliable and precise diagnosis. Nevertheless, due to the large amount of information and its heterogeneity, determining these variants is not easy. The data quality problems require the use of methods like SILE to simplify the identification of relevant variants.

The identification starts with a list of variants that are initially related to EOAD. These variants have been extracted from ClinVar [2], which is a well-known and widely used database. Clinvar has been chosen as the source of information because: i) it makes a previous validation of all of the information that is submitted into the database (as a previous verification of the information's quality); ii) it is continuously updated (at least once a month); and iii) it fulfills all of the requirements defined in the Search Stage of the SILE method (believability, relevance, reputation, currency, and accessibility) [12, 13].

In this case study, we have obtained and compared the results of the SILE method application at two different time points. As time points, we have selected May 18, 2020 and July 9, 2020 to determine whether different results are obtained even considering such a short amount of time. Our intention was to confirm that using such a minimum distance between the time points was sufficient to get results that are significant enough to allow us to make a valuable comparison. The objective was to determine how fast knowledge evolves and to evaluate the impact of the temporal dimension in providing accurate and reliable genomic diagnosis.

The list of variants to be analyzed was obtained by using the following query in the ClinVar website:

((alzheimer[Disease/Phenotype] AND "early onset" [Disease/Phenotype])) OR ((alzheimer[Disease/Phenotype] AND ("type 1" [Disease/Phenotype] OR "type 3"[Disease/Phenotype] OR "type 4" [Disease/Phenotype]))

Only the variants related to Early Onset Alzheimer's Disease and the corresponding Alzheimer's subtypes (type 1, type 3, and type 4) were selected with the query. The results were downloaded in tabular format. By repeating the same process, in July 40 new variants associated with the disease have been added to the database, resulting in 316 variants. These first results clearly indicate that genomic information increases rapidly and changes over time.

A detailed analysis of the differences between the two lists of variants shows the number of variants grouped by clinical significance of both time points (Fig. 3).

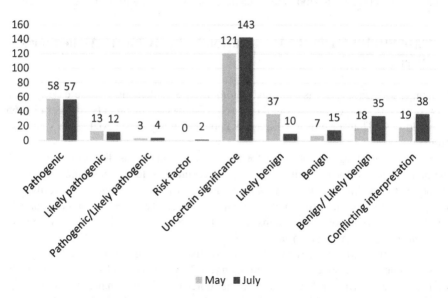

Fig. 3. Number of variants grouped by clinical significance

Figure 3 shows the differences between the distribution of the variants between May and July and the number of variants (grouped by their clinical significance) in the selected time points. First, one Pathogenic variant (rs63750450) is missing in July compared to May. Upon further analysis, we noticed that this variant is classified in July as pathogenic/likely pathogenic because a new submission that interprets the variant as likely pathogenic led to this change in clinical significance. The remaining 57 variants did not change in July since May. The case of this pathogenic variant is also a justification for the increase in pathogenic/likely pathogenic variants. There were no other changes on the pathogenic/likely pathogenic list of variants in July with respect to May. Second, when comparing the lists of likely pathogenic variants, we found that a likely pathogenic variant (rs1566630791) was also missing in July. In this case, the variant changed its clinical significance to conflicting interpretation. The other 12 variants remain unchanged in May and July.

Another difference to take into consideration is the two new risk factor variants. These two variants (rs1800562 and rs547447016) were classified in May as conflicting interpretation, but by July their clinical significance had changed to risk factor.

Finally, the main difference between the two lists is in benign, likely benign, benign/likely benign, and conflicting interpretation variants. In the benign/likely benign and the benign variants there are differences because new variants have appeared. In likely benign variants, the differences can mostly be justified as being misclassified as conflicting interpretation. The differences found in likely benign variants and conflicting interpretation variants are interrelated.

All of these differences are a clear sign that the knowledge in the genetic domain evolves and grows quickly. It is also an indicator that the temporal dimension could have an important impact on the number of variants considered to be relevant. Let us see the results of the identification stage in order to study the impact of this temporal dimension.

In the first workflow steps, Steps (F1–F2), the clinically actionable variants (pathogenic, likely pathogenic, pathogenic/likely pathogenic, and risk factor) are selected. The results presented in Fig. 3. show that 74 variants in May and 75 variants in July would pass the filters. But these results do not take into account the variants that are incorrectly classified as conflicting interpretation, which is something that commonly occurs in databases and repositories such as ClinVar.

When analyzing the conflicting interpretation variants in Steps F10 to F12, we noticed that some clinically actionable variants had been misclassified as conflicting interpretation. Specifically, 4 variants in May and 3 variants in July that ClinVar classifies as conflicting interpretation were considered as clinically actionable for the studied phenotype. In the two cases, the misclassification of the variants is explained by the way in which ClinVar treats the conflicts. This supports the need for a careful review of the interpretations to identify these situations. When added to those that had been correctly classified the misclassified variants, yield 78 variants from May and 78 variants from July which fulfills the requirements of Step F2.

The misclassification as conflicting interpretation also explains the great increase in these variants and the decrease in likely benign variants. After applying the Steps F10 to F12, in July, we noticed that 20 likely benign variants had been misclassified as conflicting interpretation. Also, 2 benign variants and 3 benign/likely benign variants had also been misclassified. These results indicate that the decrease in the number of likely benign variants is highly related to the misclassification of these variants as conflicting interpretation.

For clinically actionable variants (up to 78 at each lists), at the end of the identification, these 78 variants were classified as Accepted with Limited Evidence, Accepted with Moderate Evidence, Rejected, or To Follow Up. Figure 4 shows the number of variants for each classification:

First, a new variant appeared as classified To Follow Up (rs63750687). Second, the variants classified as Accepted with Limited Evidence coincide in both months.

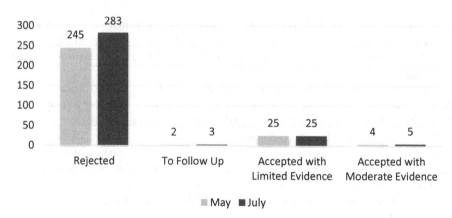

Fig. 4. Results obtained after the identification stage of the SILE method

The most important finding is that a new variant classified as Accepted with Moderate Evidence (rs63750687) appeared in July. This variant also appeared on the May list but was classified as Rejected. After studying the information available for this variant by analyzing the method used in the two different submissions, we noticed a mistake in ClinVar's own filters: the variant did not appear in May if we filtered the variants by the clinical testing method, but the variant actually did have a submission that has a method clinical testing. This is an unclear situation that is related to an undetected mistake in ClinVar's engine, which justifies the absence of this variant on the May list and serves as an example of the importance of reviewing the results periodically.

It is also noteworthy that at each time point most of the variants were classified as Rejected. Either way, most of the variants were rejected because they have no clinically actionable interpretations (e.g., benign variants, likely benign variants, and uncertain significance variants). The aim of ClinVar is to determine the clinical significance of variants, whatever may be, in order to have evidence about the role of variants in the development of disease. Databases such as ClinVar allow variants from studies that have been previously found to be unrelated to the disease of interest to be quickly discarded. The reduced number of interesting variants for clinical purposes highlights the complexity of the biological processes associated with disease. Figure 3 shows that 202 variants in May and 203 variants in July are not clinically actionable. This justifies the high number of rejected variants, together with the number of clinically actionable variants that are not classified as accepted because they do not have enough quality to be considered in a clinical setting.

All of the results presented highlight how the number of relevant variants to be considered in a genomic diagnosis had changed in a short period (two months). Since these variants are oriented to facilitating the diagnosis of EOAD (and other diseases), experts must be able to understand how the variants on which they base their diagnose change over time and why. The SILE method easily lets us compare and understand the evolution of the information, because the changes in the variants' classification can be easily tracked and justified. The transparency of the process provides clear explanations about the results obtained. This increases the trust of the users in the method and helps to evolve its accuracy as new knowledge and diseases are explored.

These results clearly support the need for taking into account the temporal dimension in the development of methods such as SILE in order to provide support for a more accurate and up-to-date genomic diagnosis. When we talk about clinical information that affects genomic diagnosis, keeping track of changes over time and allowing these differences in the obtained results to be automatically displayed becomes a must. This work shows that these changes exist and can be concretized, which is a first step in designing a software platform that can provide a general solution to this problem.

4 Conclusions and Future Work

One important dimension of genomic data is its growth and evolution over time [14]. As the results of the workflow application in Sect. 3 show, a new To Follow Up variant and a new Accepted with Moderate Evidence variant appeared just two months apart. Other changes, such as the number of variants found in the database and changes in the variants' classification and interpretation also appeared. This demonstrate that this dimension of the genomic data should be considered when using this information for clinical diagnosis.

If a diagnosis is made in July based on the results obtained in May, important information could be missing. This could crucially affect the goal of providing a reliable diagnosis. Because the SILE method provides a clear explanation for whether or not a variant should be considered for genomic diagnosis, the results and their evolution over time can be easily compared. The results presented in this work support this claim since all of the differences detected on the lists of May and July variants have been easily explained and justified.

A clearer view of this data evolution over time must be included in the identification stage. Further work associated with the SILE method must study new features related to the temporal evolution of genomic data such as reporting changes in the clinical significance of the variants over time (not only the current significance). To do this, the workflow in this work has been automatized and is ready to be incorporated into a future software platform that will exploit the results obtained by the workflow application in an understandable, traceable way. This will facilitate the automatic display of the results of the differences found over time. We plan to apply the method at different time points to other diseases in order to gain a more accurate perspective of how information evolves in different contexts.

Acknowledgements. This work has been developed with the financial support of the Spanish State Research Agency and the Generalidad Valenciana under the projects TIN2016-80811-P and PROMETEO/2018/176, co-financed with ERDF.

References

1. Cacace, R., et al.: Molecular genetics of early-onset Alzheimer's disease revisited. Alzheimer's Dement **12**(6), 733–748 (2016)

2. Landrum, M.J., et al.: ClinVar: improving access to variant interpretations and supporting evidence. Nucleic Acids Res. **46**(D1), D1062–D1067 (2018)
3. Hunt, S.E., et al.: Ensembl variation resources. Database **2018**, 1–12 (2018)
4. Buniello, A., et al.: The NHGRI-EBI GWAS catalog of published genome-wide association studies, targeted arrays and summary statistics 2019. Nucleic Acids Res. **47**(D1), D1005–D1012 (2019)
5. Cariaso, M., et al.: SNPedia: a wiki supporting personal genome annotation, interpretation and analysis. Nucleic Acids Res. **40**(D1), D1308 (2012)
6. Duzkale, H., et al.: A systematic approach to assessing the clinical significance of genetic variants. Clin. Genet. **84**(5), 453–463 (2013)
7. Sefid Dashti, M.J., et al.: A practical guide to filtering and prioritizing genetic variants. Biotechniques **62**(1), 18–30 (2017)
8. Panoutsopoulou, K., Walter, K.: Quality control of common and rare variants. In: Evangelou, E. (ed.) Genetic Epidemiology. MMB, vol. 1793, pp. 25–36. Springer, New York (2018). https://doi.org/10.1007/978-1-4939-7868-7_3
9. León Palacio, A., et al.: Smart data for genomic information systems: the SILE method. Complex Syst. Inf. Model. Q. (17) 1–23 (2018)
10. Lane, C.A., et al.: Alzheimer's disease. Eur. J. Neurol. **25**, 59–70 (2018)
11. Van Cauwenberghe, C., et al.: The genetic landscape of Alzheimer disease: clinical implications and perspectives. Genet. Med. **18**(5), 421–430 (2016)
12. León Palacio, A., et al.: Genomic information systems applied to precision medicine: genomic data management for alzheimer's disease treatment. Int. Conf. Inf. Syst. Dev. (2018)
13. León Palacio, A., Pastor López, Ó., Casamayor Ródenas, J.C.: A method to identify relevant genome data: conceptual modeling for the medicine of precision. In: Trujillo, J.C., Davis, K.C., Du, X., Li, Z., Ling, T.W., Li, G., Lee, M.L. (eds.) ER 2018. LNCS, vol. 11157, pp. 597–609. Springer, Cham (2018). https://doi.org/10.1007/978-3-030-00847-5_44
14. Pastor, O.: Conceptual modeling meets the human genome. In: Li, Q., Spaccapietra, S., Yu, E., Olivé, A. (eds.) ER 2008. LNCS, vol. 5231, pp. 1–11. Springer, Heidelberg (2008). https://doi.org/10.1007/978-3-540-87877-3_1

Towards the Generation
of a Species-Independent Conceptual
Schema of the Genome

Alberto García S.$^{(\boxtimes)}$ and Juan Carlos Casamayor

PROS Research Center, Universitat Politècnica de València, Valencia, Spain
{algarsi3,jcarlos}@pros.upv.es

Abstract. Understanding the genome, with all of its components and intrinsic relationships, is a great challenge. Conceptual modeling techniques have been used as a means to face this challenge, leading to the generation of conceptual schemes whose intent is to provide a precise ontological characterization of the components involved in biological processes. However, the heterogeneity and idiosyncrasy of genomic use cases mean that, although the genome and its internal processes remain the same among eukaryote species, conceptual modeling techniques are used to generate conceptual schemes that focus on particular scenarios (i.e., they are species-specific conceptual schemes). We claim that instead of having different, species-specific conceptual schemes, it is feasible to provide a holistic conceptual schema valid to work with every eukaryote species by generating conceptual views that are inferred from that global conceptual schema. We report our preliminary work towards the possibility of generating such a conceptual schema by ontologically comparing two existing, species-specific conceptual schemes. Those changes that are necessary to provide an expanded conceptual schema that is suitable for both use cases are identified and discussed.

Keywords: Conceptual Modeling · Genomics · Conceptual Schema

1 Introduction

Conceptual Modeling (CM) is the activity of describing aspects of the world for the purpose of understanding and communication [12]. It answers fundamental questions regardless of the research area by identifying what concepts are relevant and the relationships among them. Conceptual models make mental representations of the world explicit, which helps to establish common ontological frameworks that facilitate both communication and knowledge evolution in complex domains [4].

An example of such a convoluted and vast domain is genomics, where understanding the genome with all the intrinsic relationships that should allow to decipher the code of life conforms a huge challenge. The complexity of the genomic domain has two main reasons. The first one is the existence of relevant concepts

© Springer Nature Switzerland AG 2020
G. Grossmann and S. Ram (Eds.): ER 2020 Workshops, LNCS 12584, pp. 61–70, 2020.
https://doi.org/10.1007/978-3-030-65847-2_6

that are not clearly defined. Even the definition of the most elemental concepts, like the concept of "gene", are open to discussion [15]. The second one is that it is an ever-changing domain, with new knowledge emerging continuously [18]. Therefore, the genomic domain is a particularly good candidate to apply CM techniques.

In the last years, our research group has developed the Conceptual Schema of the Human Genome (CSHG) as proof of how CM can help improving domain understanding and communication. Our main research line has focused on the human case, and the CSHG has been intended to provide a more explicit and precise understanding of the human genome. Moreover, the CSHG has probed to be valid and useful for its purpose in multiple real-world use cases [13,14,17].

The genome is what explains what we -humans- understand by life on our planet. Sharing a common conceptual background, genome representation is a problem that affects any species of living beings. However, having a Conceptual Schema (CS) that only focuses on the human genome can be seen as a limitation in this context. Facing a study of any different species could mean that a new CS has to be created, or adapted, to cover its particularities adequately. We encountered this problem when working with geneticists that focus on the study of citrus, having to consider a particular CS of the Citrus Genome. As a result, our research group ended up having two conceptual schemes: the CSHG and the Conceptual Schema of the Citrus Genome (CSCG) [6], even if in both cases we are talking about "genome", and their conceptual background is supposed to be the same.

Although the scenarios that has motivated the generation of these schemes were different, with their particularities, a question prowled our mind: Does each species need a specific CS adapted to the problem under investigation, or is it possible to have a single, holistic CS that works for every species, adequately adapted to the idiosyncrasy of individual studies? Our work has been constrained to the particularities of the selected working domains (human genome, citrus genome,...) where different genome components have been taken as relevant depending on the corresponding data analytics purpose. Nevertheless, we have always kept in mind that the genome is the same for every *eukaryote* species, and we have been convinced that it should be possible to design a holistic conceptual schema of the genome (CSG). To move in that direction is the main goal of this work, with the final intention of facilitating that any particular working domain could have its own conceptual view that is inferred from that global CSG.

This paper reports our preliminary work towards the possibility of generating a CS that is not species-specific: the CSG. To do so, the CSHG has been compared with the CSCG to identify their similarities and differences. Those changes that are needed to provide an expanded, more generic version of the CSHG are analyzed. The final goal is to design a holistic CSG that is ready to be adapted to any particular working genome-based context (corresponding to studies affecting different species of what we mean by life on our planet). To achieve this goal, the identification of those different pieces of genome information used in different genomic cases of study, becomes an essential task.

The rest of this work is described as follows: Sect. 2 describes the evolution of the CSHG since its creation and how it is structured. Section 3 reports the use case that motivated the need for a new CS when a new working domain was explored (the citrus genome), which led us to the generation of the CSCG. Section 4 discusses the needed changes that would allow us to design a holistic CSG that, at the same time, i) is built on the experience accumulated with the CSHG, extending it accordingly, and ii) can be adapted to be used in the citrus use case, creating the corresponding conceptual view. Furthermore, this CSG could be seen as a universal conceptualization of the relevant genome properties, not exclusively linked to any particular species, but with the capability of providing any required conceptual view to be applied to any genome-based study. Lastly, Sect. 5 addresses conclusions and future work.

2   Conceptual Schema of the Human Genome

For years, the creation of a CSHG has been the main goal and a fundamental tool for our work [16]. The result has been a CS divided into multiple views that provided us with a foundational tool to communicate more effectively with domain experts and develop Model-Driven Development (MDD) Genome Information Systems (GeIS). As more knowledge about the genomic fundamentals of life is accumulated, the CSHG has evolved in parallel, with two major updates:

1. From version 1 to 1.1: The first update added phenotypic information to the CSHG in a new view called "phenotype view". This addition increased the consistency and completeness of the existing concepts.
2. From version 1.1 to 2: The second update changed how the genome sequence is comprehended and represented. While version 1 focused on structuring the genome sequence in genes, version 2 structured it in "chromosome elements". Consequently, not only genes but any relevant genome component can be modeled.

This last version of the CSHG is divided into five views: **i)** the "structural view" describes the structural parts that determines the sequence of the genome, **ii)** the "transcription view" models the elements that take part in the protein-coding process, **iii)** the "variation view" focuses on the structural changes in the genome sequence, **iv)** the "pathway view" breaks down metabolic pathways into their fundamental events, specifying the entities that take part in them, **v)** the "bibliography and databank view" provides with information regarding the origin of the data.

3   Conceptual Schema of the Citrus Genome

Unlike the CSHG, which has been developed as generic as possible to serve multiple use cases, the CSCG has been developed for a specific use-case. Because of that, the modeling process and the philosophy of the resulting CS differ notably.

The use case that motivated the generation of the CSCG consists of establishing reliable links between variations and phenotypes of interest, which is significantly different from how human genomic studies are performed. The human genomic studies we faced focused on identifying relevant variations (i.e., variations that are known to cause a given condition) in populations, especially with clinical purposes in a medicine of precision context, where early diagnosis and selection of the right treatment become the main goals. But the experts of the citrus domain focus on identifying which variations are relevant (i.e., which variations cause a given condition). The identification process is composed of four tasks:

1. Plant genome sequencing. The genome sequence of citrus plants of interest is obtained and compared to a reference sequence. A set of identified variations are obtained for each citrus variety.
2. Identification of variations of interest. Those variations that have feasible links with phenotypes of interest are identified through orthology prediction and statistical methods.
3. Characterization of genes of interest. Genes of the sequenced citrus varieties that have their expression, efficiency, or functionality modified in a disruptive way by variations of interest, are identified and analyzed. As a result, assumptions regarding potential genes of interest that require experimental validation emerge. Genes of interest are those that have a significant role in a phenotype of interest.
4. Application of genetic modifications. The previously obtained assumptions are validated by applying genetic modification through molecular techniques.

A secondary aspect is to study the implications of relevant variations in citrus varieties (i.e., different species) at an evolutionary level (i.e., how and when relevant variations were originated). It is the first time that we have to consider the existence of more than one species, pertaining to the same genus, and how they are related at an evolutionary level.

Citrus domain experts also work with more technological-oriented data rather than purely biological data. For instance, they rely on the use of variant annotations and functional effect prediction software. This data mixes biological and non-biological information, being much more format-file oriented. Thus, the information is tied to the used technologies and their limitations. Consequently, there is a loss of the semantics that difficults domain understanding.

We are perfectly aware that -generally speaking- the genome provides the common, holistic knowledge to understand life as we perceive it in the Earth, our planet, independently of any particular species. At the same time, our experience in the real working domains of human genome-based applications (in a medicine of precision context) in the CSHG case, and in the case of analyzing links between genome variations and their associated phenotypes in the CSCG case, has clearly shown us that the conceptual views that are used in these different working environments are different. Depending on the peculiarities of the problem under investigation, the relevant data that must be considered changes, hiding the conceptual homogeneity of the whole genome concepts.

In the citrus case, to deal with these particularities the CSCG has been developed following a CM method that emphasizes to explicitly separate biological and non-biological data by adopting a multi-model oriented approach. It proposes to start with a purely-biological CS to which append additional non-biological conceptual schemes. The resulting CS takes into account the intricate relationships between these two types of data, allowing us to recover the previously hidden semantics of the data. A full view of the CSCG can be seen in [5].

The experience accumulated with the analysis of both human genome data and citrus genome data has lead to enter the problem of designing an unified conceptual schema of the genome, intended to capture the essentials of the genome structure by identifying all the relevant conceptual concepts that could represent the holistic knowledge associated to the genome, in a species-independent way. We envision this Conceptual Schema of the Genome (CSG) as a holistic artifact intended to provide a common conceptual background that could be projected into any particular species by creating the conceptual view projection that satisfies the needs of any working domains (as in particular the ones supported by our CSHG and CSCG that we refer to in this paper).

4   Conceptual Schema of the Genome: A New Horizon

A new horizon opens when considering having a CSG that could be used for any species. So far, we have identified and detailed our two existing conceptual schemes: the CSHG to work with humans and the CSCG to work with citrus. Being the CSHG the most mature of both, it has been used as a basis to identify which parts need to be improved (i.e., generalized or specialized) to transform it into a potentially species-independent CSG. To do so, the CSHG has been compared with the CSCG, and the findings are reported on a per-view basis (as preserving the view structure facilitates to manage the diversity and complexity of the involved data). To conclude the section, additional considerations are addressed.

Structural View

The CSHG offers an abstraction mechanism that allows modeling any existing element contained in the genome sequence, like genes or intergenic regions. This approach equals the one used in the CSCG as the "chromosome element" concept of the CSHG corresponds to the "sequence part" concept of the CSCG. This approach allows us to include any eventual species-specific genomic element. It is a generic enough approach to achieve our goal and does not need any change. But we have identified a significant difference: the CSHG misses two relevant concepts of the CSCG, the scaffold and the ortholog group.

It is important to note two points regarding the concept of scaffold in the CSHG. The first one is that the existence of this concept is the result of the current sequencing technology limitations. Real-life sequencing is far from perfect, and it is not possible to correctly obtain the whole genome sequence at once. Sequencing machines break the genome sequence into many smaller sequences that are read multiple times and then joined. The result is a genome sequence that has gaps of known length. The second one is that every species has scaffolds that compose their genome sequence. This concept is an example of how core concept definitions can be fuzzy and hard to model. The scaffold concept is a conflicting one even between geneticists: some define it as the sequence of a chromosome while others define it as a part of it with gaps of known length.

An ortholog group, the second concept that the CSHG misses, is defined as a set of genes that are presupposed to have evolved from a single gene in a common ancestral species. Contrary to paralogue groups, which are genes created by duplication events, ortholog groups are created by speciation events. The CSCG models the concept of the orthologous group as a collection of genes that are evolutionary related and, optionally, a set of the enzymes coded by these genes. For example, an ortholog group can contain a set of genes from three different citrus varieties and the enzyme that these genes produce.

We conclude that the CSHG should incorporate: i) the concept of scaffold because some genomic domains rely on analyzing specific scaffold sequences [9] and ii) the ortholog group concept, as orthologous gene identification is fundamental to all aspects of biology [11] and allows to study hundreds of years of evolution by applying phylogenetics and comparative analysis [19].

Transcription View

When the genomic components that structure the transcription view of both the CSHG and the CSCG are compared, we concluded that they share a high degree of similarity. But the identified genomic components are more detailed regarding transcription regulators in the CSHG case. In the citrus case, the level of knowledge associated to the study of transcription regulator elements is less strong than in the human case.

However, three elements that exist in the CSCG do not exist in the CSHG and need further clarification. The first one is the concept of intron. The concept of intron was present in the first version of the CSHG but, as geneticists started using it, we found that this concept was never used, and we decided to remove it. However, in the case of citrus, intron-located variations are much more relevant and studied.

The second one is the concept of domain. A domain is defined as the basic, independent unit of protein folding, evolution, and function [2]. The CSHG represents proteins as a unique block with a given functionality, ignoring that they are composed of multiple smaller, interconnected parts. Domains are included in the CSCG because they are compared to infer evolutionary closeness of citrus species.

The third concept is the mRNA concept. The CSHG models the transcription process so that genes produce transcripts, with "protein-coding" being a type of transcript that produces proteins. This way, only those transcripts that are "protein-coding" produce proteins and transcripts that do not produce proteins can exist. The CSCG modes the transcription so that genes produce mRNAs and mRNAs produce proteins. Consequently, those transcripts that do not produce proteins cannot be modeled. The "protein-coding" concept in the CSHG is ontologically equivalent to the mRNA concept of the CSCG. We determined that this concept should be renamed to mRNA to explicit its representations in the CSHG. Besides, the CSCG also defines the structure of the mRNA because variations located in these regions are particularly studied in this domain. An mRNA is composed of three elements: the 5' untranslated region (5' UTR), the coding sequence (CDS), and the 3' untranslated region (3' UTR). On the one hand, the CSHG is a more generalizable solution because it allows us to model transcripts that do not produce proteins. On the other hand, the CSCG models the concept of mRNA in a more detailed way because it specifies the structural parts that compose it.

Consequently, the CSHG should include i) the concept of intron to perform analysis that specifically studies structural changes in introns [7], ii) the concept of domain because decomposing each protein into modular domains is a basic prerequisite for accurate functional classification of biological molecules [8], and iii) the concepts of 5' UTR, CDS, and 3' UTR to be able to locate structural changes in these regions and study their consequences [20].

Variation View

The CSHG represents variations with an appropriate level of genericity, but we identified two limitations after comparing it to how the CSCG represents variations. The first one is that the CSHG has been used in genomic studies that focus on studying genotype frequencies of SNP variations. As a result, the modeling process of the CSHG prioritized representing genotype frequencies of SNP variations over other type of variations. On the contrary, the citrus use case focuses on studying both the genotype frequency of SNP and INDEL variations. The reason is that the study of genotype frequencies of INDEL variations is relevant because their high degree of heterozygosity is used to establish taxonomic relationships [10].

Our approach consisted of identifying what parts of the CSHG are candidates to be improved (i.e., extend, generalize, or specialize) and discuss the potential benefits of improving them. We have identified three potential improvements. The first one is the identification of eight genomic components that can extend the CSHG: scaffolds, ortholog groups, introns, protein domains, and the structural components of the mRNA (5' UTR, CDS, and 3' UTR). The second one is the generalization of the genotype frequency, from being a property of SNP variations only, to be a property of every type of variation. The third one is the specialization of the concept of variation, which is represented at two different levels (general and population), into a third level so that it can represent information regarding its appearance in individuals.

As a side note, this exercise also allowed us to discover elements that are relevant in the citrus domain but were not initially considered because they are not studied in the working use case. An example is the concept of haplotype, which is defined as a set of variations that statistically appear together [1]. The identification of haplotypes in citrus is an important topic that is being studied [3] and should be included in the CSCG for future studies.

As a result, i) the concept of genotype frequency should be generalized so that it is represented for every type of variation, and ii) the CSHG should include the individual level when representing variations.

Pathway View

The CSHG has a highly generic and flexible representation of pathways and their inner processes. It allows representing the specific events that occur on each pathway, how they are related, and the biological entities that take part in them. The CSCG represents entire pathways as indivisible blocks, ignoring their internal processes. Instead of any biological entity, the CSCG only allows specifying what enzymes take part in a pathway, and only at a general level rather than at a pathway-specific process level. We conclude that, in this case, no changes in this view are required.

Bilbiography and Databank View

The CSHG allows us to represent both bibliography of the represented genomic components and how they are identified in external data sources. The CSCG includes neither information regarding the bibliography of the data nor their origin. Therefore, No changes in the CSHG are needed.

Additional Considerations

We want to emphasize that one of the main strengths of the CSCG is how well it integrates technological-oriented data since the citrus use case relies much more upon these data than the human genomic studies that we have faced. The CSCG has been modeled using a methodological approach that explicitly separates technological-related data into independent conceptual schemes that can be assembled like puzzle pieces depending on the needs of specific use cases. The main benefits of this approach are that data integration is straightforward and automated, there is a direct mapping between biological and technological-oriented concepts, and the final CS has a more complete was of representing those elements whose significance is biased by technological-oriented data. Apart from the changes proposed, reformulating the CSHG so that its generation process uses this approach can be a rightful approach to gain the benefits previously mentioned.

5   Conclusions

Our reported experience shows that the genomic domain is complex, and some of their core concept definitions are fuzzy. Although the genomic cases that we have worked with share a common ontological background, their specific particularities result in too diverse data analytic purposes. This fact has been illustrated with the generation of multiple species-specific conceptual schemes where different genomic components have been identified as relevant, depending on the working context.

However, we claim that it is feasible to have a single, holistic CS (CSG) that is valid to work with every *eukaryotic* species because, even if they are unique and diverse, their genome and how it behaves is the same. This CSG could work as a global, generic element from which conceptual views to work with any particular domain can be inferred. Herein, we reported the first steps towards this direction by intersecting two conceptual schemes that have been developed to work with different species: the CSHG for working with humans, and the CSCG for working with citrus.

Our approach has been to identify what parts of the CSHG have to be improved (i.e., extend, generalize, or specialize) and discuss the potential benefits of applying them. Eight genomic components that can extend the CSHG have been identified: scaffolds, ortholog groups, introns, protein domains, and the structural components of the mRNA (5' UTR, CDS, and 3' UTR). A concept that can be generalized: the genotype frequency, from being related to a specific type of variation to be related to every type of variation. A concept that can be specialized: the variation, which is represented at two different levels (general and population), can be represented in a third level so that it can represent information regarding its appearance in individuals.

These results, being preliminary, are a useful starting point so that the CSHG can be a candidate to be used in the citrus use case and, potentially, in more use cases that work with other species. Future works include working towards the obtaining of the so-wanted species independent CS and its reformulation so that it explicitly separates purely biological data from technological-oriented data.

Acknowledgment. This work was supported by the Spanish Ministry of Science and Innovation through Project DataME (ref: TIN2016-80811-P) and the Generalitat Valenciana through project GISPRO (PROMETEO/2018/176).

References

1. Belmont, J.W., et al.: A haplotype map of the human genome. Nature **437**(7063), 1299–1320 (2005). https://doi.org/10.1038/nature04226
2. Campbell, P.N.P.N., Smith, A.D.A.D., Peters, T.J.: Biochemistry Illustrated: Biochemistry and Molecular Biology in the Post-genomic Era, 5th edn. Elsevier Churchill Livingstone, Edinburgh (2005). https://searchworks.stanford.edu/view/5961093
3. Chen, C., Gmitter, F.G.: Mining of haplotype-based expressed sequence tag single nucleotide polymorphismsin citrus. BMC Genom. **14**(1) (2013). https://doi.org/10.1186/1471-2164-14-746
4. Delcambre, L., Liddle, S., Pastor, O., Storey, V.: A reference framework for conceptual modeling: focusing on conceptual modeling research. Technical report, November 2018. https://doi.org/10.13140/RG.2.2.33041.07521

5. García S., A., Pastor, O.: CSCG: conceptual schema of the citrus genome. Technical report (2020). http://hdl.handle.net/10251/144234

6. García S., A., Reyes Román, J.F., Casamayor, J.C., Pastor, O.: Towards an effective and efficient management of genome data: an information systems engineering perspective. In: Cappiello, C., Ruiz, M. (eds.) CAiSE 2019. LNBIP, vol. 350, pp. 99–110. Springer, Cham (2019). https://doi.org/10.1007/978-3-030-21297-1_9

7. Ghada, B., Amel, O., Aymen, M., Aymen, A., Amel, S.H.: Phylogenetic patterns and molecular evolution among 'True citrus fruit trees' group (Rutaceae family and Aurantioideae subfamily). Scientia Horticulturae **253**, 87–98 (2019). https://doi.org/10.1016/j.scienta.2019.04.011

8. Heger, A., Holm, L.: Exhaustive enumeration of protein domain families. J. Mol. Biol. **328**(3), 749–767 (2003). https://doi.org/10.1016/S0022-2836(03)00269-9

9. Heinzelmann, R., et al.: Chromosomal assembly and analyses of genome-wide recombination rates in the forest pathogenic fungus Armillaria ostoyae. Heredity **124**(6), 699–713 (2020). https://doi.org/10.1038/s41437-020-0306-z

10. Janzen, G.M., Wang, L., Hufford, M.B.: The extent of adaptive wild introgression in crops (2019). https://doi.org/10.1111/nph.15457

11. Miller, J.B., Pickett, B.D., Ridge, P.G.: JustOrthologs: a fast, accurate and user-friendly ortholog identification algorithm. Bioinformatics **35**(4), 546–552 (2019). https://doi.org/10.1093/bioinformatics/bty669

12. Mylopoulos, J.: Conceptual modelling and Telos, pp. 49–68 (1992)

13. Palacio, A.L., Fernández, I.P., López, O.P.: Genomic information systems applied to precision medicine: genomic data management for Alzheimer's disease treatment. In: International Conference on Information Systems Development (ISD), October 2018. https://aisel.aisnet.org/isd2014/proceedings2018/eHealth/6

14. Palacio, A.L., López, Ó.P.: Towards an effective medicine of precision by using conceptual modelling of the genome. In: Proceedings - International Conference on Software Engineering, pp. 14–17. IEEE Computer Society, New York, May 2018. https://doi.org/10.1145/3194696.3194700

15. Pearson, H.: What is a gene?, May 2006. https://doi.org/10.1038/441398a

16. Reyes Román, J.F.: Diseño y Desarrollo de un Sistema de Información Genómica Basado en un Modelo Conceptual Holístico del Genoma Humano. Ph.D. thesis, Universitat Politècnica de València (2018). https://riunet.upv.es/handle/10251/99565

17. Reyes Román, J.F., Martínez, D.R., Simón, A.G., Rueda, U., Pastor, Ó.: VarSearch: annotating variations using an e-genomics framework. In: Proceedings of the 13th International Conference on Evaluation of Novel Approaches to Software Engineering, ENASE 2018, vol. 2018-March, pp. 328–350. SCITEPRESS - Science and Technology Publications (2018). https://doi.org/10.5220/0006781103280334

18. Smirnov, A., Schneider, C., Hör, J., Vogel, J.: Discovery of new RNA classes and global RNA-binding proteins, October 2017. https://doi.org/10.1016/j.mib.2017.11.016

19. Train, C.M., Glover, N.M., Gonnet, G.H., Altenhoff, A.M., Dessimoz, C.: Orthologous matrix (OMA) algorithm 2.0: more robust to asymmetric evolutionary rates and more scalable hierarchical orthologous group inference. Bioinformatics **33**(14), i75–i82 (2017). https://doi.org/10.1093/bioinformatics/btx229

20. Whiffin, N., et al.: Characterising the loss-of-function impact of 5' untranslated region variants in 15,708 individuals. Nat. Commun. **11**(1), 1–12 (2020). https://doi.org/10.1038/s41467-019-10717-9

Conceptual Human Emotion Modeling (HEM)

Mohammed R. Elkobaisi[✉][iD], Heinrich C. Mayr[iD],
and Vladimir A. Shekhovtsov[iD]

Alpen-Adria-Universität Klagenfurt, Klagenfurt, Austria
M3mohammed@edu.aau.at, {Heinrich.Mayr,Volodymyr.Shekhovtsov}@aau.at

Abstract. Human emotions are considered as decision factors in specific knowledge-based systems. However, there is neither a consolidated conceptualization of the emotion domain nor a widely used modeling language, let alone a method. To close this gap, this paper presents such a language and first steps to a method. An essential aspect is that we have not conceived this language as a "stand-alone" one. Rather, it is designed for being embedded into other modeling standard or domain specific languages. For illustration purposes we use the Active and Assisted Living (AAL) domain as a running example. We conducted a first evaluation of our approach by implementing a modeling tool using the ADOxx® metamodeling framework.

Keywords: Domain-specific modeling language · Human emotion · Metamodeling · Aspect-Oriented Metamodeling

1 Introduction

In this paper we present a conceptualization and a domain-specific modeling language for the description of *human emotions* and related aspects. This language is designed to be embedded in both contextual description and interface modeling languages defined for domains where emotions play a role.

Human emotion is a biological state influenced by a situation and associated with behaviour, thought, and feeling. Emotions affect human activities in a significant way: from evoking a significant cognitive boost (feeling 'inspired' and/or empowered) that even can strengthen physical capabilities to the opposite (feeling 'depressed'), making usual routines very difficult or impossible to perform.

In the domain of cognitive psychology, the term emotion refers to *"specific sets of physiological and mental dispositions triggered by the brain in response to the perceived significance of a situation or object"* [6]. Emotions and behavior of an individual are influenced by the individual's interpretation of a given situation [16]: guided by their beliefs, different people may interpret the same events differently. Emotional expression is also an important part of emotional function, as human emotions can influence a person's physical reactions [24]. These

© Springer Nature Switzerland AG 2020
G. Grossmann and S. Ram (Eds.): ER 2020 Workshops, LNCS 12584, pp. 71–81, 2020.
https://doi.org/10.1007/978-3-030-65847-2_7

emotional reactions are mediated by speech, facial expressions, body gestures or physiological signals [29].

In addition to cognitive psychology, also other domains deal with the recognition and assessment of emotions and appropriate reactions to them. For instance, think of the domains of Recommender Systems, Monitoring of Public Places, or Active and Assisted Living (AAL). We call them *"emotion-influenced domains"*. Common to all these domains is the need of a comprehensive conceptualization of emotions and their "context", i.e. related phenomena like environmental conditions, social interaction etc. For it is only on the basis of such conceptualizations that emotion models and suitable representations can be systematically created allowing to deal with them in digital systems: based on these models, the emotions can be recognized, analyzed and understood, the emotion information can be processed, stored, and used in decision making or other activities.

Such an approach consequently leads to the development of a domain-specific modeling language (DSML) and method (DSMM) [13,22], where semantics are defined by the underlying conceptualisations of the language elements and not only by element names borrowed from natural language, as is the case with the use of general purpose languages. (Think, for example, of a domain specific concept "person" versus a UML class named "person"). DSMLs thus allow the user to specify a domain of discourse directly in concepts related to the given application domain [32]. Consequently, when specifying software solutions, the user can focus on the problem from the application perspective instead of being confronted with technical details from outside his field [5].

Regardless of the domain, *handling* (obtaining, understanding, and recording) the specific emotions which were felt by a person while performing a domain-specific activity could allow to provide better support for such activity. To illustrate our considerations, in this paper we use AAL as running example domain and discuss the embedding of our emotion modeling language in a DSML for the area of human behaviour modeling and support.

Studying emotion modeling in the field of AAL is promising because emotions have a particularly strong influence on the daily activities of people who have cognitive or other age- or capacity-related problems [31]. The support of such persons in their daily activities [15] using AAL technologies should therefore be *'emotion-aware'*, i.e. taking into account the respective emotional state of the person concerned. Within this context we aim to achieve two objectives: (1) conceptualizing the emotions of the supported persons caused by situations, and (2) conceptualizing the interface to external emotion sources (e.g., recognition systems).

The paper is organized as follows: In Sect. 2 we discuss some considerations for designing an human emotion modeling method. Section 3 introduces the essential aspects of such method. In Sect. 4 we outline a mechanism for embedding our modeling language into other DSMLs. Section 5 analyzes some related work, motivating the need for Human Emotion Modeling. Section 6 concludes the paper and gives some hints on future work.

2   Design Considerations

To be usable in practice, a DSML must be embedded in a domain-specific modeling method (DSMM). Such a method must provide, among other things, a process model for the use of the modeling language and suitable mechanisms for the analysis, management and further processing of the created models. According to [13,22], the development of a DSMM can be done in the following steps, which are only roughly outlined here:

1. **Preparation:** clarification of scope and purpose of the language, requirements analysis to reveal the focal aspects to be potentially modeled, and context analysis;
2. **Modeling Language Design:** creating a meta-model that comprises all relevant conceptualizations for the given domain, language specification, design of the notation, definition of the representation language for the instance level (see below);
3. **Modeling Process:** defining a step-wise procedure for modelers of how to act when creating models (i.e., what aspects should be modeled first);
4. **Modeling Tool:** tool requirements elicitation and specification, framework and meta-modeling language selection, view definition, tool implementation and completion by framework dependent add-ons;
5. **Evaluation.**

We have driven the development of our human emotion modeling language HEM-L and method in these steps, of course with iterations. Figure 1 shows, in accordance with the OMG Meta Object Facility [25] and the Model Centered Architecture (MCA) Paradigm [19], the model and language hierarchies that need to be taken into account in such an endeavor.

For developing the modeling tool we decided to use the ADOxx® metamodeling framework [1,12].

In order to make it easier to embed HEM-L in other modeling languages, we have kept the meta model very lean. For the embedding itself, we propose to inject the fragments of the HEM-L metamodel into the respective target metamodel, thus complementing the target language. This approach is described in Sect. 4 together with the example of embedding HEM-L into an DSML for the AAL domain, namely, HCM-L [18] which is a language describing personal and social, spatial and environmental aspects of a user's behavior (this includes the context information).

3   Human Emotion Modeling: Metamodel and Language

In this section we briefly describe the essential elements of the method we propose for Human Emotion Modeling according to the metamodeling and language definition hierarchy depicted in Fig. 5. The description follows the method development steps outlined in Sect. 2 without going into detail, as there is not enough space available for this.

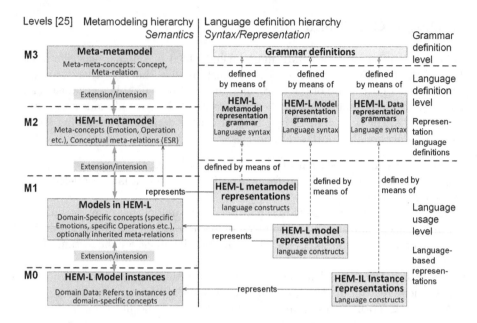

Fig. 1. Model and Language Definition Hierarchies (adapted from [20]).

Preparation. In order to identify the aspects to be considered in our modeling method, we conducted a comprehensive and in-depth literature and source analysis of ontologies, models and data sets in this area [10]. As a result of this analysis, we delimited the *HEM-L scope* within which we then defined the concepts for our metamodel. We found that the emotional aspects to be considered include capability situations involving people: Emotions can have a positive or negative influence on the ability to perform certain actions. Conversely, how well or badly a person is able to perform a certain action can have an effect on their emotional state.

Metamodel. Figure 2 shows the core concepts/elements of the HEM metamodel (for space reasons without the properties assigned to them). As is usual in literature, we present meta-classes with boxes and meta-relationships with diamonds. There are two almost symmetrical meta-relationships that conceptualize *Emotional Situations* on the one hand and *Capability Situations* on the other.

These situations consist in the association of the core meta-classes: *Emotion* conceptualizes emotion itself. *Context* conceptualizes the environmental variables related to a situation, e.g. time, weather, location, companion, occasions, etc. *Operation* conceptualizes actions that influence the respective emotional situation or are influenced by it, respectively. For example, a person might perform a certain action only in a negative emotional state, but conversely such an action might improve her/his emotional state. Operations can be composed of other Operations. *Thing* conceptualizes things involved in a situation such as a TV set, a room, an instrument. *Person*, a specialization of Thing, conceptualizes

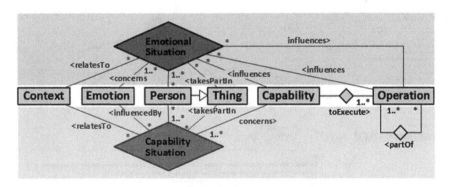

Fig. 2. HEM metamodel; due to lack of space we have omitted the attributes/properties of the metamodel elements.

the person(s) for whom the emotional and capability situations are to be modeled. *Capability* conceptualizes the capabilities of a Person to perform a certain Operation, which is expressed by the *toExecute* meta-relationship.

Modeling Language. In accordance with concepts in the metamodel, we designed the (graphical) elements of our modeling language as shown in Fig. 3. Of course, this notation can be changed at will and according to your taste - which does not involve any technical challenges, especially when using a metamodeling framework to generate the modeling tool. Note that ES stands for Emotional Situation, and CS for Capability Situation.

Basic Concepts		*Basic Relationships*
Emotion	Context	ES
Person	Thing	CS
Capability	Operation	execute

Fig. 3. Elements of the HEM-L graphical notation.

Figure 4(a) shows a simple HEM-L model (level M1) of an example situation in the AAL domain. This model has been developed using the HEM-L modeling tool (see below). It describes emotional situations in which observed persons in a certain context see something on television (within the limits of their ability to do so). Clearly, the model elements are instances of the respective meta-classes

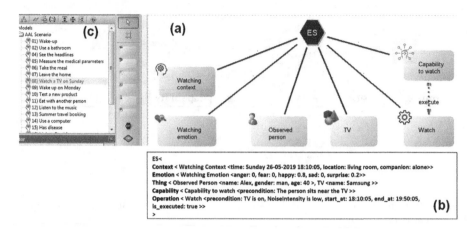

Fig. 4. a) HEM-L model, b) HEM-IL representation of an instance, c) list of emotional situations actually modeled using the HEM-L Modeler

of the metamodel. The model does (for saving space) not visualize the properties attached to the model elements, for instance *time*, *location*, and *companion* for Watching context, *emotion dimensions* (anger, fear, happiness) for Watching Emotion, *name* for TV, *pre- and post-conditions*, *start* and *end time* for Watch, or the *precondition* for the Capability to watch. For lack of space, we have also decided not to model an operator hierarchy here.

Data Level Representation Language. The Model Centered Architecture paradigm [19] treats each component of a digital ecosystem as a "model handler". Accordingly, in addition to the modeling language for Level M1, an instance representation language HEM-IL for Level M0 had to be defined. Figure 4(b) shows a possible instance of the model in Fig. 4(a), this time including the values of the associated properties: it represents a concrete emotional situation that may have been recognized with an appropriate combination of an activity recognition system and an emotion recognition system. The data is subdivided into sections corresponding to the M2 metamodel elements (Context, Emotion etc.), every section contains subsections for the M1 model elements (Watching Context, Watching Emotion etc.) each holding the instance values of their parameters. As an example, the subsection for Watching Emotion contains the values for all its dimensions. HEM-IL can be used to store emotion data in the knowledge base of an AAL system, as a means for transferring emotion data from and to external systems, or for documenting specific emotional situations (as it was designed to be as human-readable as possible without losing efficiency).

Modeling Tool. We implemented the modeling tool (*HEM-L Modeler*) by means of the metamodeling framework ADOxx® based on the metamodel as explained before. The Modeler allows to create, modify and manage HEM-L models as well as performing consistency checks. Figure 4(a) and Fig. 4(c) are screenshots from the Modeler, the latter showing a list of models designed within an AAL scenario.

4   Towards Embedding HEM-L into DSMLs

As stated in Sect. 2, one of the design goals for HEM-L is to make it an "embeddable DSML" [9]. This will allow it to be combined with other DSMLs to extend these with means for emotion modeling.

We observe that the relationship between the emotion domain and other domains, where emotions play a role, fits the aspect-oriented paradigm in the form defined in the body of work on Early Aspects [4]. For, the emotions could be considered as a *crosscutting concern*, i.e., as an area of interest appearing in various non-related contexts, belonging to the same or different domains [27].

Based on this observation, in defining the process of embedding HEM-L we propose to follow the paradigm of Aspect-Oriented Metamodeling [8] by treating the HEM-L metamodel as a *crosscutting* one: its elements are injected into the *target metamodels* through a *metamodel weaving process*. This process follows a *weaving specification*, i.e. a set of rules which define the *injection points* within the target metamodel, and control the process of extending the target metamodel by the elements of the crosscutting metamodel at the injection points.

For a small example we take a look at the weaving of elements of the HEM-L metamodel into the metamodel of the *Human Cognitive Modeling Language HCM-L* [21]. The goal is to expand the HCM-L to support emotions. This should enable the *Human Behavior Monitoring and Support System HBMS* [23] to deal with emotions (HBMS aims at assisting people with cognitive impairments to live independently at home.) For this purpose, the HCM-L metamodel [18] is extended, and the graphical notation for the corresponding emotion conceptualization constructs become a part of HCM-L Modeler (tool). Figure 5 shows only a small part of this, and only the involved fragments of the metamodels are shown: the "Emotion Weaving specification" defines the rule to inject the HEM-L meta-class `Operation` into the HCM-L target meta-class `OperationInBehavioralUnit` (representing an activity in a behavioral scenario) to reflect the fact that such activities are affected by emotions. As a result the relations involving HEM-L `Operation` are copied and, iteratively, the `Emotion` meta-class is copied as well.

Currently, we are developing a tool supporting this process in the sense of metamodel composition [11] using the ADOxx® ALL API library [2].

The advantage of this approach is that *no changes of the involved metamodels are necessary*. This way, it is possible to extend a legacy metamodel defined without knowledge of future extensions. A set of more advanced name-matching or content-matching rules is a topic for a separate publication.

After weaving the metamodels, the next step is to weave the models (*M1-level weaving*), and then to merge the data (*M0-level weaving*). Implementing such steps is a target for future research.

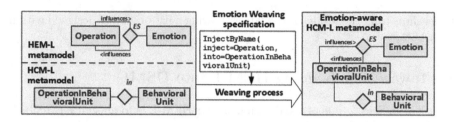

Fig. 5. Injecting HEM-L metamodel elements into HCM-L metamodel

5   Related Work

Recent research and industrial projects resulted in a number of languages to represent emotions. This section describes some of such languages and the purpose behind their development.

We start with two projects focusing on the emotion domain. Emotion Markup language (EmotionML) [7] is a general-purpose XML-based language for emotion description. Emotion Annotation and Representation Language (EARL) [28] is designed specifically for representing emotions in technological contexts such as speech synthesizers or embodied conversational agents [26].

Other projects implement emotion support within languages defined in other domains. Such support is available for (1) Extensible Multi-Modal Annotation Language (EMMA) [14] - a markup language for annotating the user input, (2) Virtual Human Markup Language (VHML) [17] - a markup language for human-computer interaction scenarios, and (3) Speech Synthesis Markup Language (SSML) [3] - an XML-based language for speech synthesis.

The existing emotion languages have limitations: i) most of them encode raw emotion data with XML markup, without offering higher level semantic concepts or a graphical representation; as a result, they are not suitable for modeling emotional situations on the conceptual level; ii) they cannot be extended with custom emotion properties: this lack of flexibility can be critical as the languages do not cover all emotion properties (e.g. type, label, intensity, etc.) by default; iii) they lack the notions of context or capability of the person, which limits their applicability for describing context- or capability-related situations.

HEM-L addresses the above-mentioned shortcomings by enabling tool-supported conceptual modeling of emotional situations, by its extensibility to include user-defined properties and by supporting contextual and personal capabilities.

Besides using emotion languages, it is possible to use general-purpose modeling tools (e.g. UML-supporting tools such as Visual Paradigm or Visio) to model emotions by exploiting the wide availability of such tools and their support for conceptual modeling. However, such approach has limitations as well: i) general-purpose tools cannot properly express all emotion properties; ii) they are based on general-purpose metamodels (such as the UML metamodel) lacking support for specific emotion concepts, as a result, the modelers cannot use notions specific to the emotion domain, and the models cannot be properly validated. As a result, modeling of human emotions with such tools may produce invalid or poor quality results, and be error-prone and time-consuming.

HEM-L addresses the shortcomings of general-purpose tools by being based on a metamodel representing key concepts and abstractions from the human emotion domain. As a result, it provides a set of modeling constructs specific to this domain, and allows for validating the models to conform to a domain-specific metamodel containing proper conceptualizations. Of course, field tests must be carried out to determine whether our modeling language is complete and detailed enough.

6   Conclusions and Future Work

In this paper, we proposed HEM-L, a domain specific modeling language for modeling human emotions. Following a systematic development procedure, we defined the language scope, designed the set of concepts for its metamodel, elaborated their graphical representation in the models, and implemented its tool support. We also defined the ways of representing the instances of emotion situations by means of a text-based language. Furthermore, we outlined how to embed HEM-L into other DSMLs.

What we reported on here is work in progress. Consequently, a comprehensive evaluation of the proposed approach is pending. However, we can rely on the experience we have gained in our laboratory with successfully completed projects and will apply the evaluation procedures used to the project in question. For now, we performed an initial evaluation of our modeling method by implementing the HEM-L Modeler, and using it to build models covering emotional situations in a set of common AAL scenarios collected within our Human Behavior Monitoring and Support project [23] and from the available literature.

For future research, we first plan to evaluate the proposed modeling language with more complex emotional situations and to complete the means for weaving HEM-L and HCM-L (see Sect. 4) on three levels of the metamodeling hierarchy (i.e. including model weaving and data merging).

Further, we plan to address the issue of obtaining emotion information from external emotion recognition systems. As such systems are heterogeneous, interfacing with them in a flexible manner requires defining an *emotion interface description language* on the conceptual and implementation levels. As the information about the emotional response itself, and its context can come from different sources (e.g. the context can be recognized by means of Human Activity Recognition systems), it is also required to combine the interface description language and existing DSMLs for interfacing with context recognition systems. This requirement may lead to applying the aspect-oriented approach in a way described in Sect. 4. We plan to elaborate the means for weaving the interface description language metamodel and a metamodel for a DSML that describes the interfaces to external human activity recognition systems [30].

References

1. ADOxx® metamodeling framework. https://www.adoxx.org
2. ADOxx® ALL Java API. https://www.adoxx.org/live/adoxx-java
3. Baggia, P., et al.: Speech synthesis markup language (SSML) version 1.1 (2010)
4. Baniassad, E., Clements, P.C., et al.: Discovering early aspects. IEEE Softw. **23**(1), 61–70 (2006)
5. Bock, A., Frank, U.: Multi-perspective enterprise modeling—conceptual foundation and implementation with ADO*xx*. In: Karagiannis, D., Mayr, H., Mylopoulos, J. (eds.) Domain-Specific Conceptual Modeling, pp. 241–267. Springer, Cham (2016). https://doi.org/10.1007/978-3-319-39417-6_11
6. Brader, T.: Campaigning for Hearts and Minds: How Emotional Appeals in Political Ads Work. University of Chicago Press (2006)
7. Burkhardt, F., et al.: W3C Emotion Markup Language (EmotionML) (2014)
8. Clark, T., Evans, A., Kent, S.: Aspect-oriented metamodeling. Comput. J. **46**(5), 566–577 (2003)
9. Dinkelaker, T., Eichberg, M., Mezini, M.: An architecture for composing embedded domain-specific languages. In: Proceedings of the AOSD 2010, pp. 49–60 (2010)
10. Elkobaisi, M.R., Machot, F.A., Mayr, H.C.: Human Emotion Recognition - A Survey focusing on Ontologies, Datasets, and Systems, under revision
11. Estublier, J., Vega, G., Ionita, A.D.: Composing domain-specific languages for wide-scope software engineering applications. In: Briand, L., Williams, C. (eds.) MODELS 2005. LNCS, vol. 3713, pp. 69–83. Springer, Heidelberg (2005). https://doi.org/10.1007/11557432_6
12. Fill, H.G., Karagiannis, D.: On the conceptualisation of modelling methods using the ADOxx meta modelling platform. EMISAJ **8**(1), 4–25 (2013)
13. Frank, U.: Domain-specific modeling languages: requirements analysis and design guidelines. In: Reinhartz-Berger, I., Sturm, A., Clark, T., Cohen, S., Bettin, J. (eds.) Domain Engineering, pp. 133–157. Springer, Heidelberg (2013). https://doi.org/10.1007/978-3-642-36654-3_6
14. Froumentin, M.: Extensible multimodal annotation markup language (EMMA): invited talk. In: NLPXML 2004, p. 33 (2004)
15. Katz, S.: Assessing self-maintenance: activities of daily living, mobility, and instrumental activities of daily living. Journal (JAGS) **31**(12), 721-7 (1983)
16. Lench, H.C., Darbor, K.E., Berg, L.A.: Functional perspectives on emotion, behavior, and cognition. Behav. Sci. **3**, 536–540 (2013)
17. Marriott, A.: VHML-virtual human markup language. In: Talking Head Technology Workshop, at OzCHI Conference, pp. 252–264 (2001)
18. Mayr, H.C., et al.: HCM-L: domain-specific modeling for active and assisted living. In: Karagiannis, D., Mayr, H., Mylopoulos, J. (eds.) Domain-Specific Conceptual Modeling, pp. 527–552. Springer, Cham (2016). https://doi.org/10.1007/978-3-319-39417-6_24
19. Mayr, H.C., Michael, J., Ranasinghe, S., Shekhovtsov, V.A., Steinberger, C.: Model centered architecture. In: Cabot, J., Gómez, C., Pastor, O., Sancho, M., Teniente, E. (eds.) Conceptual Modeling Perspectives, pp. 85–104. Springer, Cham (2017). https://doi.org/10.1007/978-3-319-67271-7_7
20. Mayr, H.C., et al.: A model centered perspective on software-intensive systems. In: EMISA, pp. 58–64 (2018)
21. Michael, J., Mayr, H.C.: Conceptual modeling for ambient assistance. In: Ng, W., Storey, V.C., Trujillo, J.C. (eds.) ER 2013. LNCS, vol. 8217, pp. 403–413. Springer, Heidelberg (2013). https://doi.org/10.1007/978-3-642-41924-9_33

22. Michael, J., Mayr, H.C.: Creating a domain specific modelling method for ambient assistance. In: ICTer 2015, pp. 119–124. IEEE (2015)
23. Michael, J., et al.: The HBMS story. EMISAJ **13**, 345–370 (2018)
24. Nummenmaa, L., Glerean, E., Hari, R., Hietanen, J.K.: Bodily maps of emotions. Proc. Natl. Acad. Sci. **111**(2), 646–651 (2014)
25. Object Management Group: Meta Object Facility (MOF) Specification. www.omg. org/cgi-bin/doc/?formal/02-04-03.pdf
26. Prendinger, H., Ishizuka, M.: Life-Like Characters: Tools, Affective Functions, and Applications. Springer, Heidelberg (2013). https://doi.org/10.1007/978-3-662-08373-4
27. Rashid, A., Moreira, A.: Domain models are NOT aspect free. In: Nierstrasz, O., Whittle, J., Harel, D., Reggio, G. (eds.) MODELS 2006. LNCS, vol. 4199, pp. 155–169. Springer, Heidelberg (2006). https://doi.org/10.1007/11880240_12
28. Schröder, M., et al.: First suggestions for an emotion annotation and representation language. In: Proceedings of LREC, vol. 6, pp. 88–92 (2006)
29. Sebe, N., et al.: Multimodal approaches for emotion recognition: a survey. In: Internet Imaging VI, vol. 5670, pp. 56–67 (2005)
30. Shekhovtsov, V.A., Ranasinghe, S., Mayr, H.C., Michael, J.: Domain specific models as system links. In: Woo, C., Lu, J., Li, Z., Ling, T.W., Li, G., Lee, M.L. (eds.) ER 2018. LNCS, vol. 11158, pp. 330–340. Springer, Cham (2018). https://doi.org/10.1007/978-3-030-01391-2_37
31. Williams, B.: Consideration of Function & Functional Decline, Current Diagnosis and Treatment: Geriatrics, 2nd edn., pp. 3–4 (2014)
32. Wolf, M.: Cyber-physical systems. In: High-Performance Embedded Computing, pp. 391–413. Newnes (2014)

Towards an Ontology for Tertiary Bioinformatics Research Process

Pietro Crovari[✉][iD], Sara Pidò[iD], and Franca Garzotto

Department of Electronics, Information and Bioengineering, Politecnico di Milano, via Ponzio 34/5, 20133 Milan, Italy
{pietro.crovari,sara.pido,franca.garzotto}@polimi.it

Abstract. Next-generation sequencing techniques made possible enormous steps in the sequencing of genomic material. These advancements were not supported by similar progress in developing of tools for extracting knowledge from these data: interfaces used to analyze genomic data require high Computer Science expertise, being not suitable for most researchers with a biological or clinical background. As a consequence, these tools impose cognitive barriers to bioinformatics research. An ontology of the research process has to be used as a reference during the development of new tools to overcome these barriers. In this work, we run a user study to elicit a hierarchical task tree of the tertiary bioinformatics research process. Then, we show how such a model can be exploited to design interfaces that are not only focused on the data treated but keep in consideration both the research workflow and the researchers' requirements. Our work has profound implications on designing new, accessible bioinformatics tools that can enhance genomic research.

Keywords: Ontology · Bioinformatics · Tertiary analysis · Hierarchical task analysis · Hierarchical task tree

1 Introduction

Due to the large amount of genomic data that has been generated in recent years, storing and processing biological information has created new challenges. In this context, bioinformatics and computational biology have tried to overcome such challenges [9]. Bioinformatics has been defined as "the application of computational tools to organize, analyze, understand, visualize, and store information associated with biological macromolecules" [14].

Typically, bioinformatics can be subdivided into primary, secondary, and tertiary analysis [21]. The primary data analysis consists of identifying and evaluating raw data, focusing on generating readable sequencing reads (base calling), and ranking the basis's consistency. The outputs are usually FASTQ files (Illumina) that are inputs of the secondary analysis, consisting of aligning the reads against the human genome and variant calling [21]. Finally, tertiary analysis is

---

P. Crovari and S. Pidò—These authors contributed equally to this work.

G. Grossmann and S. Ram (Eds.): ER 2020 Workshops, LNCS 12584, pp. 82–91, 2020.
https://doi.org/10.1007/978-3-030-65847-2_8

considered the most challenging step since it allows us to study the sequencing results. More in detail, it focuses on understanding the raw data using statistical algorithms, machine learning, and data mining ones [16].

Today, there exist many different bioinformatics tools that allow us to perform these three types of analysis. Though, the vast majority of these tools are designed, keeping in consideration exclusively constraints arising from data processing but neglecting the ones coming from the user and the ones regarding the interaction design. In the tertiary analysis, this problem is amplified, since data and operations become even more complex. The resulting design of the interface requires a deep understanding of Computer Science concepts to process data correctly.

As a consequence, the usability is a severe issue. As Bolchini states, problems that current bioinformatics tools suffer from severely impact advancements in this discipline [5]. In fact, in today's panorama, researchers must spend a tremendous cognitive effort interacting with the platform, being distracted from the interaction's goal: the biological interpretation of the data processed. In other cases, researchers are also discouraged from using the tools because of their lack of computer science skills.

For these reasons, bioinformatics research must tackle the challenge of creating tools that result usable for the final users. It is necessary to start thinking about these tools from the researcher's perspective, keeping into consideration user requirements in the software's design and development phases. Thus, it is necessary to have a deep understanding of the bioinformatics research process: this can give a clearer idea of the operative pipeline, where to insert the developed tools, and, consequently a clearer understanding of the user requirements. Even if many designers understood the importance of basing the design of such tools on ontologies of the process [6], to the best of our knowledge, no studies focused on the elicitation of such a process.

In this context, our research takes place. We want to elicit the complete tertiary analysis process to create an explicit model of the pipeline. To do so, we run a user study to gather information on the process and then conceptualize it using the hierarchical task analysis framework. Our work brings two major contributions:

1. an ontology, in the form of a hierarchical task tree, representing the complete bioinformatics tertiary process, and
2. a concrete example of the application of the elicited ontology to design a tool for data retrieval and extraction.

2   State of the Art

In the beginning, bioinformaticians analyze and study genomic data through command lines. Due to bioinformatics research progress, many tools have been developed to help bioinformaticians during the analysis.

Particularly, it is possible to identify two main types of interfaces used for bioinformatics analysis: the traditional graphical user interfaces and, recently, the conversational ones that have started to be developed. Among all the available GUI, some worth mentioning are Galaxy [2], OrangeBioLab [8], UCSC Xena [11], Globus Genomics [15] or GenePattern [24]. Galaxy [2] is a scientific workflow, data integration, and data analysis platform focused on the secondary bioinformatics analysis. It provides a quite simple graphical user interface. OrangeBioLab [8] is a data visualization tool that allows us to analyze the uploaded data using data mining, machine learning, predictive modeling, feature scoring. UCSC Xena [11] or Globus Genomics [15] are two visual programming interfaces to analyze genomic data. GenePattern [24] is a powerful scientific workflow system that provides access to hundreds of genomic analysis tools: it is composed of many modules that allow the bioinformatics analysis through both a web interface or a command-line one.

While it is a lot of years that graphical interfaces have been used to make bioinformatics more user-friendly, conversational interfaces have recently become more and more employed.

To make some examples, we can mention Ava [13] and Iris [10], two chatbots developed to help data scientists to compose data analytic pipelines. Both can build the workflow through the dialogue and transform it into an executable Jupyter Python notebook. The first one guides the user through the execution of a pre-defined work pipeline. At each step, it invites the user to choose the desired operations and their parameters. Whereas, Iris acts as a conversational wrapper for data science functions that allows users to combine them as they like.

Even if in bioinformatics, conversational agents are not yet common, there are some first attempts to use them for retrieval of biological data through natural language processing. Some examples are Maggie [20], BioGraphBot [18] and Ok DNA! [7]. Particularly, Maggie is a conversational interface to extract data from BioCatalog. The interaction in natural language facilitates users, but the agent does not actively support them. BioGraphBot is instead a chatbot that allows users to translate queries in natural language to Gremlin queries to extract biological data from BioGraphDB. The last one, Ok DNA! has the idea of helping biologists and clinicians in extracting genomic data without knowing querying languages.

In order to design usable and efficient platforms, it is fundamental to have a clear idea of the tasks to support [3]. Human-Computer Interaction research spent a considerable effort to produce many frameworks for task model elicitation [1]. The GOMS framework is one of the most known and adopted ones [12]. GOMS have been designed to describe task analysis in User Interaction through the means of four fundamental elements of the interaction: *Goals*, *Operators*, *Methods*, and *Selection Rules*. In the years, many variants have been developed. MECANO [22], MOBI-B [23], TRIDENT [4] and TADEUS [25] are other spread framework; in these cases, though, the models preclude the integration of the knowledge of the user [1].

Among the available framework, a considerable number adopted a tree-based representation for the elicited model. Most of them follow the assumption that tasks are not atomic and individuals but can be decomposed into sub-tasks, therefore originating a hierarchy. This representation facilitates the elicitation process; on top of that, produced trees enable the comparison of different approaches used to support the same task, both in terms of the types and the number of steps the approaches require. One of the most popular tree-based frameworks is Concur-TaskTree [19], which is capable embeds inside the topology of the model also the temporal dependencies of the tasks. To the scope of this paper, we will use Hierarchical Task Analysis, given its suitability for being adopted in user studies [26].

3   Empirical Study

In order to construct the conceptual model of the bioinformatics tertiary analysis research process, we ran a user study to understand researchers' work routines. We conducted interview sessions that terminated in the construction of a hierarchical task tree. Then, we confronted and integrated the various sessions' outcomes to create a unique tree able to generalize all the individuals' research process.

Population. We interviewed eight bioinformatics expert, recruited on a volunteer basis. The population was balanced in gender (4M, 4F) and heterogeneous in Academia's role (3 Ph.D. students, 2 research assistants, 2 postdoctoral researchers, and 1 assistant professor). All the volunteers were recruited through emails. No sensitive information of the participants was stored to guarantee the anonymity of the collected data.

Setting. The study took place in a room where the participants and the interviewer could sit around a table. Both the interviewed and the researcher had their personal computer in front of them. Due to the current pandemic emergency outbreak, some of the interviews were held with the same protocol and online through a video conferencing software.

Protocol. The study consisted of a semi-structured individual interview, divided into three phases. During the whole process, the volunteers could use a virtual whiteboard to help themselves with sketches.

In the beginning, the participants had to describe the steps that constitute their typical research process. No constraints were given about the granularity of the steps, neither on their number. The researcher intervened to ask for a description of the steps or to ask for any clarification. Once formulated the pipeline, the volunteers had to classify the process elements according to their abstraction level. Finally, participants had to create a hierarchical task tree starting from the elicited actions and integrating them with parents and child tasks to complete the hierarchy.

Results. All the participants successfully concluded the interview session. Comparing the first phase outcomes, we notice that the research flow is similar for most participants. Despite different abstraction levels that the interviewed people adopted, a comparison of the results shows that similar actions have the same ordering in the different pipelines. In particular, four typical macro-phases results: the retrieval of the data, their exploration, the data analysis, and the visualization and validation of the results, both from a computational and biological perspective. On the other hand, different participants focused more on different workflow sections, therefore providing complementary perspectives on the tertiary analysis.

During the second phase, the volunteers' classification was very similar, showing similar perceptions on the abstraction of the various operations.

The final phase resulted in a set of trees with very similar topology. Comparing the trees created few conflicts, all of them in the deepest nodes, showing how the researchers implicitly agree on how the research process is carried out. As in the first phase, different areas of the trees were stressed during the interviews.

4   Ontology

We create a hierarchical task tree as an ontology to describe the bioinformatics tertiary research process from user study outcomes.

The tree-based representation has many advantages. First, the research process can be analyzed at different abstraction levels according to the need for specificity. Consequently, a unique hierarchical structure can describe tools that operate at a different level. Simultaneously, the hierarchy embeds essential information, like the *part of* relationship, useful for the design and the specification of a tool functionalities. For example, if a tool predicates on a task, it must allow the user to perform all the children operations.

To elicit the ontology, we iteratively integrated the trees described by the study participants in a unique structure. When conflicts arose, we opted for the solution adopted by the majority of the participants. In the case of a tie, we asked an expert bioinformatician not involved in the interviews to resolve the conflict, providing his perspective.

The Fig. 1 illustrates the final tree. From the interviews, it comes out that the main phases that compose a tertiary bioinformatics analysis are shared with most data science applications. Indeed, they are: *defining objectives, data extraction, data analysis*, and *results analysis*. The peculiar task of bioinformatics research emerges going in-depth in the tree, that means looking at the process more in detail.

Defining objectives is the first step computed by every interviewed person. It is characterized by the definition of the research question, followed by a state of the art analysis to understand related advancements and existing procedures. In this step, a bioinformatician also wants to understand which are the deliverables needed to answer to the research question; for example, which are the data, tables, or plots necessary to verify the research hypothesis.

After having defined the goal of the research, bioinformatics analysis proceeds with the data extraction. This phase is, in turn, composed of three parts. The first one is the data retrieval: after looking at the different public available biological data, a bioinformatician selects the datasets of interest. The chosen data are explored: first, their format and meaning are studied, then there is a first preprocessing. The data are analyzed to assess their quality, clean them, remove the noisy or wrong ones, and then normalize them according to the most suitable metric. Sometimes, a user selects more than one dataset, thus, the data needs to be integrated.

The third phase is the core of the process. Data analysis is the part in which the extracted data are studied and passed through the algorithm selected to answer the biological question. First, some preliminary analyses are computed to choose the algorithm. Then the data has to be prepared and organized into training and test sets to be passed to the chosen algorithm. Eventually, the analysis is executed with a parameter tuning, and, if needed, it is optimized.

Finally, the last step is the analysis of the results. The results of a computational biology analysis are divided into computational and biological ones. The first ones are evaluated through performances and robustness. Furthermore, comparative analysis and testing is computed on them. The biological results are instead validated through commonly used analysis, such as enrichment analysis.

Even if we represent the tertiary analysis as a streamlined process, we do not have to forget that this process is a continuous iteration between the phases. Indeed, researcher iteratively refines their hypothesis to draw scientifically significant conclusions.

5   Example Application

From our research process ontology, it is possible to develop tools that can be easily used by bioinformaticians and biologists. For example, we would like to build a conversational agent that allows us to extract the required genomic data, i.e., the Data Extraction task. As the ontology suggests, the tool must allow users to perform three macro operations, retrieving the datasets, exploring the retrieved data, and, if necessary, their integration. Consequently, we design a conversation formed by three main moments that represent the three macro operations. The same reasoning must be applied iteratively at every part of the conversation, breaking each operation in its sub-tasks, until the leaves of the ontology are reached and mapped to dialogue units.

Following the Data Extraction branch, the resulting agent starts by providing all the publicly available data, and the user decides which datasets to select. Users can apply filtering operations to refine the research. Then, the chatbot allows us to explore the data starting from providing the user the data meaning and format and proceeding with asking if the user wants to compute some quality assessment, data cleaning, and normalization. In particular, for this last part, the agent must ask the user which metrics she would like to use. The agent is

Fig. 1. Resulting tree that represents the ontology of the typical bioinformatics tertiary analysis.

able to create the workflow for the Data Retrieval from the conversation with the user, and it allows the user to download the datasets for the following analysis.

Figure 2 shows an instance of the conversation. Knowing the underlying process flow, the agent does not limit itself to execute the requested operations requested, but actively support and guide them through the pipeline. In fact, at every moment, the chatbot exactly knows what the user is doing in that specific moment and what they will have to do to accomplish their goals.

The output of one operation must be the input accepted by the following one, to allow users to pass from an operation to the other smoothly. Indeed, the selected datasets in the Data Retrieval phase are passed to the Data Exploration and, after the cleaning and normalization to the Data Integration one.

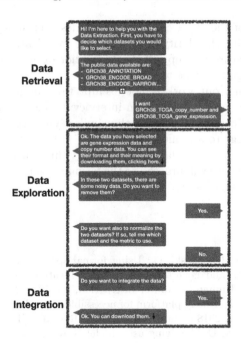

Fig. 2. Example of a dialogue built using our ontology.

6   Conclusion

In this work, we ran a user study to elicit an ontology of the bioinformatics tertiary analysis process systematically. With our research, we bring two major contributions:

- an ontology of the bioinformatics research process, and
- an example of exploitation of the elicited ontology for the design and development of a new tool

Even if the elicited ontology is still at an embryonic level, since it does not fully exploit the potentialities ontologies modeling languages, it paves the ground to profound implications for the bioinformatics research panorama. Such a model allows tools designers to have a complete overview of the process in which the tool is inserted, therefore seeing the tools not as stand-alone pieces of software, but as part of a broader pipeline. In this way, the ontology can provide the platform requirements from a functional perspective (such as input data format, expected output, and required operations) and facilitate the integration of tools with complementary capabilities. A tree-based model has the advantage of being usable at every level of abstraction, resulting in more flexibility for its adoption. Keeping in mind the pipeline, the designer can truly understand the problem from the users' point of view and have a complete overview of the motivations that drive a user to use such a method.

A clear model of the research process provides a clear way of stating tool capabilities, improving the clarity of the software specifications. Simultaneously, a standard nomenclature can support the description of the platform capabilities, removing any ambiguity in the terminology.

Even if promising, our work is not exempt from limitations. The current pandemic emergency prevented us from interviewing bioinformatics researchers on a larger scale. On the other hand, the similarity of the collected responses allowed us to converge to a unified model.

In the future, we aim at validating our ontology through a bottom-up analysis of existing tools. Then we will proceed to the formulation of the ontology through standard notations, such as OWL [17].

References

1. Abed, M., Tabary, D., Kolski, C.: Using formal specification techniques for the modelling of tasks and generation of HCI specifications. In: The Handbook of Task Analysis for Human Computer Interaction, pp. 503–529 (2003)
2. Afgan, E., et al.: The galaxy platform for accessible, reproducible and collaborative biomedical analyses: 2018 update. Nucleic Acids Res. **46**(W1), W537–W544 (2018)
3. Benyon, D., Murray, D.: Applying user modeling to human-computer interaction design. Artif. Intell. Rev. **7**(3–4), 199–225 (1993)
4. Bodar, F., Hennebert, A.M., Leheureux, J.M., Provot, I., Vanderdonckt, J., Zucchinetti, G.: Key activities for a development methodology of interactive applications. In: Benyon, D., Palanque, P. (eds.) Critical Issues in User Interface Systems Engineering, pp. 109–134. Springer, London (1996). https://doi.org/10.1007/978-1-4471-1001-9_7
5. Bolchini, D., Finkelstein, A., Perrone, V., Nagl, S.: Better bioinformatics through usability analysis. Bioinformatics **25**(3), 406–412 (2009)
6. Cannataro, M., Veltri, P.: MS-analyzer: preprocessing and data mining services for proteomics applications on the grid. Concurr. Comput. Pract. Exp. **19**(15), 2047–2066 (2007)
7. Crovari, P., et al.: Ok, DNA!: a conversational interface to explore genomic data. In: Proceedings of the 2st International Conference on Conversational User Interfaces, to be published
8. Demšar, J., et al.: Orange: data mining toolbox in python. J. Mach. Learn. Res. **14**, 2349–2353 (2013). http://jmlr.org/papers/v14/demsar13a.html
9. Diniz, W., Canduri, F.: Bioinformatics: an overview and its applications. Genet. Mol. Res. **16**(1) (2017)
10. Fast, E., Chen, B., Mendelsohn, J., Bassen, J., Bernstein, M.S.: Iris: a conversational agent for complex tasks. In: Proceedings of the 2018 CHI Conference on Human Factors in Computing Systems, pp. 1–12 (2018)
11. Goldman, M.J., et al.: Visualizing and interpreting cancer genomics data via the Xena platform. Nat. Biotechnol. 1–4 (2020)
12. John, B.E., Kieras, D.E.: The GOMS family of user interface analysis techniques: comparison and contrast. ACM Trans. Comput.-Hum. Interact. (TOCHI) **3**(4), 320–351 (1996)
13. John, R.J.L., Potti, N., Patel, J.M.: Ava: from data to insights through conversations. In: CIDR (2017)

14. Luscombe, N.M., Greenbaum, D., Gerstein, M.: What is bioinformatics? A proposed definition and overview of the field. Methods Inf. Med. **40**(04), 346–358 (2001)
15. Madduri, R.K., et al.: Experiences building Globus Genomics: a next-generation sequencing analysis service using Galaxy, Globus, and Amazon web services. Concurr. Comput.: Pract. Exp. **26**(13), 2266–2279 (2014)
16. Masseroli, M., et al.: Processing of big heterogeneous genomic datasets for tertiary analysis of next generation sequencing data. Bioinformatics **35**(5), 729–736 (2019)
17. McGuinness, D.L., Van Harmelen, F., et al.: Owl web ontology language overview. W3C Recomm. **10**(10), 2004 (2004)
18. Messina, A., Augello, A., Pilato, G., Rizzo, R.: BioGraphBot: a conversational assistant for bioinformatics graph databases. In: Barolli, L., Enokido, T. (eds.) IMIS 2017. AISC, vol. 612, pp. 135–146. Springer, Cham (2018). https://doi.org/10.1007/978-3-319-61542-4_12
19. Mori, G., Paternò, F., Santoro, C.: CTTE: support for developing and analyzing task models for interactive system design. IEEE Trans. Softw. Eng. **28**(8), 797–813 (2002)
20. Paixão-Côrtes, W.R., Paixão-Côrtes, V.S.M., Ellwanger, C., de Souza, O.N.: Development and usability evaluation of a prototype conversational interface for biological information retrieval via bioinformatics. In: Yamamoto, S., Mori, H. (eds.) HCII 2019. LNCS, vol. 11569, pp. 575–593. Springer, Cham (2019). https://doi.org/10.1007/978-3-030-22660-2_43
21. Pereira, R., Oliveira, J., Sousa, M.: Bioinformatics and computational tools for next-generation sequencing analysis in clinical genetics. J. Clin. Med. **9**(1), 132 (2020)
22. Puerta, A.R.: The Mecano project: enabling user-task automation during interface development. In: Proceedings of AAAI, vol. 96, pp. 117–121 (1996)
23. Puerta, A.R., Maulsby, D.: Management of interface design knowledge with MOBI-D. In: Proceedings of the 2nd International Conference on Intelligent User Interfaces, pp. 249–252 (1997)
24. Reich, M., Liefeld, T., Gould, J., Lerner, J., Tamayo, P., Mesirov, J.P.: GenePattern 2.0. Nat. Genet. **38**(5), 500–501 (2006)
25. Schlungbaum, E.: Support of task-based user interface design in TADEUS. Universitat Rostock (1998)
26. Stanton, N.A.: Hierarchical task analysis: developments, applications, and extensions. Appl. Ergon. **37**(1), 55–79 (2006)

Using BioPAX-Parser (BiP) to Annotate Lists of Biological Entities with Pathway Data

Giuseppe Agapito[1,2]([⊠]) [iD] and Mario Cannataro[2,3] [iD]

[1] Department of Legal, Economic and Social Sciences,
University "Magna Graecia" of Catanzaro, Catanzaro, Italy
agapito@unicz.it
[2] Data Analytics Research Center,
University "Magna Graecia" of Catanzaro, Catanzaro, Italy
cannataro@unicz.it
[3] Department of Medical and Surgical Sciences,
University "Magna Graecia" of Catanzaro, Catanzaro, Italy

Abstract. Proteins and genes are widely involved in activation or inhibition of the communication flow between a receptor and a transcription factor within a biological pathway. The key to fully understand proteins' functional roles is the deduction of the relationship between pathways and proteins. To facilitate the understanding of the complex flow of interactions characterizing biological pathways, in the last years, several public and private databases have been built to store, represent, visualize, and share pathways information. *Pathway Enrichment Analysis (PEA)* makes it possible to take advantage of the pathway databases information to discover connections with biological mechanisms. PEA methods help researchers to overcome the problem of interpreting gene lists, or other biological entity lists of interest, disconnected from the biological context, facilitating and validating their findings. Here, we introduce the BioPAX-Parser (*BiP*), an automatic and graphics-based tool aimed at performing PEA by using pathways data encoded in BioPAX format. BiP is fully developed using *Java 8*, and it helps the researcher to perform pathways enrichment analysis, merely loading a list of proteins/genes of interest. Enrichment in BiP has been performed by implementing *Hypergeometric* test, along with False Discovery Rate (FDR) and Bonferroni multiple-test statistical correctors. A case study of using BiP to annotate endometrial cancer gene list is also presented.

Keywords: Pathway Enrichment Analysis · Biological pathway · Statistical analysis · BioPAX

1 Introduction

Main experimental high throughput (HT) technologies such as Single Nucleotide Polymorphisms (SNPs) and gene expression microarrays, Next Generation

© Springer Nature Switzerland AG 2020
G. Grossmann and S. Ram (Eds.): ER 2020 Workshops, LNCS 12584, pp. 92–101, 2020.
https://doi.org/10.1007/978-3-030-65847-2_9

Sequencing (NGS), Genome Wide association Studies (GWAS), having made it possible to study thousands or hundreds thousands biological entities in the same experiments. HT assays brought up the complex molecular interactions network among the involved biological entities such as proteins, small molecules or microRNAs connected by interactions such as activation or synthesis, producing huge amount of data per single experiment.

Although the capacity of HT assays to produce data is advancing rapidly, the biological interpretation of those data remains a challenge, especially when interpretation regards connecting genetic discovery with known biological processes. Regardless of the HT assays used, they commonly yield a list of entities e.g., differentially expressed genes, proteins, SNPs, or microRNAs. This list is remarkably useful in recognising genes that may have roles in a given phenomenon or phenotype.

Complex diseases, such as cancers, or Alzheimer are due to the effects of the complex interaction among multiple genes, proteins, and other molecules, and are not due to the impact of a single mutated gene, for example. Biological pathways play an essential role in understanding the flow of multiple actions among molecules in a cell leading to a specific product or a variation in the cell. To facilitate the understanding of the complex flow of interactions characterizing biological pathways, in the last years several public and private databases have been built to store, represent, visualize and share pathways information. Pathway databases comprise KEGG [10], MetaCyc [2], PantherDB [8], Pathway-Commons [3], Reactome [6], and WikiPathways [11]. MetaCyc and KEGG provide information about metabolic pathways from several organisms, Reactome and Panther collect and share signaling and metabolic pathways information including human, WikiPathways contains information about metabolic, signaling, and regulatory pathways from multiple species. Finally, PathwayCommons is a collection of publicly available pathway data from multiple organisms.

Pathway Enrichment Analysis (PEA) makes it possible to take advantage of the pathway database information and the data yielded by HT assays, to discover connections with biological mechanisms. PEA methods can be classified into three classes: (1) Over Represented Analysis (ORA); (2) Gene Set Enrichment Analysis (GSEA); and (3) Topological Enrichment Analysis (TEA). The first two categories of methods perform enrichment analysis using as input a list of genes, proteins, SNPs, or mRNA. Whereas, the third class takes into account the topology information available from the pathways. PEA methods attempt to help researchers to overcome the problem of interpreting gene list or other biological entity lists of interest disconnected from the biological context, facilitating and validating their findings. Analyzing lists of genes, proteins, SNPs, or microRNAs at the functional pathway level, can provide more descriptive power than analyzing a list of disconnected entities.

We developed BioPAX-Parser (BiP) [1], a novel software tool able to compute PEA from a list of genes or proteins. BiP allows researchers to graphically dig with information from biological pathways represented in BioPAX (Biological Pathway Exchange) Level 3 format. The proposed approach is based on the following steps: *(i)* initially we load the input list containing the biological entities of interest; *(ii)* then, we compute enrichment by using a customized version of Hypergeometric test, along with the False Discovery Rate (FDR) and Bonferroni correctors, to correct the *p*-value from errors due to multiple statistical tests. BiP is freely available at https://gitlab.com/giuseppeagapito/bip, where users may download the software user guide and some toy datasets to familiarize with the BiP functions. To execute PEA, BiP integrates several pathways databases that are preliminary loaded into the system.

The remainder part of the paper is structured as follows: Sect. 2 describes PEA approaches and the main pathway databases. Section 3 discusses BiP methodology and implementation, Sect. 4 presents a case study of PEA and discusses the results of the application of BiP on a genes list of interest using different pathway databases. Finally Sect. 5 concludes the paper and outlines future work.

2   Background

This section presents main concepts related to the pathway databases and PEA approaches.

2.1   Pathway DataBases

The number of pathway databases is growing quickly in recent years. This is advantageous because biologists often need to use information from many sources to support their research. Here we report a short list of well-known pathway databases.

– KEGG[1] (Kyoto Encyclopedia of Genes and Genomes) is a collection of 19 databases, including genomic, chemical, pathway, and phenotypic information [7]. KEGG collects pathways in classes, including metabolic pathways, genetic information pathways, and signaling pathways. KEGG stores pathways from several organisms, including human. KEGG provides significant coverage for the human with 7, 217 annotated proteins. Pathways are manually curated from the experts through the literature. KEGG data can be accessed using the KEGG API or KEGG FTP, allowing users to download each pathway in KGML, the KEGG XML format used to encode the pathways. KEGG also provides a web interface to browse each pathway.
– MetaCyc[2] [2] is a curated database of experimentally elucidated metabolic pathways from all domains of life. MetaCyc contains 2, 847 pathways from 3, 161 different organisms. MetaCyc data can be accessed in several ways by searching pathways, enzymes, reactions, and metabolites, and by browsing MetaCyc metabolic pathways. Data can be downloaded in the following

---

[1] https://www.kegg.jp.
[2] https://metacyc.org.

formats: BioPAX, Pathway Tools attribute-value format, Pathway Tools tabular format, SBML format and Gene Ontology annotations. To access and download data, MetaCyc requires a paid subscription.

– Panther[3] (Protein Analysis Through Evolutionary Relationships Classification System) was designed to classify proteins (and their genes) in order to facilitate high-throughput analysis. The Panther Classifications are the result of human curation through the literature. Panther database includes protein sequencing, evolutionary information, metabolic and signaling pathways information. Panther in the current version [9] stores pathways from several organisms, including human, for a total of 177 pathways. Data can be accessed using the Panther API, or users may download pathways in the BioPAX, SBML and Protein Sequence Association data format.

– PathwayCommons[4] [3] is a collection of public pathway databases such as Reactome, PID and Cancer Cell Map as well as protein-protein interaction databases, such as HPRD, HumanCyc, IntAct, and MINT. The main goal of PathwayCommons is to provide an access point for a collection of public databases and includes technology for integrating pathway information. Pathway creation, extension, and curation remain the duty of the source pathway databases. PathwayCommons provides a web interface to browse pathways, as well as a web service API for automatic access to the data. Also, PSI-MI and BioPAX formats are supported for the data download. Furthermore, the complete PathwayCommons database can be automatically accessed using the PathwayCommons plugin.

– Reactome[5] is an open source, open access, manually curated, and peer-reviewed pathway database of human pathways, biological processes and biochemical reactions [4,5]. Reactome is the result of the joint efforts among several international research institutes. In the current version, Reactome contains the whole known pathways coming from 22 different organisms including the human. Reactome includes 2, 324 pathways, and 10, 923 annotated proteins for the *Homo sapiens*. Reactome allows to browse pathways through the graphical web interface, as well as to download the data in different formats comprising SBML Level 2, and BioPAX Level 2 and Level 3 and other graphical formats, for local analysis using other tools.

– WikiPathways[6] [11] is an open, collaborative platform dedicated to the curation of biological pathways. WikiPathways is a new model of pathway databases that improves and complements ongoing efforts, such as KEGG, Reactome and PathwayCommons. WikiPathways has a dedicated web page, displaying diagrams, description, references, download options, version history, and component gene and protein lists. Any pathway can be edited from the embedded pathway editor. WikiPathways data are freely available for download as image, and in GPML, a custom XML format. In addition, data can be accessed programmatically by using the available Webservice/API.

---

[3] http://www.pantherdb.org/.

[4] https://www.pathwaycommons.org.

[5] https://www.reactome.org.

[6] https://www.wikipathways.org/index.php/Help:Contents.

2.2 Pathway Enrichment Analysis Approaches

Pathway Enrichment Analysis approaches can be broadly divided in three different types:

- *Over Representation Analysis (ORA)*: it is the easiest PEA method because it can be used to analyze gene expressions, SNPs, or additional data. ORA methods perform statistical evaluation of the fraction of pathway components found among a user-selected list of biological components. They statistically evaluate the portion of genes in a particular pathway found among the set of genes. The enrichment is accomplished through an iterative methodology. It counts, for each pathway, the input genes that belong to the current pathway, repeating this process for the whole gene list, and each pathway into the database. The most used tests are based on the *hypergeometric, chi-square, Fisher's Test,* or *Binomial distribution.* The final results from an ORA method generally consist of a list of relevant pathways, ordered according to a P-value or multiple hypothesis tests corrected P-value.
- Gene Set Enrichment Analysis (GSEA): such methods exploit the hypothesis that significant change has a considerable effect on the pathway's genes. As well as, weaker but simultaneous changes in pathways' genes impact the general functioning. GSEA methods compute pathway enrichment analysis using a three steps methodology. *i)* The first step regards the computation of gene's statistical significance by using molecular measurement, e.g., the gene expression values. Gene statistics are assessed using the following methods: ANOVA, fold change, t-statistic, log-likelihood ratio, t-test, and Z-score. *ii)* The second step consists of aggregating each genes' statistics into pathway statistics. Pathway statistic is estimated using the Kolmogorov-Smirnov, Wilcoxon sum rank, and Chi-squared tests, respectively. *iii)* The last step regards the computing of the statistical relevance of the pathway. Statistical pathway relevance is assessed according to the selected *null* hypothesis. That can be done by permuting only genes' class labels (e.g., phenotype) into the pathway or permuting all the genes' class labels for each pathway.
- Topological Enrichment Analysis (TEA): it takes into account the connections/interactions among the entities, e.g., proteins, genes, or small molecules. Pathways are represented as a graph, where nodes represent pathway's component, e.g., genes, proteins, small molecules, and gene products; and edges provide information about the interactions among components, the type of interaction (e.g., activation, inhibition, and topological information) and where components interact, e.g., nucleus, membrane, etc. The main difference between ORA and GSEA methods, compared with TEA methods, is that TEA uses topological knowledge as additional information to calculate the enrichment value.

3   The BiP Algorithm and its Implementation

Here we discuss the BiP pathway enrichment analysis algorithm and the related software architecture.

3.1 BiP Algorithm

In this section, we briefly describe the *BiP* algorithm, developed to perform pathway enrichment analysis by using a gene or protein list of interest.

Algorithm 1 is a summary of the main phases of the *BiP* algorithm. The first step of BiP algorithm consists in loading the input pathway database (PD) and the transformation of each RDF-triple in *Attribute A*, to be indexed and stored into the *Attributes-Container AC*, making it possible to represent the RDF-triples in a graph-like mode. Concurrently to the loading and conversion phase, the input list of biological entities L is loaded and converted in gene name or UniprotID. Subsequently, as a results of the PEA calculation, the ranked list of enriched pathways EP is visualized to the user. Currently BiP loads the following pathways databases: Humancyc, KEGG, Netpath, Panther, PID, Reactome, and WikiPathways.

Algorithm 1. BiP Pathway Enrichment Analysis Algorithm

Require: Pathway Data PD, Entities List L
Ensure: Ranked List of Enriched Pathways EP
  1: *Data Structure initialization: AC, A, EP*

  2: $PD \leftarrow loadBioPAXdata()$
  3: $L \leftarrow loadEntities()$

  4: **for all** $rt \in PD$ **do**
  5:     $A \leftarrow convertRDF(rt)$
  6:     $AC \leftarrow A$
  7: **end for**

  8: $EP \leftarrow computePEA(AC, L)$

  9: $visualizeEnrichment(EP)$
10: **end.**

3.2 BiP Implementation

BiP has a layered architecture as depicted in Fig. 1 which is composed of 5 modules.

The *BiP-Core* module receives the user requests e.g., the biological entities' list of interest, the pathway datasets, and in addition it acts as controller for the other modules. The *Input Reader* module is composed of two submodules, the *BioPAX Reader* and the *Biological Entities List Reader*. The Input Reader module is implemented using the *Master-Slave* approach that is realized by using the *Java Threads package*, to achieve better performance in loading input files. The submodule *BioPAX Reader* is internally implemented by using the *RDF-Reader* component available within the *Jena* library version 3.1.0, that allows to load the *rdf-statements* represented in the form of ontological triples:

subject, *predicate* and *object*, used to define the pathway's features, making BiP independent from the pathway data source, as well as to speed-up the loading and extraction process from BioPAX files. Characteristic that allows BiP to perform PEA by using any pathway database compliant with the BioPAX format.

The *Biological Entities List Reader* submodule loads and translates the provided biological entities list using gene name, or Uniprot identifier.

The *RDFTripleHandler* module is responsible for improving the triples' handling. RDF triples in BioPAX are used to represent the complex biological interactions among the involved biological entities, e.g., genes, small molecules and mRNAs. Internally in BiP we have developed two customized data structures called *Attribute* and *Attributes-Container*. An *Attribute* stores in a compact way the rdf-triples through a hash function providing a twofold advantage: first it allows to compress the data saving space both in central and secondary memory; second, *Attributes* are indexed by the *Attributes-Container* data structure, allowing to get better performance in loading and handling flat BioPAX data, for the subsequent analysis. *Attributes-Container* indexes and stores the *Attribute* elements using a linked data structure emulating a graph-based representation, taking advantage from the graph structure encoded in the BioPAX format to represent the pathway's elements. Linking data such as a graph, let the algorithm to take advantage of the Depth First Search (DFS) or Breadth First Search (BFS), allowing to recursively scan the graph making it more efficient to go across the pathway and to improve the information handling.

The PEA module provides the calculation of the enrichment for each gene, protein, or microRNA loaded. It uses a customized version of the *Hypergeometric* test implemented in Java. The GUI module is based on Java Swing Technology (http://docs.oracle.com/javase/tutorial/uiswing/) and provides to the user transparent access to all the implemented functionalities. BiP is fully developed using *Java 8*, and it is available for download at https://gitlab.com/giuseppeagapito/bip.

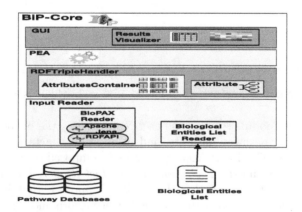

Fig. 1. BiP's modular architecture.

4   Case Study Results

Here we compare the enrichment results of BiP with respect to the pathDIP PEA software tool. pathDIP[7] is an annotated database of signaling cascades in human and non-human organisms, comprising core pathways from major curated pathways databases, allowing user to perform pathway enrichment analysis [12]. Conversely from pathDIP, BiP, in addition to PEA, allows to retrieve information enclosed in pathways compatible with the BioPAX format. For instance, users can automatically select proteins and genes enclosed in the pathway under analysis, and automatically annotate them with information from Uniprot database.

The gene list of interest were downloaded from the TCGA database available online at https://portal.gdc.cancer.gov/projects/TCGA-UCEC. We downloaded the Endometrial cancer mutated genes list that contains about 7,443 mutated genes. To perform pathway enrichment we used the pathway data from KEGG and Reactome databases.

BiP enriched 266 Reactome pathways, and 73 KEGG pathways, whereas pathDIP enriched 225 Reactome pathways, and 232 KEGG pathways. The comparison between the first 10 enriched pathways considering p-value lower than 0.05 from both databases using BiP and pathDIP provided the results discussed in the following. Figure 2 shows the enrichment overlap between BiP and pathDIP using Reactome and the endometrial genes list. Both tools show an enrichment overlap of 40% for pathways related to the cell activities such as, *Extracellular matrix organization, Ion channel transport, Gene expression (Transcription)*, and *RNA Polymerase II Transcription* pathways well known to contribute in endometrial cancer.

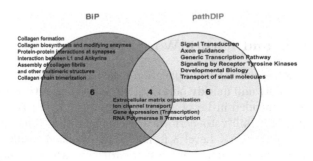

Fig. 2. The overlap between the first 10 enriched pathways obtained by BiP and pathDIP, by using Reactome pathways database.

Figure 3 shows the enrichment overlap between BiP and pathDIP using KEGG and the endometrial genes list. The enrichment results obtained by using KEGG database does not provide any overlap between the two tools. The non-overlap between the pathways enriched by the two tools requires further analysis

---

[7] http://ophid.utoronto.ca/pathDIP/.

to identify whether all the enriched pathways are involved in endometrial cancer (maybe, this can be due to the use of different versions of KEGG pathway database).

The obtained results show good performance in term of the number of relevant enriched pathways, and specificity. In particular, BiP enriched more pathways than pathDIP respect computing PEA by using Reactome database. In particular, BiP enriched 266 pathways with a mean p-value less than E^{-22}, whereas pathDIP enriched 224 pathways with a mean p-value less than E^{-15}. On the other hand, pathDIP enriched more pathways than BiP by using KEGG database. In particular, pathDIP enriched 232 pathways with a mean p-value less than E^{-24}, whereas BiP enriched 72 pathways with a mean p-value less than E^{-16}.

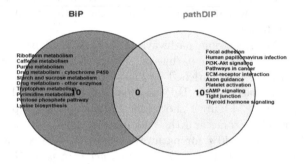

Fig. 3. The overlap between the first 10 enriched pathways obtained by BiP and pathDIP, by using KEGG pathways database.

5   Conclusion and Future Work

In this work we presented a Java application called BioPAX Parser (BiP), with which users can simply and quickly perform PEA, as well as retrieve information from BioPAX files encoded in Level 3. The main advantage of BiP in pathway enrichment is the possibility to perform enrichment from different databases compatible with the BioPAX Level 3 format. The obtained results show good performance in term of the number of relevant enriched pathways, and specificity. As future work, we are extending BiP in order to make it possible to compute enrichment by using as additional information the pathway topology.

In addition, we plan to extend BiP to deal with the majority of the available files format employed to represent pathway data, such as XML, SBML, GMTL.

References

1. Agapito, G., Pastrello, C., Guzzi, P.H., Jurisica, I., Cannataro, M.: BioPAX-Parser: parsing and enrichment analysis of BioPAX pathways. Bioinformatics (2020). https://doi.org/10.1093/bioinformatics/btaa529

2. Caspi, R., et al.: The MetaCyc database of metabolic pathways and enzymes and the BioCyc collection of pathway/genome databases. Nucleic Acids Res. **36**(Suppl. 1), D623–D631 (2007)

3. Cerami, E.G., et al.: Pathway commons, a web resource for biological pathway data. Nucleic Acids Res. **39**(Suppl. 1), D685–D690 (2010)

4. Fabregat, A., et al.: The reactome pathway knowledgebase. Nucleic Acids Res. **46**(D1), D649–D655 (2017)

5. Fabregat, A., et al.: Reactome pathway analysis: a high-performance in-memory approach. BMC Bioinform. **18**(1), 142 (2017). https://doi.org/10.1186/s12859-017-1559-2

6. Joshi-Tope, G., et al.: Reactome: a knowledgebase of biological pathways. Nucleic Acids Res. **33**(Suppl. 1), D428–D432 (2005)

7. Kanehisa, M., Goto, S.: KEGG: Kyoto encyclopedia of genes and genomes. Nucleic Acids Res. **28**(1), 27–30 (2000)

8. Mi, H., et al.: The panther database of protein families, subfamilies, functions and pathways. Nucleic Acids Res. **33**(Suppl. 1), D284–D288 (2005)

9. Mi, H., Muruganujan, A., Ebert, D., Huang, X., Thomas, P.D.: Panther version 14: more genomes, a new panther go-slim and improvements in enrichment analysis tools. Nucleic Acids Res. **47**(D1), D419–D426 (2019)

10. Ogata, H., Goto, S., Fujibuchi, W., Kanehisa, M.: Computation with the KEGG pathway database. Biosystems **47**(1–2), 119–128 (1998)

11. Pico, A.R., Kelder, T., Van Iersel, M.P., Hanspers, K., Conklin, B.R., Evelo, C.: WikiPathways: pathway editing for the people. PLoS Biol. **6**(7), e184 (2008)

12. Rahmati, S., et al.: pathDIP 4: an extended pathway annotations and enrichment analysis resource for human, model organisms and domesticated species. Nucleic Acids Res. **48**(D1), D479–D488 (2019). https://doi.org/10.1093/nar/gkz989

Relational Text-Type for Biological Sequences

Cristian Tristão[1] , Antonio Basilio de Miranda[2] , Edward Hermann
Haeusler[1] , and Sergio Lifschitz[1(✉)]

[1] Dep. Informática - (PUC-Rio), Rio de Janeiro, Brazil
`sergio@inf.puc-rio.br`
[2] Lab. Genética Molecular de Microrganismos, Fundação Oswaldo Cruz (FIOCRUZ),
Rio de Janeiro, Brazil

Abstract. DNA sequencers output very long biological data strings that
we should persist in a database system. In this paper, we first propose a
conceptual schema for representing the core biological information, which
may be inferred from biological data and necessary function manipulations. We also present a possible extension of the relational text data
type-specific to manipulate biological sequences and their derivatives.

1 Introduction and Motivation

One of the relevant open problems concerns the way to store and manipulate
biological sequence data. Information inherent to this domain, such as nucleotide
and its derivatives and relations (central dogma of molecular biology), are currently represented as simple character strings with no concern for their meaning.
To access the data, some index structures for manipulating sequences have been
proposed, especially the suffix tree [4,5]. It is a versatile and very efficient data
structure that can be built in linear time if it can be stored in main memory [3].

We claim that there is no standard to represent, store and manipulate appropriately a biological sequence. Moreover, even the derived information, such as
the relationship between the sequences that are part of the central dogma of
molecular biology and protein alignment are not appropriately considered.

Also, there is still no specific structure for the storage and manipulation
of biological data. Most systems persist data in files in text format, e.g. the
BLAST family [2] and SSEARCH [6]. Systems that use a relational database
persist sequences in structures of type string or BLOBs (Binary Large OBjects),
in its original form. This practice facilitates loading of repositories from text
files. However access to data is limited to traditional operators.

It is natural to use a DBMS such as relational ones to manage large volumes
of data. However, the available data structures are not suitable for managing
biological sequences. The problem with treating a biological sequence as a word
(string) or BLOB, used to store any data, files in general, is the loss of semantic
information. A "biological string" has well-defined interpretations, e.g. amino
acids, proteins, coding regions, etc., and specific characteristics that differ from

G. Grossmann and S. Ram (Eds.): ER 2020 Workshops, LNCS 12584, pp. 102–112, 2020.
https://doi.org/10.1007/978-3-030-65847-2_10

a word string, e.g. comparison and similarity are not simple pattern matching. Just to mention a few examples, there are no appropriate mechanisms to answer queries related to the identification homologous (analogues and orthologs) genes.

This paper proposes a biological conceptual schema to represent information related to the central dogma of molecular biology, as well as an abstract data type (ADT) specific to the manipulation of biological sequences and their derivatives. We have been inspired by dedicated system already adopted in Temporal Databases [7].

Section 2 brings our proposal comprising a conceptual schema of biological sequences and some common requirements for accessing and manipulating them. Section 3 we discuss the use of the relational string-type that, together with a relational schema with specific functions, may add semantics to our data. Finally, Sect. 4 is dedicated to the conclusions and future work.

2   Conceptual Modeling and Initial Data Manipulation

The great difficulty in representing and manipulating biological sequences is related to its origin. Everything we know today about molecular biology is abstractions of how things are. Second, a biological sequence, taken in isolation, has no meaning of its own. The information is "hidden" in the set of letters that make up the sequence, requiring a manipulation on it to extract such information.

We represent all the genetic information of a living organism in its linear sequence of the four bases. Therefore, a four-letter alphabet (A, T, C, G) must encode the primary structure (i.e., the number and sequence of the 20 amino acids) of all proteins. We may realize that representing biological sequences, quite simply, as a blob or string relational database type, does not make sense. Every set of information contained in a nature-based sequence is lost.

Furthermore, analyzing the behavior and some phenomena (manipulation), represented by the central dogma of molecular biology, that a biological sequence can suffer, we can define some rules (R) and functions (F) that an abstract type of data must consider.

In nature, there are two types of nucleic acids: DNA (deoxyribonucleic acid) and RNA (ribonucleic acid). Analogously to a communication system, this information is kept inside the cell in what we call a genetic code. In their primary structure, we see both DNA and RNA as a linear chain composed of simple chemical units called nucleotides. A nucleotide is a chemical compound with three parts: a phosphate group, a pentose (five-carbon sugar molecule), and an organic base. In DNA molecules, pentose is deoxyribose, while in RNA molecules, pentose is ribose. The organic base, also known as the nitrogenous base, characterizes each nucleotide. We may either refer to a nucleotide or base sequence. The bases are Adenine, Guanine, Cytosine, Timine, and Uracil, the first two are purines, and the last three are pyrimidines. In DNA, we find bases A, G, C, and T. In RNA, base U is observed instead of base T. Our first rule **R1** states that biological sequences are stored as nucleotides.

DNA molecules are made up of two strands, which bond together, forming a helical structure, known as a double helix. The two tapes are merged by the stable connection of their nucleotide bases. Base A always binds base T, and base G binds base C. Thus, the nucleotide sequence in one strand ultimately determines the DNA molecule. It is precisely this property that allows for DNA self-duplication.

Function F1 – complement (sequence)

Given a sequence, it returns its complement.

Ex.: complement ('ACGGCTATTTAGAC') = TGCCGATAAATCTG

Each strand of DNA has two ends, called 3′ and 5′, in an allusion to the carbon atoms free in the sugar that make up each nucleotide. The two tapes are antiparallel; that is, the tapes have a 5′ 3′ orientation opposite each other. The convention adopted worldwide to represent DNA molecules is to write only one of the strips in the 5′ 3′ direction. Therefore, our rule **R2** states that we will represent every nucleotide sequence in the 5′ 3′ direction. In this case, another function might be useful to obtain both directions:

Function F2 – reverse (sequence)

Given a sequence, the function returns its inverse.

Ex.: reverse ('ACGGCTATTTAGAC') = CAGATTTATCGGCA

Although the base composition varies from one species to another, the adenine amount is always equal to that of thymine ($A = T$). The number of guanine and cytosine bases is also the same ($G = C$). Consequently, the total amount of purines is equivalent to pyrimidine (i.e., $A + G = C + T$). On the other hand, the AT/GC ratio varies considerably between species.

Function F3 – getGCcontent (sequence)

Given a sequence, it returns the GC content that is present.

Ex.: getGCcontent('ACGGCTATTTAGACT') = 6

In the DNA nucleotide chain, a set of 3 nucleotides corresponds to an amino acid: they are the triplets. Through the transcription process, the DNA triplets are converted into RNA codons. These codons are, like triplets, sets of 3 nucleotides in the messenger RNA chain.

Function F4 – transcript (sequence)

Given a DNA sequence, its transcript (mRNA) is returned.

Ex.: transcript('ACGGCTATTTAGACT') = ACGGCUAUUUAGACU

It migrates to the cell's cytoplasm, where it binds to a ribosome and a carrier RNA molecule. Through the translation process and using the genetic information of the individual's DNA with the RNA molecule, the ribosome produces the amino acids to form the proteins.

> **Function F5 – translation (position, sequence)**
>
> *Given a nucleotide sequence, the amino acid sequence is*
> *returned using the genetic code translation table*
> *Ex.: translation (2, 'ACGGCTATTTAGACT') = RLFR*

ORF (Open Reading Frame) is a nucleotide sequence in a DNA molecule that can encode a peptide or a protein. Every protein originates from an ORF, but not every ORF originates from a protein.

An ORF is bounded by the AUG initiation codon, which encodes the amino acid Methionine (Met), indicating where the protein's amino acid sequence encoding begins. Also, the termination codons (UAA, UGA, and UAG) suggest that the amino acid sequence destined for that protein ends there. In this way, all proteins begin with the amino acid Met. ORF that does not have the identified protein product is called URF (unidentified reading frame).

> **Function F6 – searchORF (position, sequence, size)**
>
> *Given a nucleotide sequence, it returns a set of*
> *ORFs (possibly proteins) with a minimum size*
> *Ex.: searchORF (1, 'ACGAUGCUAUUUAGAUAGCUG', 10) = AUGCUAUUUAGAUAG*

This set of two rules and six functions is enough to generate an enormous amount of information. Besides, it facilitates users who do not have a domain, both in the database area and in the biology area. In the next section, we will discuss its implementation into a relational database.

A protein is generated from a gene, which is a region in a genomic sequence. A gene that encodes a protein produces a primary transcript that, after some processing, generates a mature transcript containing the protein-coding sequences (CDS). This mature transcript is formed by concatenating substrings containing information for proteins (exons) and untranslated regions (RTUs). An ORF is a series of nucleotides with a start codon (AUG) and extends to the first terminal codon (UAA, UGA, or UAG). ORFs may not be encoded in proteins. In this way, all coding sequences (CDS) are ORFs, but not every ORF encodes a protein.

The protein entity represents the amino acid sequence of a protein with the nucleotide sequence of a CDS and the CDS with the gene and the genomic sequence that contains it, maintaining only an external reference to its transcription. Thus, the CDS is an entity whose primary property is to keep the relationship between the protein, gene, and genomic sequence entities. This is done by placing a given gene coding region (exons) in the coordinate system of the genomic sequence that contains it. Each exon in a gene corresponds to a subsequence CDS, defined by a starting and ending position mapped in a genomic sequence coordinate system.

The nucleotide sequence of a gene that encodes a protein is part of a genomic sequence having sub-regions of codons (exons) and non-codons (introns and untranslated regions). The reading and transcription of a gene generate the mRNA, which in the future will be processed and transcribed into an amino acid sequence, which occurs in a specific direction in vivo (5' to 3').

The gene entity has an identifier, and we will use the NCBI identifier - Entrez Gene [Entrez Gene 2010], the geneId. We may define its corresponding region in the genomic sequence by a start and stop position, a sense of reading, a transcription identifier (from RefSeq), and the GC content. An ORF_T amino acid sequence is analogous. It relates to the genomic nucleotide sequence through an ORF_region delimited by a start and stop position within the genomic sequence, with the RefSeq identifier of the genomic sequence, the reading direction, its position concerning its neighboring gene, and the sequence itself.

A genomic nucleotide sequence (derived from a RefSeq) refers to the genes containing CDSs that code for the protein amino acid sequence. These genomic sequences have a status, which refers to the current stage of the sequencing project. The possible values for this property are:

- Complete, which typically means that each chromosome is represented by a single scaffold of a very high-quality sequence;
- Assembly, which typically means that scaffolds have been built not at the chromosome level or are of a low-quality sequencing project; and
- In Progress indicates that both the sequencing project is in the pre-assembly or the completed (assembled fragments) strings have not yet been submitted to public databases as the GenBank or EMBL.

The Genomic Sequence entity has a RefSeq identifier, definition and the length of the sequence, the type of organic molecule (DNA or RNA), status, type of sequence (chromosome, organelle, plasmid), an optional identifier of the respective genome project, GC content and an identifier of the original taxon.

The taxonomy of organisms is an essential organizing principle in the study of biological systems. Inheritance, homology by common descent, and the conservation of sequence and structure in determining function are all central ideas of biology directly related to the evolutionary history of any group of organisms. Taxonomic classification follows a hierarchy structure. We call this path from the root node to any other particular taxon a "lineage."

Regarding similarity information, there are three possible combinations of hits involving translated ORFs and proteins: (1) ORFs x ORFs; (2) proteins x ORFs; and (3) proteins x proteins. The minimum cardinality for all relationships is zero if the comparison does not generate significant hits. The maximum cardinality is n, as there may be several significant hits between the comparisons.

The translated amino acid sequences (ORF) are represented by another entity - ORF_T - because they do not have a previous identifier. Information about these strings includes the reference to the original organism, location, and size. There are three distinct types of relationships between hits, proteins, and translated ORFs.

- $hit_O O$ - result of the comparison between translated ORFs;
- $hit_O P$ - result of the comparison between ORFs translated with proteins derived from SwissProt. Proteins derived from RefSeq were not used in the comparison process with the translated ORFs;
- $hit_P P$ - result of the comparison of RefSeq proteins with RefSeq and SwissProt proteins.

These relationships have attributes that specify the comparison process's result, based on the information obtained using the Smith-Waterman algorithm. These are query gi, subject gi, SW score (gross score of the comparison), bit score (score normalized), e-value (alignment significance), % identity, alignment length (alignment size), query start, query end, subject beginning, subject end, query gaps, subject gaps. Figure 1 presents an overview of the proposed conceptual schema based on the entity-relationship model.

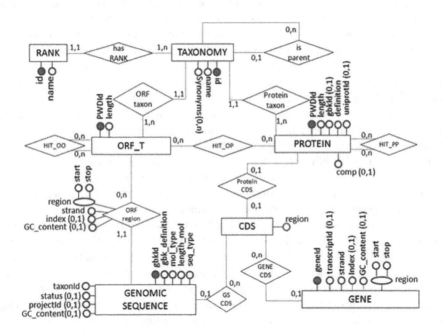

Fig. 1. A conceptual biological data schema

3   Sequences as Relational Text-Type

Once one has a conceptual schema, we must think about a corresponding logical schema looking forward to actual manipulations for biological applications and users. We claim that a straightforward mapping from our conceptual schema may quickly be obtained considering standard rules for transformations to the logical-relational model due to space limitations. Therefore, we might focus on the significant problem of representing biological sequences.

We will show that our data and functional requirements can be modeled directly in a robust and well-known relational system. However, there is no direct correspondence from very long biological sequences to relational data types. Moreover, those very long strings and sub-strings actually carry some semantics with them, and ideally, this should be taken into account.

Concerning any possible Abstract Data Type (ADT), we usually have two alternatives: (i) the creation of a new data structure that addresses all requirements and defines a new way of storing and manipulating the data, or (ii) the extension of an existing data type, enforcing the list of requirements to match only the user needs. If we think in terms of implementation, both alternatives have their pros and cons. On the one hand, creating a new type has the advantage of thinking and generating an appropriate structure and mechanisms for this new data type, which may have superior performance compared to an extended type. On the other hand, the effort to generate this new type is considerably higher. We need to create all the structures and mechanisms involved for storage and manipulation, which must run within an existing system. For the extended type, the scenario is reversed. Depending on the type used, the adaptation can be simplified, using any base already defined and developed. On the other hand, in terms of performance, the result may not be as satisfactory.

We claim that it may not be a problem to manage biological sequences in the relational model but, instead, the lack of semantics in the existing data structures. We propose and discuss in this paper the idea of a *bio-string* type, which is an extension of the *text* or *string* type. The main reason is the complexity of storing and representing biological sequences in BLOB structures concerning expressiveness. As BLOBs are designed to hold any possible data, there are no appropriate access and manipulation mechanisms.

The string type structure has a well-defined storage pattern and mechanisms for accessing and manipulating data. Nevertheless, if we use the string storage structure for biological sequences, we must create or rewrite functions or operators specific to the molecular biology domain. Common string functions such as *lower*, *upper* and *convert* do not make any sense for a biological applications.

A straightforward case study was carried out using the DBMS PostgreSQL [1], in its version 9.1, for prototyping of the solutions presented. The implemented functions proposed here, concerning explicitly biological data, are the only functions and operators available in the core DBMS implementation. The idea is to simulate an actual ADT.

As stipulated in Sect. 2, biological sequences will be stored as nucleotides (Rule R1). Besides, any nucleotide sequence will be considered in the 5'3' direction (Rule R2). In order to validate Rule 1, we need a function that verifies that the character set reported as a sequence of nucleotides is composed only of bases A, C, G, and T. For this, we may define the function isDNA (sequence), which it takes as a parameter a sequence of characters and returns TRUE if the sequence is formed only by nucleotides, FALSE otherwise.

The complement function returns a new nucleotide sequence, which corresponds to the other strand of the DNA molecule. This function's construction is based on the principle of *ligands* and base pairs: base A always connects to base T, and base G always attaches to base C and vice versa. Therefore, we must go through the input sequence, replacing each base with its pair. The reverse function returns the reverse sequence of an input nucleotide sequence. It makes it possible to read a DNA sequence in the 3′ 5′ direction. The basic idea for the construction of this function is to traverse the chain of nucleotide sequences by inverting the nucleotide bases' position.

Knowledge about the GC content of a DNA sequence is vital for determining the physical properties of DNA. The function for obtaining the GC content returns the number of bases G and C of a given input sequence. Unlike the other functions, which had to go through the nucleotide sequence to obtain the desired information, the getGCcontent function had its implementation simplified using predefined functions in the relational TEXT type, such as the *replace* function.

For the construction of the getGCcontent function, we use the replace function to return the occurrences of bases A and T with an empty character (" "), eliminating the sequence's bases. Subsequently, to obtain the GC content from the biological sequence, we must only get the resulting sequence's size, which now has only bases G and C (Fig. 2).

```
- Name: getGCcontent
- Input: sequence - nucleotide sequence
- Output: integer - amount of GC content
- Description: returns the amount of GC content of DNA sequence
CREATE OR REPLACE FUNCTION getGCcontent(TEXT) RETURNS INTEGER AS
$$
    DECLARE
        original ALIAS FOR $1;
        modify TEXT := '';
        length   INTEGER;
    BEGIN
        SELECT REPLACE(original,'A','') INTO modify;
        SELECT REPLACE(modify,'T','') INTO modify;
        SELECT LENGTH(modify) INTO length;
        RETURN length;
    END
$$
LANGUAGE plpgsql IMMUTABLE RETURNS NULL ON NULL INPUT;
```

Fig. 2. GC content relational function

The function that transforms a DNA sequence into an mRNA sequence is the transcript function. Its implementation is based on the getGCcontent function, requiring minor changes.

- **Name:** searchORF

- **Input:** position – integer

    sequence – nucleotide sequence (RNA)

    length - minimum size of ORF

- **Output:** sequence Collection – amino acid sequence (Protein)

- **Description:** search ORFs in a nucleotide sequence (RNA).

```
CREATE OR REPLACE FUNCTION searchORF(INTEGER,TEXT,INTEGER)
RETURNS SETOF TEXT AS
$$
    DECLARE
        pos ALIAS FOR $1;
        seq ALIAS FOR $2;
        size ALIAS FOR $3;
        tam INTEGER;
        tamORF INTEGER;
        sub character varying(3);
        orf TEXT := '';
        found BOOLEAN := false;
    BEGIN
        SELECT TRANSCRIPT(seq) INTO seq;
        SELECT LENGTH(seq) INTO tam;
        LOOP
            EXIT WHEN pos+2 > tam;
            SELECT substring (seq FROM pos FOR 3) INTO sub;
            IF (sub = 'AUG') THEN
                found := true;
            END IF;
            IF (found) THEN
                orf := orf || sub;
            END IF;
            IF (sub = 'UAA' OR sub = 'UGA' OR sub = 'UAG') THEN
                found := false;
                SELECT LENGTH(orf) INTO tamORF;
                IF (tamORF >10) THEN
                    RETURN QUERY SELECT orf;
                END IF;
                orf := '';
            END IF;
            pos := pos +3;
        END LOOP;
    END
$$
LANGUAGE plpgsql IMMUTABLE RETURNS NULL ON NULL INPUT;
```

Fig. 3. Search ORF function

To carry out the translation function, we must go through the nucleotide sequence of an mRNA molecule and convert them into an amino acid at each sequence of three bases. The translation function depends on a translation table of the genetic code. Two approaches are possible: (1) storing the translation table information in an auxiliary storage structure, or (2) inserting the mapping of nucleotide sequences into amino acids directly into the function body. For simplification, we have used the first alternative.

The transcribed DNA region is called an ORF (Open Read Frame). The main characteristic of an ORF is that it is a subsequence of transcribed DNA delimited by the initiation (AUG) and termination (UAA, UGA, and UAG) codons. As with the translation function, we must inform the starting position for reading (1, 2, or 3) to identify codons. Another parameter is the minimum size of the ORF. Like translation, the search for ORFs is performed on an RNA sequence. To avoid user errors (e.g., use a DNA sequence instead of RNA), the function transcribes the input sequence before actually performing the search. Figure 3 illustrates this function.

4   Conclusions

We have proposed a conceptual schema and extended data type structure for the representation of biological data. We have also presented a set of functions that manipulate and extract biological information from sequences based on information from molecular biology's central dogma.

The idea of proposing a *generic* biological conceptual schema helps reinforce some biological concepts, regardless of specific research projects. We have shown that an actual implementation of sequence-oriented functions on *bio-strings* type is feasible and effective. The set of proposed rules and functions maps the intrinsic semantic information from the very long character sequence representing biological concepts.

Our implementation also shows that it is quite feasible to deal with biological data within a relational database system. The relational model is not a problem but, rather, the lack of semantics in existing data structures and types. Our next steps include the idea of creating an actual Abstract Data Type for the biological domain. We look forward to enabling this extension as a PostgreSQL DBMS *contrib* publicly available.

References

1. PostgreSQL. http://postgresql.org
2. Altschul, S., Gish, W., Miller, W., Myers, E., Lipman, D.: Basic local alignment search tool. J. Mol. Biol. **215**(3), 403–410 (1990)
3. Cheung, C.F., Yu, J.X., Lu, H.: Constructing suffix tree for gigabyte sequences with megabyte memory. IEEE Trans. Knowl. Data Eng. **17**(1), 90–105 (2005)
4. Hunt, E., Atkinson, M., Irving, R.: A database index to large biological sequences. In: Proceedings of the International Conference on Very Large Databases, pp. 139–148 (2001)

5. Hunt, E., Atkinson, M., Irving, R.: Database indexing for large DNA and protein sequence collections. VLDB J. **11**(3), 256–271 (2002)
6. Pearson, W.: SSearch. Genomics **11**, 635–650 (1991)
7. Simonetto, E., Ruiz, D.: A proposal model to incorporation of temporal aspects to the relational DBMS using active databases concept. In: Proceedings IEEE 4th International Workshop on DBs and IS, pp. 52–59 (2000)

Conceptual Modeling, Ontologies and (Meta)data Management for Findable, Accessible, Interoperable and Reusable (FAIR) Data (CMOMM4FAIR) 2020

Preface

João Moreira[1], Luiz Olavo Bonino da Silva Santos[1],
Maria Luiza Machado Campos[2], Barbara Magagna[3], Peter Mutschke[4],
and Robert Pergl[5]

[1] University of Twente, The Netherlands
j.luizrebelomoreira@utwente.nl
[2] Federal University of Rio de Janeiro, Brazil
[3] Environment Agency, Austria
[4] Leibniz Institute for the Social Sciences, Germany
[5] Technical University of Prague, Czech Republic

The FAIR principles condense decades of work and challenges on data usage into four main aspects. The guidance provided by the principles on how to make data, or any other digital object findable, accessible, interoperable, and reusable is being seen as the basis on how organizations are tackling their modern informational challenges. The goal of FAIR is to promote optimal reusability of digital assets, mainly through the use of machines. A common expression is that "in FAIR, the machine knows what I mean." In other words, we would like to have computation systems that can properly interpret information found in their self-guided exploration of the data ecosystem.

Before machines are able to "know what we mean," the meaning in our informational artefacts should also be clear for us, thus, addressing semantic interoperability. Here enters conceptual modeling as a means to improve semantic interoperability by capturing knowledge about a particular universe of discourse in terms of various semantic artefacts such as ontologies, semantic data models, and semantic metadata models. The workshop on Conceptual Modeling, Ontologies and (Meta)Data Management for Findable, Accessible, Interoperable, and Reusable Data (CMOMM4FAIR) aims at investigating, discussing, and improving conceptual modeling practices towards improved FAIRness.

In this 2nd edition of the CMOMM4FAIR workshop, co-located with the 39th International Conference on Conceptual Modeling (ER 2020), we accepted the papers "Evaluating FAIRness of Genomic Databases," "Mapping the Web Ontology Language to the OpenAPI Specification" and "Reusable FAIR Implementation Profiles as Accelerators of FAIR Convergence." These papers discuss methods to evaluate adherence to the FAIR principles of genetics data repositories, an approach to map OWL ontologies and OpenAPI Specification facilitating the exploration of semantic-rich services by web developers, and a conceptual model for profiling FAIR implementation choices made by communities on how to realize the FAIR principles, respectively.

Apart from the paper presentations, the program includes invited talks to steer the discussions on FAIR and conceptual modeling. We would like to express our deepest appreciation to the authors of the submitted papers and to all Program Committee members for their diligence in the paper review and selection process. We would also like to thank the Organizing Committee of ER 2020, in particular the workshop chairs for all their support.

Mapping the Web Ontology Language to the OpenAPI Specification

Paola Espinoza-Arias[1]([⊠]) [iD], Daniel Garijo[2] [iD], and Oscar Corcho[1] [iD]

[1] Ontology Engineering Group, Universidad Politécnica de Madrid, Madrid, Spain
{pespinoza,ocorcho}@fi.upm.es
[2] Information Sciences Institute, University of Southern California, Los Angeles, USA
dgarijo@isi.edu

Abstract. Many organizations maintain knowledge graphs that are organized according to ontologies. However, these ontologies are implemented in languages (e.g. OWL) that are difficult to understand by users who are not familiar with knowledge representation techniques. In particular, this affects web developers who want to develop ontology-based applications but may find challenging accessing ontology-based data in knowledge graphs through SPARQL queries. To address this problem, we propose an accessible layer for ontology-based knowledge graphs through REST APIs. We define a mapping specification between the Web Ontology Language (OWL) and the OpenAPI Specification (OAS) to provide ontology-based API definitions in a language well-known to web developers. Our mapping specification identifies key similarities between OWL and OAS and provides implementation guidelines and examples. We also developed a reference mapping implementation that automatically transforms OWL ontologies into OpenAPI specifications in a matter of seconds.

Keywords: OWL · OpenAPI · REST API · Ontologies

1 Introduction

Many public and private organizations have adopted a knowledge-driven approach to make publicly available their knowledge graphs. Ontologies [10] play a crucial role in this approach, as they describe the knowledge about a domain in an agreed and unambiguous manner; and they allow organizing data, ease its reusability, and facilitate its interoperability. Ontologies are usually formalized in the Web Ontology Language (OWL) [6], a W3C recommendation to represent the semantics of a domain in a machine-readable way. However, OWL has a steep learning curve due its inherent complexity [12], and newcomers may get confused with the meaning of constraints, axioms or the Open World Assumption.

This problem has become evident in the case of developers who have an interest in taking advantage of the data available in existing knowledge graphs but are not used to Semantic Web technologies. Instead, developers are familiar with REST APIs as a resource-access way which hides details about the

© Springer Nature Switzerland AG 2020
G. Grossmann and S. Ram (Eds.): ER 2020 Workshops, LNCS 12584, pp. 117–127, 2020.
https://doi.org/10.1007/978-3-030-65847-2_11

implementation of operations for resource management or how such resources have been described according to the data models. To describe APIs, several Interface Description Languages have been defined to document their domain, functional and non-functional aspects. The OpenAPI Specification[1] (OAS) is a broadly adopted de facto standard for describing REST APIs in a programming language-agnostic interface. OAS allows both humans and computers to understand and interact with a remote service. Due to its wide adoption, OAS has a big community behind, wich has provided tools to allow developers to generate API documentation, server generation, mockup design, etc.

In this paper we describe additional work in the direction of making ontology-based data available though REST APIs. We define a mapping specification between OWL and OAS to facilitate the work of those who are interested in using data represented by semantic technologies and have to face the challenging task of developing ontology-based applications. Our mapping also aims to enhance adherence to the FAIR data principles [13] by facilitating: Findability, as it provides a template for finding types of available resources in knowledge graphs; Accessibility because it allows translating the ontology to an interface that developers are used to; Interoperability because the mapping matches two recommendations, the OWL W3C recommendation and OAS de facto standard; and Reusability because the mapping also translates explicit and understandable data definitions available in the ontology and generates an HTML document with the API details that may be published on the Web.

Our work has the following contributions: 1) A mapping specification between OWL and OAS to provide ontology-based API definitions (Sect. 2); and 2) A reference implementation to automatically transform OWL ontologies into an OAS document according to our mapping specification (Sect. 3). We also present work related to our approach in Sect. 4 and discuss conclusions and future work in Sect. 5.

2 Mapping OWL to OAS

In this section we provide the details about our mapping specification. First, we explain the methodology followed to generate the mapping. Then, we present a summarized description of the main characteristics of the specification. Finally, we give an example on how an OWL ontology is translated into OAS according to our mapping specification.

2.1 Method for Mapping Generation

The method followed to generate the mapping included the following steps:

1. Manual analysis of the OWL constructs. We analyzed the constructs from the OWL 2 Web Ontology Language [4]. We also analyzed the RDFS [1] constructs and the XSD datatypes [8] that are used in OWL 2.

---

[1] https://github.com/OAI/OpenAPI-Specification.

2. Manual analysis of the OAS definitions. We analyzed the definitions provided by the OpenAPI specification v3.0.3.[2]
3. Manual generation of the mapping specification. Once the analysis of OWL and OAS constructs and definitions had been completed, we selected the OAS definitions which allow representing the OWL constructs. Then, we wrote a specification document to describe the equivalences found. To show how these equivalences could be implemented, we developed a sample OWL ontology and its corresponding OAS representation. The mapping specification and the examples are available online.[3]

2.2 Mapping Definitions

We summarize below the main concepts of OAS that we use in this mapping:

1. A `Schema Object` allows defining input and output data types. For example, we may specify objects such as *Person*, or any concept that has its own attributes, primitives, or any expression to specify types of values.
2. A `Component Object` holds a set of reusable definitions of schemas, parameters, responses, etc. that may be referenced from somewhere in the API definition. For example, a component may hold a *Person* schema definition.
3. A `Reference Object` allows linking to other components in the specification instead of defining them inline. For example, to reuse the *Person* schema definition we reference it from its definition specified in the `Component Object`.
4. A `Path Object` holds the resources exposed in an API. For example, the path of the *Person* resource may be */persons*. It contains `Path Item Objects`.
5. A `Path Item Object` describes the available operations (HTTP methods to manage the resource) on a single path. For example, we may specify that the */persons* path allows the GET method.

Figure 1 illustrates these concepts with an example of a *Person* schema. Each number in the figure corresponds to the number shown in the enumeration list presented above. Table 1 describes the prefixes that we use throughout this paper. Regarding the mapping specification details, we present them in three main sets corresponding to classes and properties, restrictions, and boolean combinations. Table 2 shows the similarities between OWL classes and properties and OAS definitions.

In general, OWL classes are similar to a `Schema Object` that must be defined as an object type. OWL object and data properties are similar to the `Schema Object`'s properties and depending on the property type its value can be a data type or an object. Also, when a property is functional it must be defined as an array with 1 as the maximum number of array items. Additional details about similarities between OWL and OAS data types are provided in our online specification,[4] including a naming strategy for `Schema Objects` and `Paths`. Each

---

[2] http://spec.openapis.org/oas/v3.0.3.

[3] https://w3id.org/OWLToOAS.

[4] https://owl-to-oas.readthedocs.io/en/latest/mapping/#data-types_1.

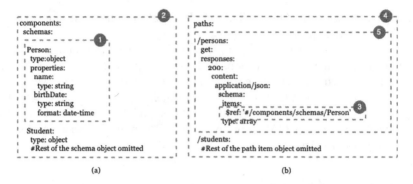

Fig. 1. Example of OAS definitions: a) A `Component Object` which contains some `Schema Object` definitions; b) A `Path Object` which includes some `Path Item Objects`.

Table 1. Prefixes used in this document

Prefix	Namespace
`owl`	http://www.w3.org/2002/07/owl#
`rdfs`	http://www.w3.org/2000/01/rdf-schema#
`rdf`	http://www.w3.org/1999/02/22-rdf-syntax-ns#
`xsd`	http://www.w3.org/2001/XMLSchema#
`ex`	https://w3id.org/example#

OWL class has a `Path Item Object` (as shown in Fig. 1). Depending on the method used (GET, POST, PUT or DELETE), a class may be referenced as part of the `Response` or `Request Body`.

Table 3 shows the similarities between OWL restrictions and OAS. In general, properties must be defined as an array, except for properties with a specific value restriction (`owl:hasValue`). If that is the case, the property must be defined as `default` and it must specify its corresponding literal (for data properties) or its individual URI value (for object properties). When a property is restricted to `owl:someValuesFrom` or `owl:allValuesFrom`, a type of value must define the type of array items as a data type or as a `Reference Object`. When a property has a cardinality restriction, the maximum or minimum number of array items should be adjusted accordingly. Note that we used a Close World Assumption for translating the existential constructs because it is what developers expect when inserting and retrieving instances from an API.

Table 4 presents the translation of OWL boolean combinations into OAS. In general, these combinations may be applied to the `Schema Object`'s properties. Depending on the combination, it is allowed to represent that a property value must be compliant with all or any schema type, or that it must not be valid against a certain schema. Also, a property may have one value included in an enumeration list.

Table 2. Classes and properties mapping

OWL	OAS	Implementation details
Classes		
`owl:Class`	`Schema Object`	The `Schema Object` must be defined as a `type: object` in the `Component Object`
`rdfs:subClassOf`	`Schema Object` and `allOf`	The `Schema Object` must be defined in the same manner as the `owl:Class`. The `allOf` field must also be included referencing to the parent class defined as a `Reference Object`
Properties		
`owl:DatatypeProperty`	`properties`	Defined as a `Schema Object`'s property
`owl:ObjectProperty`	`properties`	Defined as a `Schema Object`'s property
`rdfs:domain`	`Schema Object`	Defined as the `Schema Object` where the property should be defined
`rdfs:range`	`type`	Defined as the property type value
`owl:FunctionalProperty`	`maxItems`	The property must be defined as a `type: array` with 1 as the maximum number of items (`maxItems: 1`)

Table 5 summarizes the coverage of our mapping specification in terms of SROIQ expressiveness, the description logic underlying OWL 2 DL. The mapping covers functional properties (F), concept negation (C), hierarchies (H), nominal values (O), cardinality (N) and qualified cardinality restrictions (Q), and data types (D). Role disjointness (R) and inverse properties (I) are not covered because OAS does not have a similar definition to represent them. OAS can represent unions (U), but we consider to be partially covered, as OWL allows defining complex combinations that are not possible in OAS, like the union of the intersection between concepts. Similarly, the existential qualification expression (E) is also partially covered in our mapping, except when complex combinations are included in OWL.

2.3   Mapping Example

To showcase our mapping, we provide a code snippet of an example ontology and its OAS representation. The OAS definitions are provided in YAML and the OWL constructs in Turtle. Listing 1.1 presents an ontology snippet with the *Professor* class and its data and object properties, e.g. *Professor* has a degree (*hasDegree*) from a list of values. *Professor* is subclass of *Person*, thus it inherits all the restrictions from the *Person*. Restrictions defined over properties, e.g. a *Professor belongsTo* a *Department*, must be also taken into account as part of the *Professor* class definition.

Table 3. Restrictions mapping

OWL	OAS	Implementation details
owl:onProperty	properties	The restriction must refer to the property name where it is applied
owl:onClass	Schema Object	The restriction must refer to the schema name where it is applied
owl:hasValue	default	The restriction must be defined as a default property. Depending on whether it is on a data or object property, it will be a literal or an indvidual URI value
owl:someValuesFrom	type, nullable	The property must be defined as a not nullable (nullable: false) array (type: array). Depending on whether it is on a data or object property the item's type value will be the restricted data type or Reference Object
owl:allValuesFrom	type, nullable	The property must be defined as a nullable (nullable: true) array (type: array). Depending on whether it is on a data or object property the item's type value will be the restricted data type or Reference Object
owl:minCardinality	minItems	The restriction must be defined as the minimum number of array items (minItems)
owl:maxCardinality	maxItems	The restriction must be defined as the maximum number of array items (maxItems)
owl:cardinality	minItems and maxItems	The restriction must be defined as the same minimum (minItems) and maximum (maxItems) number of array items
owl:minQualifiedCardinality	minItems	The restriction must be defined as the minimum number of array items (minItems)
owl:maxQualifiedCardinality	maxItems	The restriction must be defined as the maximum number of array items (maxItems)
owl:qualifiedCardinality	minItems and maxItems	The restriction must be defined as the same minimum (minItems) and maximum (maxItems) number of array items

Table 4. Boolean combinations

OWL	OAS	Implementation details
owl:intersectionOf	allOf	The combination must be defined as **allOf** which validates the property value against all the schemas
owl:unionOf	anyOf	The combination must be defined as **anyOf** which validates the property value against any (one or more) of the schemas
owl:complementOf	not	The combination must be defined as **not** which validates that the property value is not valid against the specified schema
owl:oneOf	enum	The combination must be defined as **enum** which holds the possible property values

Table 5. Mapping OWLToOAS specification coverage ($\checkmark$ = covered, – = partially covered, and x = not covered)

Expressivity	Coverage	Expressivity	Coverage
F	$\checkmark$	O	$\checkmark$
E	–	I	x
U	–	N	$\checkmark$
C	$\checkmark$	Q	$\checkmark$
H	$\checkmark$	D	$\checkmark$
R	x		

```
1  ex: Professor  rdf:type  owl:Class ;
2      rdfs:subClassOf  :Person ,
3      [ rdf:type  owl:Restriction ;
4          owl:onProperty :hasDegree ;
5          owl:someValuesFrom [ rdf:type owl:Class ;
6          owl:oneOf (<https://w3id.org/example/resource/Degree/MS>
7          <https://w3id.org/example/resource/Degree/PhD>)]] .
8  ex:Person  rdf:type  owl:Class ;
9      rdfs:subClassOf [ rdf:type owl:Restriction ;
10         owl:onProperty :address ;
11         owl:maxQualifiedCardinality "1"^^xsd:nonNegativeInteger ;
12         owl:onDataRange xsd:string] ;
13     rdfs:comment "A human being regarded as an individual."@en ;
14     rdfs:label "Person"@en .
15 ex:belongsTo  rdf:type  owl:ObjectProperty ;
16     rdfs:domain :Professor ;
17     rdfs:range :Department ;
18     rdfs:label "belongs to"@en .
```

Listing 1.1. Ontology code excerpt

Listing 1.2 shows the OAS definitions corresponding to the previous ontology. This snippet was obtained from the YAML generated by our mapping implementation (described in Sect. 3). The `Component Object` includes the *Professor* schema (a `Schema Object`) which represents the *Professor* class including its own properties and those inherited from the *Person*.

```
 1  components:
 2    schemas:
 3      Professor:
 4        type: object
 5          description: A university academic.
 6          properties:
 7            address:
 8              items:
 9                type: string
10              maxItems: 1
11              nullable: true
12              type: array
13            belongsTo:
14              items:
15                $ref: '#/components/schemas/Department'
16              nullable: true
17              type: array
18            hasDegree:
19              items:
20                enum:
21                - <https://w3id.org/example/resource/Degree/MS>
22                - <https://w3id.org/example/resource/Degree/PhD>
23                format: uri
24                type: string
25              type: array
```

Listing 1.2. OAS snippet of a `Component Object` that includes the *Profesor* schema

Listing 1.3 shows the path assigned to *Professor* in the API. This `Path Item` defines a GET operation, including a successful response which delivers a *Professor* schema:

```
 1  paths:
 2    /professors:
 3      get:
 4        description: Gets a list of all instances of Professor
 5        responses:
 6          200:
 7            content:
 8              application/json:
 9                schema:
10                  items:
11                    $ref: '#/components/schemas/Professor'
12                  type: array
```

Listing 1.3. OAS snippet of a `Path Item Object` generated from the OWL ontology

3   Mapping Implementation

We implemented our mapping specification by extending the Ontology Based APIs Framework (OBA) [3], an existing tool for helping users create REST APIs from ontologies. OBA generates a server with a REST API based on an OpenAPI specification, and includes the automated management of SPARQL query templates for common operations; but has a limited support for OWL constructs (mostly limited to `rdfs:Class`, `rdfs:domain` and `rdfs:range`).

We extended the OBA Specification Generator module, which takes the ontology code and generates the OAS document in YAML, to support our mapping specification. It is worth mentioning that OBA does not check for consistency or syntactic correctness of an ontology, assuming that it has been evaluated before. The implementation release is available at the OBA's GitHub repository.[5]

Our implementation allows generating API definitions for ontologies of different sizes with a reasonable overhead. We tested our implementation in an average laptop (Intel Core i7 2.6 Ghz with 16 GB of RAM) with the example ontology we defined to illustrate our mapping specification,[6] an ontology which contains 119 logical axioms, including 36 class axioms, 42 object property axioms, and 37 data property axioms. The corresponding OAS was generated in 6 s. We also tested the DBPedia ontology,[7] which contains over 6000 logical axioms, including over 700 class axioms, over 2000 object property axioms, and over 2000 data property axioms. The DBpedia OAS took 64 s to build. In both cases, we generated only GET operation for each path in the specification.

4   Related Work

Several efforts have attempted to promote and facilitate Semantic Web technology adoption by web developers, providing Web APIs to allow developers accessing and managing data from knowledge graphs. Specifications like the Linked Data API[8] (LDA), the Linked Data Platform (LDP) [9], and the Triple Pattern Fragments (TPF) [11] have been proposed to describe how to define such interfaces. LDA details how to define read-only interfaces to Linked Data, LDP describes how to design read/write HTTP interfaces to RDF data, and TFP defines read-only interfaces to specific triples from a dataset to provide an efficient client-side querying execution. However, they do not use ontologies as templates for the API generation, hence developers have to deal with them to manage APIs. Works like BASIL [2] and GRLC [7] have been proposed to generate Web APIs on top of SPARQL endpoints; both generate Swagger specifications for the resulting APIs. However, these specifications are generated from the SPARQL queries, GitHub query repositories and SPARQL decorator notation which have to be defined manually by developers. Thanks to our mapping implementation, a full OAS can be generated from an ontology without human intervention.

Other recent approaches focus on generating API definitions from ontologies. In this regard, two efforts have recently appeared: the Ontology Based APIs Framework (OBA) [3] (which we extended with our mapping implementation) and the OWL2OAS Converter.[9] Both efforts generate OAS documents from OWL, and were efforts developed in parallel. The main differences between them and our implementation are summarized in Table 6. On the one hand, OBA

---

[5] https://github.com/KnowledgeCaptureAndDiscovery/OBA/releases/tag/3.4.0.

[6] http://tiny.cc/3eyjsz.

[7] https://wiki.dbpedia.org/services-resources/ontology.

[8] https://code.google.com/archive/p/linked-data-api.

[9] https://dev.realestatecore.io/OWL2OAS.

Table 6. Comparison ontology-based APIs approaches ($\checkmark$ = included, x = not included, $-$ = less coverage, and $+$ = more coverage of OWL constructs)

Proposal	OWL2OAS	OBA	Our approach
OWL to OAS mapping available	X	$\checkmark$	$\checkmark$
Expressiveness	$+$	$-$	$++$
REST Server	X	$\checkmark$	$\checkmark$

provides an initial mapping to describe details on translation of OWL constructs into OAS. However, the expressiveness covered by OBA is basic; restricted to the translation of classes, subclasses, object and data properties with singleton ranges. Despite its basic expressiveness, OBA provides extra functionality for implementing the API as a REST API server which allows validating requests from users, generating tests for API calls, etc. On the other hand, OWL2OAS does not include a specification of its coverage from OWL into OAS. By manually inspecting the OWL2OAS's code repository we can see that, in addition to OBA's coverage, it includes support for functional properties, class and property restrictions (`owl:onClass`, `owl:onProperty`), existential and some cardinality restrictions. However, it does not support specific values (`owl:hasValue`) and boolean combinations (`owl:oneOf`, `owl:unionOf`, `owl:intersectionOf`, `owl:complementOf`) which we cover (partially) in our mapping.

Our contribution proposes a detailed mapping between OWL and OAS, aimed at facilitating a specification, including examples on how to transform an ontology into an API definition, and an implementation to automatically generate an OAS document based on this mapping. Our mapping and its implementation have been built on top of OBA, reusing the work previously done.

5   Conclusions and Future Work

In this work, we proposed a mapping specification to translate OWL ontologies into OAS. This specification facilitates the creation of REST APIs that enables developers to access ontology-based data. Our mapping includes examples and details on how to define each OWL construct as an OAS definition using a Close World Assumption. Since manually editing OAS definitions can be tedious, time consuming, and error-prone, we extended the Ontology Based API framework to automatically translate OWL constructs into OAS. However, not all OWL constructs are covered in our specification, because they do not have an equivalent OAS definition. For example we cannot represent the equivalence between classes or restrictions that include complex unions and intersections.

As future work, we plan to extend OBA to improve the schema and path naming strategy used in the API. We would like to generate these names from the ontology class and property labels instead of the URI fragments as OBA currently does. We also plan to use the smartAPI specification [14], an extended version of OAS for defining key API metadata, to annotate our resulting APIs to maximize their FAIRness. This way, API providers may publish their APIs into the smartAPI registry to make them more discoverable, connected and reusable. Finally, given the limitations of OAS to represent some OWL constructs, we will explore how to combine our API definitions with the Shapes Constraint Language (SHACL) [5]. SHACL was created for data validation and therefore allows defining the restrictions that data from knowledge graphs must fulfill. With SHACL, those OWL constructs that are not covered in our mapping may be defined as shapes to validate the requests received by an API.

Acknowledgments. This work has been supported by a Predoctoral grant from the I+D+i program of the Universidad Politécnica de Madrid and the Spanish project DATOS 4.0: RETOS Y SOLUCIONES (TIN2016-78011-C4-4-R).

References

1. Brickley, D., Guha, R.V., McBride, B.: RDF Schema 1.1. W3C recommendation (2014)
2. Daga, E., Panziera, L., Pedrinaci, C.: A BASILar approach for building web APIs on top of SPARQL endpoints. In: CEUR Workshop Proceedings, vol. 1359, pp. 22–32 (2015)
3. Garijo, D., Osorio, M.: OBA: An Ontology-Based Framework for Creating REST APIs for Knowledge Graphs, July 2020. https://arxiv.org/abs/2007.09206
4. Hitzler, P., et al.: OWL web ontology language primer. WC Recommendation **27**, 123 (2009)
5. Knublauch, H., Kontokostas, D.: Shapes constraint language (SHACL). W3C Recommendation (2017)
6. McGuinness, D.L., et al.: OWL web ontology language overview. W3C Recommendation **10**(10), 2004 (2004)
7. Meroño-Peñuela, A., Hoekstra, R.: grlc makes GitHub taste like linked data APIs. In: Sack, H., Rizzo, G., Steinmetz, N., Mladenić, D., Auer, S., Lange, C. (eds.) ESWC 2016. LNCS, vol. 9989, pp. 342–353. Springer, Cham (2016). https://doi.org/10.1007/978-3-319-47602-5_48
8. Peterson, D., Gao, S., Malhotra, A., Sperberg-McQueen, C.M., Thompson, H.S., Biron, P.: W3C XML schema definition language (XSD) 1.1 part 2: datatypes. W3C Recommendation **5** (2012)
9. Speicher, S., Arwe, J., Malhotra, A.: Linked data platform 1.0. W3C Recommendation (2015)
10. Studer, R., Benjamins, V.R., Fensel, D.: Knowledge engineering: principles and methods. Data Knowl. Eng. **25**(1–2), 161–197 (1998)
11. Verborgh, R., et al.: Triple pattern fragments: a low-cost knowledge graph interface for the web. J. Web Semant. **37**, 184–206 (2016)
12. Vigo, M., Bail, S., Jay, C., Stevens, R.: Overcoming the pitfalls of ontology authoring: Strategies and implications for tool design. Int. J. Hum.-Comput. Stud. **72**(12), 835–845 (2014)
13. Wilkinson, M.D., et al.: The FAIR Guiding Principles for scientific data management and stewardship. Sci. Data **3**, 1–9 (2016)
14. Zaveri, A., et al.: smartAPI: towards a more intelligent network of web APIs. In: Blomqvist, E., Maynard, D., Gangemi, A., Hoekstra, R., Hitzler, P., Hartig, O. (eds.) ESWC 2017. LNCS, vol. 10250, pp. 154–169. Springer, Cham (2017). https://doi.org/10.1007/978-3-319-58451-5_11

Evaluating FAIRness of Genomic Databases

Matheus Pedra Puime Feijoó[1][(✉)] [iD], Rodrigo Jardim[3] [iD],
Sergio Manuel S. da Cruz[1,2] [iD], and Maria Luiza M. Campos[1] [iD]

[1] Federal University of Rio de Janeiro (PPGI/UFRJ), Rio de Janeiro, Brazil
feijoo@ufrj.com, {serra,mluiza}@ppgi.ufrj.br
[2] Federal Rural University of Rio de Janeiro (UFRRJ), Seropédica, Brazil
[3] Oswaldo Cruz Foundation (LBCS/IOC), Rio de Janeiro, Brazil

Abstract. Several studies show the difficulty experienced for the reuse of the ever increasing amount of genomic data. Initiatives are being created to mitigate this concern; one of the most well-known is the FAIR Data Principles. Nonetheless, the related works are too generic and do not describe simultaneously and properly the human and machine perspectives of the FAIRness of databases. Hence, in order to bridge this gap, our paper introduces an approach named the Bio FAIR Evaluator Framework, a semiautomated tool aimed to analyze the FAIRness of genomic databases. Furthermore, we performed experiments that analyzed selected genomic databases according to two orthogonal and complementary perspectives (human and machine). The approach uses standardized FAIR metrics and generates recommendation reports to researchers indicating how to enhance the FAIRness of databases. Our findings, when compared with related works, show the feasibility of the approach, indicating that the current genomic databases are poorly compliant with FAIR Principles.

Keywords: Genomics · Data compliance · FAIRness · FAIR

1 Introduction

Nowadays, the ever-increasing volume of research data is widely debated in the scientific fields. Today, managing, sharing, and reusing scientific data are among the main issues addressed by the research community, mainly because of the complexity and lack of general governance rules [1, 2]. One of the areas facing these problems is bioinformatics, and, more specifically, genomics, which is concerned with the study of genes and their function, applying the techniques of genetics and molecular biology to the genetic mapping sequencing of sets of genes or the complete genomes of selected organisms. The results are organized in databases, with rich applications in medicine, pharmaceutic industry, and biology, among others [3].

Genomics is in the midst of a datacentric revolution, which is causing an escalation in the size and number of genomic datasets [4]. Many archives, as highlighted by [5], are hard to be found, shared, or reused due to the lack of precise semantics and provenance. These problems are like those addressed by the FAIR data principles [6] introduced in 2016 [6]. The FAIR principles (and their 15 sub principles) were stated

© Springer Nature Switzerland AG 2020
G. Grossmann and S. Ram (Eds.): ER 2020 Workshops, LNCS 12584, pp. 128–137, 2020.
https://doi.org/10.1007/978-3-030-65847-2_12

as goals aiming to provide guidelines for creating digital resources such as datasets, databases, code, workflows, and research objects, in a way that makes them (F)indable, (A)ccessible, (I)nteroperable, and (R)eusable, strongly relying on metadata publication and management.

However, the sole existence of the FAIR principles is not enough to aid the researcher in evaluating the FAIRness of genomic databases. We advocate that it should be conducted under two orthogonal and complementary perspectives (human and machine) because humans and machines deal with distinct obstacles when attempting to find and access data on the databases [6]. As far as we are concerned, the human perspective is about the upper level of abstraction and the diffuse sense of "semantics". Humans can identify and interpret a wide variety of signs and make intuitive decisions on the selection of useful data. On the other hand, the machine perspective is more self-guided, accurate, and even more reproducible. It concentrates on the ability to evaluate de data in the scope, scale, and speed necessity that the genomic research requires [6].

In this work, we evaluated the FAIRness of seven well known genomic databases, analyzing how close these databases are to achieve FAIRness. To do that, we developed a semi-automated tool named Bio FAIR Evaluator Framework to support researchers to evaluate the databases, considering metrics and criteria based on the interpretation of the FAIR principles. Furthermore, we discuss the tool usage performing two sets of experiments and analyzes focused on the orthogonal perspectives mentioned above. Besides, our tool additionally offers a series of recommendations about the improvements that can be made in the genomic databases.

This article is structured as follows: Sect. 2 presents the background of the genomic databases and FAIR principles; in Sect. 3 we present the core features of our contribution named Bio FAIR Evaluator Framework; Sect. 4 presents the two sets of complementary experiments and its results, showing the FAIRness of the database according to the two perspectives; Sect. 5 shows the related works; and, finally, Sect. 6 presents concluding remarks and topics for further investigation.

2 Background

2.1 Genomic Databases

Most genomic datasets are derived from legacy sequencing projects, which are frequently openly accessible to the public. This practice is evidenced by the fact that most journals require a public accession identifier for any dataset associated with a publication. Thus, to attain a broad distribution of open datasets, all subfields of genomics have also adopted the use of central, large-scale public databases [7].

The early adoption of these databases to host large amounts of all sorts of genetic data has allowed researchers to efficiently query data and promote the reuse of datasets produced by others [7, 9]. Genbank[1], EBI[2], UniProt[3], and KEGG[4] are some of the most

---

[1] https://www.ncbi.nlm.nih.gov/genbank/.

[2] https://www.ebi.ac.uk/.

[3] https://www.uniprot.org/.

[4] https://www.genome.jp/kegg/.

well-known databases in the area. However, they represent a small part of a group of more than 1,364 databases linked to the life sciences area [10]. Many of these archives are highly consolidated and have a long history, but it is also highly recognized in the academy that these same databases present issues of the most varied types [5, 11–13].

When analyzing in-depth these concerns, several inconsistencies in data and metadata are evident. In some cases, there is a lack of control in the (meta)data vocabularies, reduced use of semantic-related concepts, and even simple fields are filled with different data [13]. It is noticeable that these problems are closely addressed by the FAIR principles, where reuse is one of the main target goals. It is also natural that some of those works cite FAIR as a potential for circumventing these problems.

2.2 FAIR Principles and FAIRness

Sharing and reusing research data is not an easy task. Considering the researchers' point of view, data preservation is a critical role that supports data reuse. Data reuse can be executed either by humans or machines (a.k.a data reusers), which need time and resources to understand the data to identify whether it has value to be reused in a given context [8]. Reuse by some means focuses on the ability to understand the reuser perspective, but the main question ends up being how the data is stored, how the data producers classified it, or even how the data archive presents their data [1].

The problem of reusability is being worsened by the escalating volume of ever-increasing genomic data being produced worldwide even before the COVID-19 pandemics. To mitigate the reuse problem, in 2016, the FAIR data principles were established by Wilkinson et al. [6]. A set of stakeholders devised these principles to stress the role of Open Science with a focus on the '(meta)data', where the authors use this term in cases that must be applied to metadata and data [6]. The FAIR principles are composed of 15 sub principles (See Fig. 1), where each of these goals aims to maximize the value of digital research objects either for humans or machines.

Findable	Accessible
F1 (Meta)data with globally unique and persistent identifier.	A1 Use a standardized communication protocol.
F2 Data with rich metadata.	A1.1 Use an open, free and universally protocol.
F3 Metadata with data identifier.	A1.2 The protocol allows authentication and authorization.
F4 (Meta)data indexed in a searchable resource.	A2 Metadata accessible, even with no avaible data.
Interoperable	**Reusable**
I1 (Meta)data use formal, accessible, shared, and broadly applicable language for knowlede representation.	R1 Metadata need to be detailed.
I2 (Meta)data use vocabularies that follow the FAIR principles.	R1.1 Clear and accessible data usage license.
I3 Use of qualified reference in (meta)data.	R1.2 Use of detailed provenance.
	R1.3 (Meta)data are approved by domain-relevant community standards.

Fig. 1. The FAIR data principles

The FAIRness of digital resources (like a genomic database) is the degree to which it is Findable, Accessible, Interoperable, and Reusable not only in the Web, but in other contexts as well. Thus, increasing the FAIRness of a genomic database might maximize their reuse. Nevertheless, to evaluate its FAIRness, we need to use metrics (a.k.a criteria) to obtain an assessment that provides feedback to content creators about the resulting degree of findability, accessibility, interoperability, and reusability. This means that genomic communities should not only understand how to access the genomic data stored in these databases but also be aware that they can monitor the FAIRness of these databases, realistically and quantitatively.

3 Bio FAIR Evaluator Framework

After conducting a systematic review of the literature (not discussed in this paper due to lack of space), it has been perceived that there were no computational frameworks that aid researchers in evaluating genomic databases considering the FAIR principles according to these two orthogonal perspectives (human and machine).

We aim to contribute with the Bio FAIR Evaluator framework. Differently from previous works, described in Sect. 5, it is a semi-automated modular tool that helps scientists to check the FAIRness of databases by walking through assessments related to each of the four groups of FAIR principles [14]. The framework is composed of two self-contained and independent modules: Researcher Compliance Evaluator (RaCE) and Machine Compliance Evaluator (MaCE). RaCE is related to the human perspective; it holds a list of questions related to the process of genomic data discovery and reuse. A researcher performs the RaCE by manually answering each question based on the human perspective using pre-specified reference criteria in order to delve into the FAIRness conformity. MaCE is a Python script that dynamically loads a set of preestablish questions that were automatically answered after checking the genomic database to evaluate the FAIRness of the database.

The evaluation of the FAIRness of the databases is achieved through the execution of both modules; they check the structure of the genomic databases using several metrics (criteria) to assess compliance with each one of the FAIR sub-principles of the genomic databases.

We stress that our approach allowed us to evaluate databases FAIRness through compliance experiments according to the two orthogonal perspectives. In short, the compliance experiments represent an evaluation considering either scenarios involving humans or machines regarding the acceptance of data reuse from autonomous computer applications. Our metrics, evaluation criteria, and experiments are described in the following subsections, and all reports created to carry out this analysis are available in a GitHub repository[5].

3.1 Metrics and Criteria of FAIRness Evaluation

The development of the framework allowed us to test the alignment of genomic databases with the FAIR principles. Hence, we outlined standardized metrics to generate quantitative outputs considering the execution of compliance experiments with the assistance of RaCe and MaCE modules.

For the sake of clarity, the traffic-light colour system was chosen to categorize the scores of the two modules. We use four levels: green for exemplary databases that meet

---

[5] doi: https://doi.org/10.5281/zenodo.3949344

the compliance criteria (score = 3), yellow for average databases that partially meet the criteria (score = 2), red for poor databases that not meet the criteria (score = 1) and grey for cases that cannot be tested (score = 0). Extra attention is deserved to MaCe because the output of the script returns two types of results: green for databases that meet the criteria (score = 3) and red for those that do not meet (score = 1).

To structure the criteria, we scrutinized previous genomics analyses databases works [5, 11, 12], and also the FAIRsharing6 and re3data7 portals, in order to extract what is a trustworthy genomic database according to RaCE and MaCE. We developed the three levels of criteria that focus on how close a genomic database is to FAIR principles and linked to the metric score already described. The metrics and criteria aided then the reinforcement of the recommendation stage that is presented after the evaluation.

3.2   RaCE Module

RaCE module aims to analyze the databases considering human needs, for example, the necessities during the search of a use license or finding the last release of a (meta)data, taking as a starting point the 15 FAIR sub principles. By this, each principle is analyzed and linked with the necessities of the genomic data human reuser.

The questions of RaCE can be subdivided into two modules: the first one describes the module and its relation to the FAIR principles; the second is a set of precondition steps to be taken during the evaluation and a follow-up questionnaire linked to the aforementioned metrics and criteria.

3.3   MaCE Module

The MaCE module focuses on analyses according to a machine perspective. Differently from RaCE that uses only manual assessments, it was necessary to develop a computational environment explicitly focused on this scenario. The automated module was elaborated following previous research [13], where the FAIR principles are extended to machine vision-oriented maturity indicators called FAIR Metrics Gen2 (FM-Gen2). We adopted the same metrics, proposed by the FAIR principles developers, which will be included and discussed during the presentation of the results.

To support MaCE module, we developed Python scripts, based on the objectives of each FM-Gen2 metric, and also reformulated some of them in the view of genomic databases analysis, to evaluate genomics specific concerns and better understand the outputs results. Correspondingly to the description of the RaCE module, we developed the same analysis structure in MaCE. First, describing the module and the relation to FAIR, outlining the precondition steps, how the module should be analyzed considering the metrics and criteria, and how the support script will execute the evaluation.

4   Results and Discussion

To evaluate the FAIRness of the genomic databases, we designed and executed experiments with RaCE and MaCE. Both considered seven popular resources widely adopted by the genomics community.

The requirements for choosing these databases and repositories were to be the most representative in the genomics area and consider the use of the FAIR principles in their (meta)data. The evaluated databases were: Genbank (www.ncbi.nlm.nih.gov/gen bank/), KEGG (www.genome.jp), EBI (www.ebi.ac.uk), UniProt/Swiss-Prot (www.uni prot.org), EuPathDB (www.eupathdb.org), VirusDB (www.viprbrc.org) and MaizeGDB (www.maizegdb.com). On the follow-up section, the results of FAIRness experiments are grouped by the FAIR principle related name, as cited on Fig. 1, in addition, the MaCE receive the FM-Gen2 acronym cited before. All experimental data, tables, statistics, and graphs, accompanied by the documentation, can be accessed via the GitHub repository (See footnote 5).

4.1 FAIRness Experiments

The (F)indable RaCE module was the first executed. As a result, most of the data holdings met the requirements criteria (Fig. 2 (a)). Despite that, the F2 experiment has the most non-exemplary databases; this module evaluates if data is richly described with metadata, and perhaps this can be considered a subjective principle. Nonetheless, it is noticeable that the same databases have in common the absence of required fields or the use of incoherent/incorrect metadata.

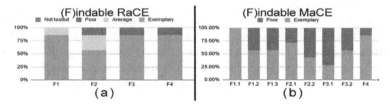

Fig. 2. Findable module results

In turn, the MaCE module (Fig. 2 (b)) have higher compliance rates concentrated on FM-Gen2 F1.1 and F4 analysis. FM-Gen2 F1.1 evaluates if there are any unique identifiers in the databases, as a Uniform Resource Identifier (URI). FM-Gen 2 F1.2 and F1.3 experiments identify the existence of standardization in persistence identifiers and obtained a result below 42.86% for poor databases. For instance, the guarantee of persistence is a problematic point for all FAIR principles; its use adds greater control and

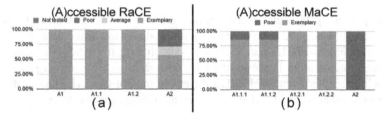

Fig. 3. Accessible module results

reusability over (meta)data. Interestingly, Genbank had lower results on these modules, which substantiates previous findings in the literature [5, 12].

FM-Gen2 F2.1 and F2.2 appraise the identification of structured language related to richly described metadata accessed by machines, and obtained 57.14% of poor databases, because they do not use a standardized structured language. Besides, FM-Gen2 F3.1 and F3.2 found the lowest compliance rate in the (F)indable MaCE module, only around 28.57% as exemplary. These evaluations refer to the explicit use of identifiers in metadata about the data and for other metadata. Consequently, non-compliance generates an obstacle for scraping data tools. However, the FM-Gen2 F4 performs the search for the (meta)data on search engines, and only one database was poor, as it does not authorize search engines to perform the scraping.

With the (A)ccessible RaCE module, the databases achieved 100% compliance on A1, A1.1, and A1.2 (see Fig. 2(a)). This result occurred because these experiments search for the use of standardized communication protocols and the use of non-proprietary software. A2 RaCE experiment obtained 42.86% of average or poor databases due to the non-use or non-specification of policies for persistence/versioning of (meta)data. The results of (A)ccessible MaCE module (see Fig. 2(b)) ended up being satisfactory in the FM-Gen2 A1.1.1, A1.1.2, A2.1.1, and A2.1.2 with 85.71% of compliance, checking if they use open free protocols and if there are authentication/authorization for access (meta)data. However, FM-Gen2 A2 revealed that all databases are non-compliant to the existence of persistence policy keys.

The most remarkable compliance rate was in (I)nteroperable module, RaCE compliance was below 42.86% (Fig. 3(a)), mainly in I2 experiment, where the (meta)data vocabularies must follow the FAIR principles. Even the data holdings that cite the use of FAIR also failed this test. Regarding I1 and I3 experiments, non-compliance comes from not using knowledge representation languages and qualified references (Fig. 4).

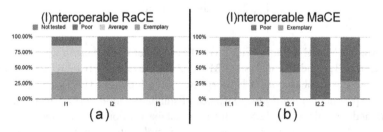

Fig. 4. Interoperable module results

Correspondingly, the same scenario is noticeable in the MaCE, with 100% of non-compliance in FM-Gen2 I2.2, because the databases do not use linked data on metadata. Nevertheless, FM-Gen2 I1.1 had 85.71% of compliance. It verifies if metadata uses knowledge representation in the most basic form, using any type of structured data, being readily accepted even for HTML. Conversely, the FM-Gen2 I1.2 has greater rigor in the analysis where only knowledge representation languages are accepted.

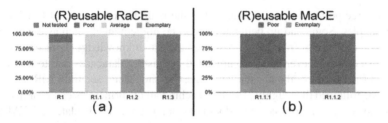

Fig. 5. Reusable module results

On the reusable module, general non-compliance is seen. In RaCE, two points stand out, and the first is R1.1, where 100% were average. Referring to the use of licenses, some databases contained the license. However, they were not complete or were hard to find. The second highlighted is the R1.3 experiment, where there is a need for certification by the data domain community. Even creating criteria for analysis, there are no documents yet or FAIR guidelines that assist this. Likewise, MaCE experiments obtained non-compliance between 57.14% and 85.71% due to the non-indexing of user licenses for automatic identification. In addition to that, there are no experiments for R1.2 and R1.3 FAIR principles because it is hard to measure from the machine point of view.

The results of RaCE and MaCE experiments were grouped to analyze compliance in general (See Fig. 5). This is because, as mentioned before, we are dealing with two complementary and orthogonal perspectives (Fig. 6).

Database	RaCE	MaCE	Final Average
Genbank	33	34	34.5
KEGG	38	52	46
EBI	38	52	46
UniProt	41	54	48.5
EuPathDB	26	28	28
VirusDB	31	36	34.5
MaizeGDB	38	46	43

Examplary

Average

Poor

Fig. 6. Final compliance result of the seven genomic databases

By this final results, interesting points can be highlighted. From the three with the highest score, only UniProt mentions the use of FAIR principles in its (meta)data. On the other hand, MaizeGDB cites the use of FAIR but ended up being the fourth in compliance. Genbank is one of the most popular genomic databases. However, it is the one that has smaller compliance with the FAIR principles.

4.2 Recommendations

After the analysis was carried out, a referenced document (See footnote 5) was made with possible recommendations that could be made for each compliance experiment's results. Among the most important recommendations, one can cite the use of persistent identifiers, the use of knowledge representation languages, and the provision of policies for the (meta)data.

These three points can be summarized as the main improvements of following the FAIR principles. Some end up being simpler to be implemented, such as the provision of policies for the use of (meta)data. Although the use of knowledge representation languages, turn out to be even more complicated in existing databases due to the need to readapt all (meta)data to the chosen language. We should not see the FAIR as a guide that must be followed thoroughly [14], but reaching all the principles can generate many benefits. However, non-completeness does not result in an 'unFAIR' database. FAIRness must be adapted in each of the realities but the principles can certainly improve reusability. Based on the compliance recommendations, it is possible to make the principles more concrete.

5 Related Work

There are some works aimed at evaluating compliance concerning the FAIR principles. Dunning, Smale, and Bohmer [16], clearly inspired our work, as they proposed a series of compliance experiments on the FAIR principles, although focused on different areas. They perform experiments from a human point of view and quoted that some of the principles are too vague. At the same time, others are more complicated to verify adherence, especially Interoperable and Reusable.

The FM-Gen2 [15] is very important as providing a view on the analysis focused on machines, due to its automatic reuse. However, it ends up not carrying out experiments on all principles, such as principles R1.2 and R1.3. The Research Data Alliance [17] gathered and compared 12 FAIR analysis tools, contemplating compliance indicators. During these analyses, the tools were grouped, considering the different FAIR principles. Comparing these tools, we noticed some interesting facts. Some have restrictions to use, in others not all the principles were analyzed (like principle A2 that was only analyzed by three tools). Some tools contemplate either the human vision or the machine vision.

All these works were essential to the development of our research, but mainly the FM-Gen2 that we used on our compliance experiments. Different from the related works, we focus on the compliance of a specific area, make compliance experiments to map all the FAIR principles, and ended up providing analysis from two points of view (human and machine).

6 Conclusions

Reusability of genomic data is utterly necessary. However, several databases face various types of shortcomings related to FAIRness. In this investigation, we presented an approach to evaluate the genomic databases, considering two orthogonal perspectives (human and machine). Bio FAIR Evaluator Framework allows researchers to perform complementary manual and automated experiments to evaluate FAIRness of genomic databases. Our results show that seven of them are poorly compliant with the FAIR principles. Besides the compliance checks, the evaluation also generated a series of recommendations to increase the FAIRness of genomic databases. Our framework may also benefit data reusers and database administrators. As future work, we intend to develop further investigations to improve the quality of compliance experiments to evaluate other fields of bioinformatics like proteomics as well as other domains.

Acknowledgements. This study was financed in part by the National Council for Scientific and Technological Development (CNPq), Programa de Educação Tutorial (PET) and Coordenação de Aperfeiçoamento de Pessoal de Nível Superior – Brasil (CAPES) – Finance Code 001.

References

1. Paquetto, I., Ranfles, B., Borgman, C.: On the reuse of scientific data. Data Sci. J. **16**, 8 (2017)
2. Hey, T., Trefethen, A.: The Data Deluge: an e-science Perspective. Grid Computing: Making the Global Infrastructure a Reality, pp. 809–824. Wiley-Blackwell (2003)
3. Bayat, A.: Bioinformatics: science, medicine, and the future: bioinformatics. Br. Med. J. **324**(7344), 1018–1022 (2002)
4. Cook, C., Bergman, M., Finn, R., Cochrane, G., et al.: The European bioinformatics institute in 2016: data growth and integration. Nucl. Acids Res. **44**(D1), D20–D26 (2016)
5. Gonçalves, R., Musen, M.: The variable quality of metadata about biological samples used in biomedical experiments. Sci. Data **6**, 190021 (2019)
6. Wilkinson, M., Dumontier, M., Aalbersberg, I., Apleton, G., Axt, M., et al.: The FAIR guiding principles for scientific data management and stewardship. Sci. Data **3**, 160018 (2016)
7. Navarro, F., Mohsen, H., Yan, C., Li, S., Gu, M., Meyerson, W.: Genomics and data science: an application within an umbrella. Genome Biol. **20**, 109 (2019)
8. Wallis, J.: Data producers courting data reusers: two cases from modeling communities. Int. J. Digit. Curation **9**(1) (2014)
9. Stephens, Z., Lee, S., Faghri, F., Campbell, R., Zhai, C., Efron, M., et al.: Big data: astronomical or genomical. PLoS Biol. **13**(7), e1002195 (2015)
10. Re3Data. https://www.re3data.org. Last accessed 06 June 2020
11. Bouadjenek, M., Verspoor, K., Zobel, Z.: Automated detection of records in biological sequence databases that are inconsistent with the literature. J. Biomed. Inform. **71**, 229–240 (2017)
12. Miron, L., Gonçalves, R., Musen, M.: Obstacles to the Reuse of Study Metadata in ClinicalTrials.gov. BioRxiv (2020)
13. Gonçalves, R., Connor, M., Romero, M., Graybeal, J., Musen, M.: Metadata in the biosample online repository are impaired by numerous anomalies. In: 1st Workshop on Enabling Open Semantic Science, pp. 39–46 (2017)
14. Mons, B., Cameron, N., et al.: Cloudy, increasingly FAIR: revisiting the FAIR data guiding principles for the European open science cloud. Info. Serv. Use **37**(1), 49–56 (2017)
15. Wilkinson, M., Dumontier, M., Sansone, S., Santos, B., et al.: Evaluating FAIR maturity through a scalable, automated, community-governed framework. Sci. Data **6**(174), 1–12 (2019)
16. Dunning, A., Smaele, M., Bohmer, J.: Are the fair data principles fair? Int. J. Digit. Curation **12**(2), 177–195 (2017)
17. Bahim, C., Dekkers, M., Wyns, B.: Results of an Analysis of existing FAIR assessment tools. RDA (2019)

Reusable FAIR Implementation Profiles as Accelerators of FAIR Convergence

Erik Schultes[1] ⓘ, Barbara Magagna[2,3](✉) ⓘ, Kristina Maria Hettne[4] ⓘ,
Robert Pergl[5] ⓘ, Marek Suchánek[5] ⓘ, and Tobias Kuhn[6] ⓘ

[1] GO FAIR International Support and Coordination Office, Leiden, The Netherlands
erik.schultes@go-fair.org
[2] Umweltbundesamt GmbH, Vienna, Austria
barbara.magagna@umweltbundesamt.at
[3] University of Twente, Enschede, The Netherlands
[4] Centre for Digital Scholarship, Leiden University Libraries, Leiden, The Netherlands
k.m.hettne@library.leidenuniv.nl
[5] Faculty of Information Technology, Czech Technical
University in Prague, Prague, Czech Republic
{perglr,suchama4}@fit.cvut.cz
[6] Department of Computer Science, Vrije Universiteit
Amsterdam, Amsterdam, The Netherlands
t.kuhn@vu.nl

Abstract. Powerful incentives are driving the adoption of FAIR practices among a broad cross-section of stakeholders. This adoption process must factor in numerous considerations regarding the use of both domain-specific and infrastructural resources. These considerations must be made for each of the FAIR Guiding Principles and include supra-domain objectives such as the maximum reuse of existing resources (i.e., minimised reinvention of the wheel) or maximum interoperation with existing FAIR data and services. Despite the complexity of this task, it is likely that the majority of the decisions will be repeated across communities and that communities can expedite their own FAIR adoption process by judiciously reusing the implementation choices already made by others. To leverage these redundancies and accelerate convergence onto widespread reuse of FAIR implementations, we have developed the concept of FAIR Implementation Profile (FIP) that captures the comprehensive set of implementation choices made at the discretion of individual communities of practice. The collection of community-specific FIPs compose an online resource called the FIP Convergence Matrix which can be used to track the evolving landscape of FAIR implementations and inform optimisation around reuse and interoperation. Ready-made and well-tested FIPs created by trusted communities will find widespread reuse among other communities and could vastly accelerate decision making on well-informed implementations of the FAIR Principles within and particularly between domains.

Keywords: FAIR principles · Convergence · FAIR-Enabling resource · FAIR implementation community · FAIR implementation considerations · FAIR implementation choices · FAIR implementation challenges · FAIR implementation profile

G. Grossmann and S. Ram (Eds.): ER 2020 Workshops, LNCS 12584, pp. 138–147, 2020.
https://doi.org/10.1007/978-3-030-65847-2_13

1   Introduction

The FAIR Guiding Principles articulate the behaviors expected from digital artifacts that are Findable, Accessible, Interoperable and Reusable by machines [1]. Although arguably an established term already, the FAIR Principles do not explicitly consider actual implementation choices enabling FAIR behaviors [2]. For example,

- Principle F2 states that data should be described with rich metadata, but leaves the definition of "rich" and other findability requirements to the discretion of the domain community (which varies from one stakeholder, domain, and application to another, e.g. CERIF, DataCite Metadata Schema or ISO 19115/ISO 19139);
- Principle I1 requests that a formal, accessible, shared, and broadly applicable language for knowledge representation be used to embed machine-actionable semantics (e.g., RDF/OWL, RuleML, CycL) but it gives no recommendation on how to select the best option in any particular use case;
- Principle R1.1 requests that data and metadata be released with clear and accessible usage licenses, but does not specify which of the many digital licensing schemes should actually be applied (e.g., Creative Commons Attribution 4.0 International Public License or Open Data Commons Public Domain Dedication and License).

In each case, the FAIR Principles leave implementation choices to the communities of practice, permitting maximum freedom to operate while at the same time ensuring a high degree of automated Findability, Accessibility, Interoperability, and Reusability. This freedom to operate, while necessary and desirable, has led to the development of a variety of technical solutions which hold the inherent risk of reducing compatibility between stakeholder communities. For example, although initiatives like the European Strategy Forum on Research Infrastructures (ESFRI) or the Research Data Alliance (RDA) are driving the adoption of FAIR practices, different domain communities nonetheless have their own, often well-established implementation preferences and priorities for data reuse. Hence, coordinating a broadly accepted, widely used FAIR implementation approach still remains a global challenge.

In an effort to accelerate broad community convergence [3] on FAIR implementation options, the GO FAIR FIP Working Group [4] launched the development of the FAIR Convergence Matrix, a collaborative online resource consisting of all the FAIR implementation choices made by different domain communities [5]. This ongoing activity aims to create a machine-actionable description of the emerging FAIR implementation landscape. This will enable stakeholders to systematically optimise implementation choices with respect to, for example, more streamlined FAIR deployments while at the same time securing some guarantees on the FAIR maturity levels of those deployments and the degree of interoperation that can be expected with Resources created by other communities.

In this paper we first describe the different components of the FAIR Implementation Conceptual Model and the workflow for the creation of community-specific FAIR Implementation Profiles (Sect. 2). In Sect. 3 we discuss the potential benefits of this approach and how the FAIR Implementation Profile relates to the FAIR Principle R1.3

and why this contribution is novel in relation to previous work. In Sect. 4 we conclude by describing upcoming activities and planned improvements to the ongoing work.

2 The FAIR Implementation Profile Conceptual Model and Its Supporting Components

2.1 FAIR Implementation Profiles

The FAIR Implementation Profile (FIP) conceptual model [6] is based on the developing GO FAIR Ontology [7] and is composed of two principal concepts: FAIR Implementation Community and the FAIR-Enabling Digital Resource.

By FAIR Implementation Community (Community) we mean a self-identified organization (composed of more than one person) sharing a common interest that aspires to the creation of FAIR data and services. Typically, a Community forms around a knowledge domain or in the participation in a research infrastructure, or in the commitment to a policy jurisdiction such as those found in a university, a hospital, a province or a county. As such, Communities can be formal (e.g., scholarly society) or informal (e.g., working groups), large or small, influential or not, long-lived (industry associations) or temporary (e.g., funded projects). It may also be useful to identify sub-communities that may be related to specific repositories when dealing with different types of resources (e.g., sensors). In any case, a Community must itself be represented with FAIR (meta)data, by procuring a globally unique and persistent resolvable identifier (GUPRI) usually via a registration process. Every Community registers a Community Data Steward (a single person representing data stewards of the Community who provides a contact point for FIP creation and who likely works in a team of experts coordinating FIP development).

By FAIR-Enabling Digital Resource (Resource) we mean any digital object that provides a function needed to achieve some aspect of FAIRness and is explicitly linked to one or more FAIR Principles. Resources include for instance datasets, metadata, code, protocols, compute resources, computed work units, data policies, data management plans, identifier mechanisms, standards, FAIRification processes, FAIRness assessment criteria and methods, data repositories and/or supporting tools. We define an Implementation Choice as the decision of a Community to reuse a Resource from among existing implementations. If, however, none of these appear suitable, the Community may then accept the Implementation Challenge to create and implement a new solution to solve the identified gap (note that every Resource that forms a Choice, was itself once a Challenge). Choices and Challenges are made on the basis of Considerations that involve numerous Community-specific factors including FAIR Requirements and various sources of Constraints endemic to the Community.

Since early 2019, prototype FIPs have been created for roughly 50 communities (including ESFRIs [8] and projects like ENVRI-FAIR [9]) as a means to achieve practical development of the conceptual model and its representation. An advanced example of a FIP created by the GO FAIR Virus Outbreak Data Network can be found in both human-readable (PDF) [10] and machine-actionable (JSON) formats [11].

2.2 FAIR Implementation Questionnaire

Although Community Data Stewards may build a FIP de novo, in practice the task can be facilitated and standardized when they are prompted via a questionnaire to systematically list the implementation choices that correspond to each of the FAIR Principles. These choices are drawn from an accumulated listing of existing or proposed Resources. The GO FAIR FIP Working Group has developed the FIP questionnaire in a series of hackathons since January 2019, carefully aligning questions and accommodating the complex space of potential answers with the aim to ensure machine-actionable FIPs. The current version 4.0 questionnaire (with 21 questions covering the FAIR Principles) is accessible on GitHub [12].

A tool in which the FIP questionnaire is currently implemented is the Data Stewardship Wizard (DSW) [13]. The DSW platform provides an efficient means to capture implementation Choices and Challenges by directly linking to canonical references for Resources issued in public registries, such as FAIRsharing.org (see Fig. 1). In turn, the DSW tool enables the FIP to be output in various file formats, both human and machine-readable including the development of custom export templates. In this case, the DSW has been repurposed from its original application as a data management/stewardship planning tool into a FIP capture tool by substituting the data stewardship knowledge model (i.e., extensible and evolvable definition of a questionnaire) with a newly created one corresponding to the FIP questionnaire. As such, we refer to the new knowledge model and interface as the "FIP Wizard" which is publicly accessible [14].

Fig. 1. An implementation choice of the VODAN Community in the FIP Wizard for F1

2.3 FIPs as FAIR Digital Objects

FIPs created in the FIP Wizard can be represented as collections of assertions having the form *<Community> <Chooses* to reuse*> <Resource>* or *<Community>* <accepts the *Challenge* to build*> <Resource>*. All assertions having the same Community as the subject compose the FIP for that Community. This graph structure where a single subject has multiple predicate-object pairs is called a Knowlet [15]. The Knowlet structure of the FIP can itself be encapsulated as a FAIR Digital Object (FDO) having GUPRIs, type specifications and other FAIR metadata components [16]. As new FIPs are created, and existing FIPs are revised with alternative choices or extended when novel technologies are introduced, the FIP FDO is updated and versioned with provenance trails. These features allow FIPs to have ownership/authorship, to be cited, and will therefore accumulate value to its creators. This will incentivise the ongoing curation and maintenance of the FIP by its Community and garner reputation and trust that engenders reuse by others when making their own FAIR implementation choices. Moreover, applications that perform automated inference over Knowlets will open a range of potential analyses assisting in the optimization of FIPs or clusters of FIPs with respect to well-defined convergence objectives. Because the FIP Wizard captures and outputs Community-specific FIPs as JSON, we have written custom pipelines to convert the FIP Wizard format to nanopublications [17] that can then be permanently published on the decentralized, federated nanopublication server network [18].

2.4   The FIP Convergence Matrix

Over time, as numerous Communities independently create FIPs (whether manually or via tools such as the FIP Wizard) it will be possible to accumulate a comprehensive listing of FAIR-Enabling Resources reflecting the current technology landscape supporting FAIR data and services. Based on patterns of use and reuse of existing Resources, transparent strategies for optimal coordination in the revision of existing, or the creation of novel FIPs could be derived.

For example, Fig. 2 depicts an idealized repository of FIPs, each column representing a Community, each row a Resource linked to the appropriate FAIR Principle(s). The list of implementation choices for each principle might be tediously long but will be filterable on a variety of criteria including the frequency of its use in other research domains, its FAIR maturity level, or its endorsement by trusted organizations such as funding agencies.

FIPs may be similar or divergent, but in any case, are likely to compose a unique 'signature' for each Community. In its simplest formulation, for each Resource listed in rows, a Community may choose to either use (1) or not use (0) that Resource. In this idealized 'binary' limit the FIP could be represented as a bit string (for example, the FIP for Community C in Fig. 2 would be represented as $\{0,1,0,1,0,1,0,1\}$). In this binary vector representation, the FIP composes a community-specific 'fingerprint' that can be used to map the similarity distribution of FAIR implementation decisions (using for example, vector matching techniques). As depicted here, Communities A-D have each created distinct FIPs. In contrast, Communities E-H have chosen to reuse the profile of Community C (red arrows). Community I has also adopted the FIP of Community C but in this case, with 2 modifications (red circles for Resource 3 and Resource 5). Community J has adopted the exact FIP of Community 4 (blue arrow). FIP reuse leads to increasing similarity among FIPs in the Matrix which can be taken as a metric for convergence. In a manner similar to the Knowlet representation of the FIP, the fingerprint can itself be treated as FAIR data, including its representation as a FAIR Digital Object.

However, in practice, responses to the questionnaire are more nuanced than binary 'use/do not use' and require additional codes or in some cases even free-text responses

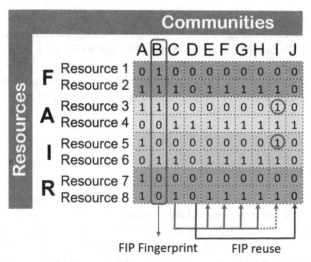

Fig. 2. FIP Convergence Matrix with registered Community Choices regarding the use of FAIR-Enabling Resources, which are made available for reuse by other Communities. (Color figure online)

(for example, from preliminary results working with roughly 50 research communities throughout Europe, it is clear that Community Data Stewards often wish to declare "we do not use this Resource yet, but have a project to implement in the next year"). Furthermore, alongside the FIP as a digital fingerprint it is vital to also publish the Considerations (captured as free text) as a separate referenceable record in order to make the reasons for the implementation choices and challenges intelligible to others and thereby making FIP reuse better fit for purpose.

The ultimate goal of this analysis is to align FIPs from different Communities in order to achieve convergence on the reuse of existing Resources and interoperation between the FAIR data and services of each Community. Hence, we refer to a FIP repository as the FIP Convergence Matrix. Although we can be confident that the FIP Wizard and the Nanopublication Server Network which currently store FIPs are reliable repositories, the FIP Convergence Matrix should eventually be sustained by a global and trusted data-mandated organization as an Open and FAIR resource, whether it be a centralized registry or a distributed network of repositories.

2.5 An Emerging FIP Architecture and Workflow

The FIP conceptual model and its various supporting components that are in development by the GO FAIR FIP Working Group compose a workflow for FIP creation and reuse.

The process of FIP creation begins by defining the Community description itself as a Resource. This includes the creation of a corresponding GUPRI and designation of a Community Data Steward. This minimal Community template has been used in the Nanobench tool [19] to mint nanopublications for a Community with a GUPRI and metadata like its research domain, time/date and versioning information [20].

Following the completion of the FIP questionnaire in the FIP Wizard, all FAIR implementation choices can be linked to the Community, creating an unambiguous machine-actionable FIP. FIPs can then be exposed as FAIR Digital Objects which in turn can be collected in the FIP Convergence Matrix repository yielding an overview of the FAIR implementation landscape. The FIP Convergence Matrix composed of FIP fingerprints facilitates systematic analyses over these landscapes leading to FIP optimization.

3   Discussion

3.1   FIPs and FAIR Convergence

Entering the FIP Wizard, confronting a complicated questionnaire that is likely to exceed the expertise of any single person, and then researching and declaring FAIR implementation decisions is a tedious and costly investment. However, once made, the FIP FDOs are reusable and can be shared with others in a number of important ways. This has the potential to lead to the rapid convergence and scaling required to realise the Internet of FAIR data and services in short time frames. This is especially true for FIPs authored or sanctioned by trusted domain authorities such as scholarly societies, scientific unions, GO FAIR Implementation Networks, or industry associations. Shareable and reusable FIPs can be used as a 'default setting' to kick-start FIP creation by other communities that aspire to adopt FAIR practices. However, organizations having cross-disciplinary or administrative mandates - such as repositories and national archives, funding agencies or publishers - may also define FIPs that would be seen as target implementation profiles by data producers. Likewise, data-related organizations, such as the GO FAIR Foundation, the Research Data Alliance, CODATA, and the World Data System could also create and endorse FIPs as they do for other best practices. As more FIPs accumulate, it should be possible to harness positive feedback where FIPs can inform the creation of other FIPs, leading potentially to easily reusable solutions and rapid convergence in this otherwise complex space. The reuse of carefully crafted FIPs has at least two important, and deeply related applications:

First, Trusted FIPs as Defaults in the FIP Convergence Matrix: The optimized FIPs composed, maintained and endorsed by trusted authorities can be offered in the Convergence Matrix as 'one-click' defaults for other communities to adopt and reuse, in whole or in part, as they see fit.

Second, Trusted FIPs as Defaults in Data Stewardship Plans: Once a FIP has been published in the FIP Convergence Matrix, it can be seen as the FAIR component of any data management/stewardship plan. The FIP could even inform community-specific 'autocomplete' functions in data management/stewardship planning tools assisting the data steward.

Community declared FIPs can be objectively evaluated on the basis of different attributes. For example, by inspecting each Resource listed in the FIP, it will be possible to calculate the degree to which the FIP maximises the reuse of existing Resources or the degree to which the FIP ensures interoperability. In addition, FIPs can be evaluated against various maturity indicators, while taking into account actual cost estimates for implementation.

As such, the FIP can itself be systematically optimized through judicious consideration and revision of implementation choices. Given the potential economic impact of "going FAIR" [21], there will likely emerge sophisticated FIP optimisation applications that could even include machine learning approaches that offer "suggestions" on how to improve a FIP for a given purpose. Advanced stages of FIP analysis will eventually lead to the identification and examination of FAIR technology 'gaps', spurring innovation of next-generation FAIR technologies.

The FAIR Principle R1.3 states that "(Meta)data meet domain-relevant Community standards". This is the only explicit reference in the FAIR Principles to the role played by domain-specific communities in FAIR. It is interesting to note that an advanced, online, automated, FAIR maturity evaluation system [22] did not attempt to implement a maturity indicator for FAIR Principle R1.3. It was not obvious during the development of the evaluator system how to test for "domain-relevant Community standards" as there exists, in general, no venue where communities publicly and in machine-readable formats declare data and metadata standards, and other FAIR practices. We propose the existence of a valid, machine-actionable FIP be adopted as a maturity indicator for FAIR Principle R1.3.

3.2 Related Work

Although the FAIR Guiding Principles are numerously cited (~3000 citations of [1]) and strongly supported by the EOSC initiative to push Europe towards a culture of open research, there are currently no broadly accepted FAIR solutions. Most of the work today is on the topic of FAIR data assessment approaches, be it quantitative measurements with Maturity Indicator tests [22] or qualitative assessment tools like those from DANS [23], CSIRO [24] or from the RDA FAIR Data Maturity Model Working Group [25]. Relevant work on the uptake of good FAIR practices is being driven by the FAIRsFAIR project that issued FAIR semantic recommendations recently [26]. Also, standardization efforts such as the CoreTrustSeal certification procedures [27] will leverage the adoption of FAIR data management practices for trustworthy data repositories. As for the tools, in [28], the authors analysed and commented on the current trends and convergence in data management tools with respect to FAIR data stewardship and machine-actionability.

Other attempts are trying to foster harmonisation on specific aspects of the FAIR Principles, or focus on a specific domain. The project ENVRI-FAIR emphasizes the need to implement common FAIR policies and interoperability solutions across environmental research infrastructures. One way to foster convergence is to provide technical demonstrators for research infrastructures that adopt FAIR implementations offered by others [29]. The RDA I-ADOPT WG is developing on Interoperability Framework for seamless cross-domain terminology alignment for observable property descriptions [30]. In an effort to support and harmonise metadata applications toward FAIR, the GO FAIR initiative has launched a systematic and scalable approach to the creation of machine-actionable metadata called Metadata for Machines (M4M) Workshops [31]. As such, the FIP approach is novel in the sense that it offers a transparent vehicle for very specific, yet open and flexible Community-based solutions for each of the FAIR Principles.

4 Conclusion

FIP creation is not a goal in itself. The ultimate objective is to accelerate convergence onto widespread FAIR implementations. This calls also for a coordinated effort to create an agreed compilation of FAIR-Enabling Resources. The practical testing and uptake of the FIP conceptual model and its supporting tools signals promising applications across a broad spectrum of knowledge domains: from environmental sciences, like in ENVRI-FAIR using the FIP approach in its recurring FAIR assessment evaluation [9] to life sciences with the GO FAIR Virus Outbreak Data Network (VODAN Implementation Network), which has now published its version 1.0 FIP [10, 11]. FIP creation also features prominently in a series of hackathons leading up to the GO FAIR/CODATA Convergence Symposium 2020 [32] where five diverse communities attempt to demonstrate FIP-mediated FAIR convergence.

Acknowledgements. This work was carried out in the context of the GO FAIR VODAN Implementation Network (supported also by the GO FAIR Foundation) and ENVRI-FAIR. ENVRI-FAIR has received funding from the European Union's Horizon 2020 research and innovation programme under grant agreement No. 824068.

References

1. Wilkinson, M., Dumontier, M., Aalbersberg, I., et al.: The FAIR guiding principles for scientific data management and stewardship. Sci. Data **3**, 160018 (2016). https://doi.org/10.1038/sdata.2016.18
2. Jacobsen, A., et al.: FAIR principles: interpretations and implementation considerations. Data Intell. **2**(1–2), 10–29 (2020). https://doi.org/10.1162/dint_r_00024
3. Wittenburg, P., Strawn, G.: Common Patterns in Revolutionary Infrastructures and Data (2018). https://www.rd-alliance.org/sites/default/files/Common_Patterns_in_Revolutionising_Infrastructures-final.pdf. Accessed 10 Aug 2020
4. FAIR Implementation Profile. https://www.go-fair.org/how-to-go-fair/fair-implementation-profile/. Accessed 10 Aug 2020
5. Sustkova, H.P., et al.: FAIR convergence matrix: optimizing the reuse of existing FAIR-related resources. Data Intell. **2**(1–2), 158–170 (2019)
6. FAIR Implementation Profile Conceptual Model. https://github.com/go-fair-ins/GO-FAIR-Ontology/tree/master/Models/FIP. Accessed 10 Aug 2020
7. GO FAIR ontology. https://github.com/go-fair-ins/GO-FAIR-Ontology. Accessed 10 Aug 2020
8. GEDE-IN Survey and Analysis. https://osf.io/jd5fp/. Accessed 10 Aug 2020
9. Magagna, B., Adamaki, A., Liao, X., Rabissoni, R., Zhao, Z.: ENVRI-FAIR D5.1 Requirement analysis, technology review and gap analysis of environmental RIs (2020). https://doi.org/10.5281/ZENODO.3884998
10. Human Readable VODAN FIP. https://doi.org/10.17605/OSF.IO/P2X7M
11. Machine Actionable VODAN FIP. https://doi.org/10.17605/OSF.IO/P2X7M
12. FIP questions. https://github.com/go-fair-ins/GO-FAIR-Ontology/blob/master/Models/FIP/FIP-MM.pdf. Accessed 10 Aug 2020
13. Pergl, R., Hooft, R., Suchánek, M., Knaisl, V., Slifka, J.: Data stewardship wizard: a tool bringing together researchers, data stewards, and data experts around data management planning. Data Sci. J. **18**(1), 59 (2019). https://doi.org/10.5334/dsj-2019-059

14. FIP Wizard: fip-wizard.ds-wizard.org, Email: guest@example.com, Password: "guest"
15. Mons, B.: FAIR science for social machines: let's share metadata knowlets in the Internet of FAIR data and services. Data Intell. **1**(1), 1–15 (2018)
16. Wittenburg, P., Strawn, G., Mons, B., Bonino, L., Schultes, E.: Digital objects as drivers towards convergence in data infrastructures (2019). http://doi.org/10.23728/b2share.b605d8 5809ca45679b110719b6c6cb11
17. Kuhn, T., et al.: Nanopublications: a growing resource of provenance-centric scientific linked data. In: 2018 IEEE 14th International Conference on e-Science (e-404Science) (2018). https://doi.org/10.1109/escience.2018.00024405
18. Kuhn, T., Chichester, C., Krauthammer, M., Dumontier, M.: Publishing without publishers: a decentralized approach to dissemination, retrieval, and archiving of data. In: Arenas, M., et al. (eds.) ISWC 2015. LNCS, vol. 9366, pp. 656–672. Springer, Cham (2015). https://doi.org/10.1007/978-3-319-25007-6_38
19. Nanobench. https://github.com/peta-pico/nanobench. Accessed 10 Aug 2020
20. VODAN Community nanopublication. http://purl.org/np/RAdDKjIGPt_2mE9oJtB3YQX6 wGGdCC8ZWpkxEIoHsxOjE. Accessed 10 Aug 2020
21. Directorate-General for Research and Innovation (European Commission): Cost-benefit analysis for FAIR research data, PwC EU Services, 16 January 2019. https://doi.org/10.2777/02999
22. Wilkinson, M.D., et al.: Evaluating FAIR maturity through a scalable, automated, community-governed framework. Sci. Data **6**, 174 (2019). https://doi.org/10.1038/s41597-019-0184-5, FAIR Evaluation Services. http://w3id.org/AmIFAIR
23. DANS: FAIR enough? Checklist. https://docs.google.com/forms/d/e/1FAIpQLSf7t1Z9IOBo j5GgWqik8KnhtH3B819Ch6lD5KuAz7yn0I0Opw/viewform. Accessed 10 Aug 2020
24. CSIRO: 5 Star Data Rating Tool. https://research.csiro.au/oznome/tools/oznome-5-star-data/. Accessed 10 Aug 2020
25. RDA FAIR Data Maturity Model Working Group: FAIR Data Maturity Model: specification and guidelines. Res. Data Alliance (2020). http://doi.org/10.15497/RDA00045
26. Le Franc, Y., et al.: D2.2 FAIR Semantics: First recommendations (Version 1.0). FAIRsFAIR (2020)
27. CoreTrustSeal Data Repository Requirements. https://www.coretrustseal.org/why-certifica tion/requirements/. Accessed 10 Aug 2020
28. Jones, S., et al.: Data management planning: how requirements and solutions are beginning to converge. Data Intell. **2**(1–2), 208–219 (2019)
29. ENVRI FAIR Gap Analysis and Demonstrators. https://envri-fair.github.io/knowledge-bas e-ui/. Accessed 10 Aug 2020
30. Magagna, B., Moncoiffe, G., Devaraju, A., Buttigieg, P. L., Stoica, M., Schindler, S.: Towards an interoperability framework for observable property terminologies, EGU General Assembly (2020), Accessed 4–8 May 2020, EGU2020-19895. https://doi.org/10.5194/egusphere-egu 2020-19895
31. Metadata for Machines Workshops. https://www.go-fair.org/today/making-fair-metadata/
32. CODATA GO FAIR Convergence Symposium 2020. https://conference.codata.org/FAIRco nvergence2020/. Accessed 10 Aug 2020

Conceptual Modeling for NoSQL Data Stores (CoMoNoS) 2020

Preface

Meike Klettke[1] ⓘ, Stefanie Scherzinger[2], and Uta Störl[3] ⓘ

[1] University of Rostock, Rostock, Germany
meike.klettke@uni-rostock.de
[2] University of Passau, Passau, Germany
stefanie.scherzinger@uni-passau.de
[3] Darmstadt University of Applied Sciences, Darmstadt, Germany
uta.stoerl@h-da.de

The objective of the First Workshop on Conceptual Modeling for NoSQL Data Stores (CoMoNoS 2020) is to explore opportunities for conceptual modeling applied to real-world problems that arise with NoSQL data stores (such as MongoDB, Couchbase, Cassandra, Neo4J, or Google Cloud Datastore). In designing an application backed by a NoSQL data store, developers face specific challenges that match the strengths of the ER community. The purpose of this workshop is to grow a community of researchers and industry practitioners working on conceptual modeling for NoSQL data stores. The workshop provides a forum for researchers to learn about the actual pain points faced by practitioners. Equally, it is our aim that practitioners benefit from the experience of the ER research community at large, and the authors of the workshop articles in particular.

Among eight submissions, the Program Committee selected three research articles. Main topics of the workshop are schema reverse engineering methods, approaches for model-based NoSQL data generation, and an overview on the current state of NoSQL modeling in industry, presented by keynote speaker Pascal Desmarets (Hackolade).

Acknowledgements. We would like to thank the members of our Program Commitee. This workshop was further supported by the Deutsche Forschungsgemeinschaft (DFG, German Research Foundation), grant #385808805.

Deimos: A Model-Based NoSQL Data Generation Language

Alberto Hernández Chillón$^{(\boxtimes)}$ ⃝, Diego Sevilla Ruiz ⃝,
and Jesús García Molina ⃝

Faculty of Computer Science, University of Murcia, Murcia, Spain
{alberto.hernandez1,dsevilla,jmolina}@um.es

Abstract. Synthetic data generation is of great interest when testing applications using databases. Some research and tools have been developed for relational systems. However there has been little attention to this problem for NoSQL systems. This work introduces Deimos, a prototype of a model-based language developed to generate synthetic data from NoSQL schemas represented as models conforming the NoSQLSchema metamodel. Requirements for the language–that become its design forces–are stated. The language is described, the generation process is analyzed, and future lines of work are outlined.

Keywords: NoSQL · Synthetic data · Data injection · Data generation

1 Introduction

Testing database applications is often difficult because of the lack of datasets wide and varied enough to test each and every desired aspect. It is difficult to work with existing datasets because they usually are of an inadequate size or variability for the purposes of testing. For example, load or performance tests of *MapReduce* operations require large databases. Also, usually it is not possible to work only with a fragment of the datasets, since referential integrity and statistic properties cannot be assured, and capturing every variation of the data is unlikely. Finally, existing datasets tend to be curated, with errors removed, and lack of an evolution history as a consequence of being mere database dumps.

The generation of synthetic datasets is then a topic of great interest for validating research results in data engineering, testing data intensive applications, deciding querying strategies, and testing a data schema and its physical layout. Past research has been focused in relational systems, and some solutions have been proposed, such as the use of restriction languages [4,14] and several other techniques described in [2].

This work was supported in part by the Spanish Ministry of Science, Innovation and Universities, under Grant TIN2017-86853-P.

G. Grossmann and S. Ram (Eds.): ER 2020 Workshops, LNCS 12584, pp. 151–161, 2020.
https://doi.org/10.1007/978-3-030-65847-2_14

Conversely, when generating NoSQL data, current approaches and existing tools have some significant limitations. They are only applicable to specific domains, or they obviate some specifics of NoSQL such as support for references among objects, referential integrity, and structural variations in entity types.

In this paper, we present an approach to tackle the issue of generating synthetic data. Our contribution is the Deimos language, aimed to specify, in a declarative way, what data should be generated. Deimos is platform-independent, but here we will focus on NoSQL data and show how we approach the limitations mentioned above. This work is defined in the *Model-based NoSQL data engineering* research line of our group [7, 8, 13]. Data generation will be defined based upon models that conform to the *NoSQLSchema metamodel* created to represent NoSQL schemas [13].

This article has been organized in the following sections: The next Section is used to discuss related work and tools on this research area and list their limitations. Section 3 is used to introduce requirements that led to the design of the language, and introduce the metamodel it is based upon. In Sect. 4 we detail the designed language and show how all the required functionality is covered. Section 5 describes the generation process. Finally, in Sect. 6, some conclusions are drawn and future work is outlined.

2   Related Work

Several research works and commercial tools have been devised to generate synthetic data. We discuss them in the field of NoSQL systems.

An approach to generate NoSQL datasets has been presented in [12]. The proposal is based on the dataset generation from JSON samples. Given an input sample, its implicit schema is inferred and the possible values to be generated are identified. With this analysis, datasets of arbitrary size can be generated, mimicking the given sample. Some limitations of this strategy are: (i) references between objects and structural variations are not supported; (ii) it needs to be provided with a sample descriptive enough; (iii) each generation only considers an entity type, and (iv) generated data values are not as realistic as desired.

Strategies to pollute existing datasets normally include a two step process as shown in [1, 6, 9]. A dataset is received as an input, some statistical analysis is performed, and invalid and duplicated tuples are generated to corrupt the input dataset. The quantity, type, and probability of the errors introduced can be configured, and some strategies require to apply a manual pre-processing. Another approach oriented to a particular domain is described in [5], where synthetic data are generated to evaluate context-aware recommendation algorithms. These works add to the limitations of the previous approach the following: (i) They are designed to be applied on a specific domain, and thus cannot be applied by supplying a generic schema, and (ii) a starting dataset is expected in order to pollute or refine it, something that cannot always be assured.

The commercial tools available to generate random data are usually designed to create data volumes against which software can be tested. They are focused on providing data generators from realistic pre-created dictionaries. One of the most popular tools is *Mockaroo* [3]. Mockaroo has a variety of pre-generated dictionaries where a primitive value can be taken from. This allows the user to test its code against certain predefined and expected values. Mockaroo supports a complete set of output formats: CSV, JSON, SQL, and XML, among others.

Generate-data [11] is similar to Mockaroo. It allows to define tuples by specifying a name and a data type, and then giving certain guidelines that map to a pre-generated dictionary from which values are taken at random. Its main advantages are that it supports exporting generated data by using several programming languages, and saving configurations for later reuse.

These tools offer little flexibility when specifying restrictions on the generated data, do not allow integrating existing datasets as parts of the output, do not take into account the introduction of random errors, or they simply do not consider the specifics of NoSQL as well as the existence of structural variations.

3   Rationale Behind Deimos

Deimos is a declarative textual language aimed to generate synthetic data. In this paper, we will show how Deimos can be used to generate aggregation-based NoSQL data (e.g. MongoDB datasets).

Hildebrandt et al. [9] list five items as desirable by any synthetic data generation tool: (i) efficiency and scalability, (ii) schema independence, (iii) realistic data values and patterns, (iv) realistic and variable error patterns, and (v) simple but adaptable configuration. These five items have been kept in mind as requirements to be fulfilled by the design of Deimos.

From our domain analysis through the study of published works and available tools, as well the recommendations shown before, we have designed the Deimos language meeting a set of requirements:

- The language is *complete*, that is, it allows to generate data for all of the elements of the model, and supports all its variability (entity types, variations, data types, references, and aggregations.)
- It is a *declarative specification* of what to generate. As so, it is *reproducible* with respect to statistic properties (seen below). This is very important to test how different query strategies, different data layouts, or distribution strategies (*sharding*, replication, etc.) in a given installation affect performance. Note that NoSQL technology is tightly linked to the physical deployment of the data. By simply changing the input data schema (e.g. converting an aggregation into a reference) the queries can be tested against the generated data to decide the best schema.
- It is capable of integrating several data sources to produce a resulting data set. This is crucial in a world where data is collected from different sources. The language supports specifying which parts of existing Internet datasets (or databases) are used as source for the generation.

- It is flexible enough to specify restrictions to the data types generated as well as to the identifiers of data elements. Applications often require for identifiers of entity elements to follow a given pattern, or that correct *referential integrity* is maintained within the dataset. This is guaranteed by Deimos.
- When generating many values, it is necessary to maintain some *statistic properties* of the data. For a given dataset, developers might know the relations between the number of data elements of one entity with respect to others (e.g. a user has, in mean, three favourite albums), so these relations must be maintained regardless of database size. Deimos allows the specification of these parameters, maintained when varying the output dataset size.
- Introduction of errors, nulls, and duplicates is possible for the generated output. These errors happen due to coding or user errors, and the applications must tolerate them, and be able to recover or fill the missing data.
- The generation must be efficient and parallelizable. It has to be able to generate batches at the same time that the previous batch is being bulk-inserted in the database. As data may depend on identifiers generated in previous batches (for instance, in references), mechanisms such as *consistent hashing* [10] are used to track the identifiers already generated for each entity.

A Deimos specification is based on a data schema that defines how data are structured. These schemas are defined according to the NoSQLSchema metamodel presented in [13]. They can be either inferred from a given database, or defined using a dedicated schema description language. The NoSQLSchema metamodel is shown in Fig. 1, slightly improved from the original by adding some new classes to the *Type* hierarchy, enriching the type a *Property* can have.

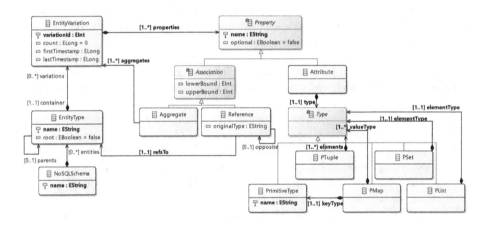

Fig. 1. The NoSQLSchema metamodel.

A NoSQLSchema model is formed by a set of entity types which can have one or more structural variations (entity variations). Each variation is defined by a set of properties or fields that can be attributes (if its value is a scalar or a collection) or associations (aggregations or references). Attributes are represented as a pair formed by a name and a data type. Aggregates and References are the basic building blocks of the relationships among entity data elements in aggregation-based data. They model, respectively, that a (sub)entity is aggregated under a given field name, and that a field is holding a reference to other entity data element. A more detailed description can be found in the original paper [13].

4 Designing the Deimos Language

A Deimos specification has four basic elements, that constitute its main four blocks: (i) The *input* elements, including the *schema* describing how data are organized, (ii) a set of data generation *rules*, (iii) a set of *mappings*, each of which bind an element of the schema to a rule, and (iv) the kind of *output* of the generation process.

An *input* block must indicate the schema against which the generation is being performed. This block can also include one or more data source declarations. A data source declaration associates a variable to the location of a data resource. A data source can be a URL of data in different formats (JSON, CSV, and plain text are supported), a relational database or even an external script or function. The type of source must be indicated in the declaration. The variables declared can be used later on to define rules. Sources may be sequentially traversed or either values can be obtained by means of a random access. In the case of relational databases, SQL queries can be specified to retrieve values.

Listing 1.1 shows an example of an input block in which a schema named *MongoSongs* is referenced, and several variables are declared. Note that in the case of complex content (CSV or queries), it is possible to map a column to an inner variable name. In the example, the first and second columns of *csvFile* would be mapped to the variables *csvFile.names* and *csvFile.phones*, respectively. Also the variable *pyFunc* refers to a Python script that uses the *Faker* library to generate numbers. For each data source it can be specified how should that data source be accessed: In a random order or sequentially.

```
Input:
    schema:     MongoSongs
    wordsFile:  text ("file://./config/txt/words.txt", order: random)
    namesFile:  csv ("https://github.com/jbencina/facebook-
        news/blob/master/fb_news_pagenames.csv", order: cycle)
    jsonFile:   json ("config/json/surnames.json")
    csvFile:    csv ("config/csv/phoneNumbers.csv", { names: $1, phones: $2 }
        )
    pyFunc:     python ("scripts/fakerYears.py")
```

Listing 1.1. Example of an input block.

Rules determine how the elements of the NoSQLSchema metamodel (e.g. entity types, variations, or values of a primitive type) are generated. Two types of rules can be defined: *Default* and *Specific*. Each rule refers to a metamodel element. Unlike default ones, specific rules are identified by a name. Default rules are automatically applied to all the instances of the metamodel elements that are part of the input schema for which a specific rule has not been defined. Instead, specific rules can be applied in the *mapping* block to any element of the schema that is an instance of the metamodel element specified in the rule. In the example shown in Listing 1.2, default rules have been defined for *Reference* and *Number*, and specific rules for *EntityType* and the *String* and *Double* types.

```
Rules:
    default:        Reference    { strange: 0.01 }
    default:        Number       { null: 0.01, distr: { poisson, mean: 3 } }
    etypeRange:     EntityType   { range: [1000..2000],
                                   duplicate: 0.05, idpattern: "album_%d"}
    simpleString:   String       { src: namesFile, null: 0.02, length: [1..10] }
    enumString:     String       { enum: ["Value 1", "Value 2", "Value 3"] }
    doubleFirst:    Double       { range: [0..1] }
    doubleSecond::doubleFirst:{ precision: 2 }
```

Listing 1.2. Example of a rule block.

A rule declaration includes one or more *modifiers*. Each modifier sets a restriction over the generation of the metamodel element specified in the declaration. In Listing 1.2, modifiers *src*, *null* and *length* have been defined for rule *simpleString*, and for the default rule applied to numbers, modifiers *null* and *distribution* have been configured. Rule inheritance is supported for specific rules in order to extend the set of modifiers of an existing rule. For example, *doubleSecond* extends *doubleFirst* with the *precision* modifier.

Modifiers applicable to elements are shown in Tables 1 and 2. On each table there is a column for each primitive type, collection type, or other NoSQLSchema element, a row for each modifier, and a check mark ($\checkmark$) to show whether a certain modifier is applicable to the corresponding element or not.

Table 1. Modifiers applicable to primitive types and collection types.

Modifiers	Primitive types					Collection types			
	String	Number	Double	Boolean	Timestamp	PList	PSet	PMap	PTuple
Fixed	$\checkmark$	$\checkmark$	$\checkmark$	$\checkmark$	$\checkmark$	–	–	–	–
Source	$\checkmark$	$\checkmark$	$\checkmark$	$\checkmark$	$\checkmark$	–	–	–	–
Regex	$\checkmark$	–	–	–	–	–	–	–	–
Range	–	$\checkmark$	$\checkmark$	–	–	–	–	–	–
Distribution	–	$\checkmark$	$\checkmark$	–	–	–	–	–	–
Enum	$\checkmark$	$\checkmark$	$\checkmark$	–	$\checkmark$	–	–	–	–
IdPattern	$\checkmark$	–	–	–	–	–	–	–	–
Null prob.	$\checkmark$	$\checkmark$	$\checkmark$	$\checkmark$	$\checkmark$	$\checkmark$	$\checkmark$	$\checkmark$	$\checkmark$
Strange prob.	$\checkmark$	$\checkmark$	$\checkmark$	$\checkmark$	$\checkmark$	$\checkmark$	$\checkmark$	$\checkmark$	$\checkmark$
Duplicate prob.	–	–	–	–	–	–	–	–	–
Precision	–	–	$\checkmark$	–	–	–	–	–	–
Length	$\checkmark$	–	–	–	–	$\checkmark$	$\checkmark$	$\checkmark$	$\checkmark$
Starting date	–	–	–	–	$\checkmark$	–	–	–	–
Format	–	–	–	–	$\checkmark$	–	–	–	–
Interval	–	–	–	–	$\checkmark$	–	–	–	–

Table 2. Modifiers applicable to other NoSQLSchema elements.

Modifiers	NoSQLSchema element			
	Entity type	Entity variation	Reference	Aggregate
Fixed	–	–	–	–
Source	–	–	–	–
Regex	–	–	–	–
Range	✓	✓	–	–
Distribution	–	–	–	–
Enum	–	–	–	–
IdPattern	✓	✓	✓	–
Null prob.	–	–	✓	✓
Strange prob.	–	–	✓	✓
Duplicate prob.	✓	✓	–	–
Precision	–	–	–	–
Length	–	–	✓	✓
Starting date	–	–	–	–
Format	–	–	–	–
Interval	–	–	–	–

The currently defined modifiers can be divided into three families depending on what use they are intended: (i) to generate a value, (ii) to replace a value, or (iii) to alter an already generated value.

Modifiers *Fixed, Source, Regex, Range, Distribution, Enum,* and *IdPattern* belong to the first family. *Fixed* sets a static value to be generated. *Source* extracts the values from a defined source in the *Input* block. *Regex* specifies the generator regular expression for the values. *Range* limits the range of the generated elements. *Distribution* uses a predefined distribution (such as *normal, geometric,* or *poisson*) to generate values. *Enum* generates a value only from among the given values. Finally, *IdPattern* shows a pattern in C `printf` format defining how IDs will be generated for a given entity type. Each rule must contain one, and only one, of these modifiers. These modifiers may be divided into two groups, depending on the quantitative or qualitative approach they follow to generate data. Deimos permits modifiers for both approaches in order to allow for each developer profile to choose the most suitable approach for each generation.

The second family is composed by modifiers *Null prob.* and *Strange prob.* *Null prob.* defines a probability by which a *null* value is generated instead of the expected value, and modifier *Strange prob.* defines a probability by which a value whose type is different than the expected one is generated. Each rule can define zero, one, or both of these modifiers.

The last family includes modifiers: *Duplicate prob.*, *Precision*, *Length*, *Starting date*, *Format*, and *Interval*. *Duplicate prob.* defines a probability of generating a duplicated entry (with different identifiers). *Precision* limits the number of decimals to be generated for Double values. *Length* limits the size of collections and Strings. *Starting date*, *Format*, and *Interval* are used to generate realistic Timestamps. A rule may include any number of modifiers from this family.

Mapping declarations associate a specific rule to an element of the input schema. Such an element must be an instance of the metamodel element specified in the rule declaration. These declarations are part of the *mapping* block. This block is ordered in a JSON-like structure for each entity type of the schema, and, by using the syntax *<property name>: <rule>* for each element, a rule can be associated. In Listing 1.3 a mapping for the entity type *Album* (belonging to the *MongoSongs* schema specified in the input block) is shown. The rule *etypeRange* is associated to *Album*, altering the number of objects generated for this entity type and defining how identifiers will be generated. Then, properties *name*, *popularity*, *score*, and *genre* are associated to a defined rule (*simpleString*, *doubleSecond*, *doubleFirst*, and *enumString*, respectively). Finally for *releaseYear* an inline rule can be created, which will not be reused later on. Those properties in *Album* without a specific rule associated, or those entity types without an entry in this block will be using the *default* rules already defined.

```
Mappings:
  Album
  {
    etypeRange,
    name:        simpleString,
    popularity:  doubleSecond,
    score:       doubleFirst,
    genre:       enumString,
    releaseYear: { src: pyFunc }
  }
```

Listing 1.3. Example of a mapping block.

The data generated can be registered in several kinds of output: (i) the standard output (*console*), (ii) CSV or JSON files (*folder*), and (iii) a *database*. As shown in Listing 1.4, several output declarations can be included in the *output* block. In the example, the data generated will be shown in the console, stored in a MongoDB database, and recorded in a folder named *results* in JSON format.

```
Output:
  name:      generated_MongoSongs
  console
  database:  mongodb ( localhost:7777 )
  folder:    json     ( "../../results/" )
```

Listing 1.4. Example of an output block.

5   The Generation Process

In this section we will describe the generation process, which is shown in Fig. 2. The process receives as inputs a Deimos model, a NoSQLSchema model detailing the schema to which the generation is being done, and a dataset output size.

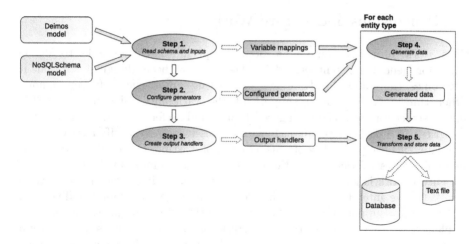

Fig. 2. Overview of the proposed process to generate data from a NoSQLSchema.

The first step makes use of the input block. It reads the NoSQLSchema model, solves the given references to dictionary files and queries to databases, and maps those inputs to variables, in order to be able to use them later on. At the end of this step several *mapping variables* have been produced.

The second step involves the rules block. For each defined rule, the process creates a data generator for the corresponding element and configures it according to each defined modifier. If no rules are provided for a certain element, then a basic default generator is created. At the end of this step several *configured generators* have been created.

The third step uses the output block. For each declared output type, an *output handler* is created and configured. Each handler is responsible for creating the needed structure for it to be used properly.

The fourth step focuses on the mapping block, and uses the previous *mapping variables* and *configured generators* to generate the synthetic data. For each entity type on the schema and for each property, a generation is performed by applying the corresponding configured generator. For each entity type and property to be generated without rule, a basic default generator of the corresponding type will be applied. At the end of this step *generated data* has been created.

The fifth and last step is not bound to any block. It receives the *generated data* from the last step, and the already created *output handlers*, and it applies each handler to store the data. Each handler will transform the data to a suitable format and store it. Output handlers are reused between steps.

As can be seen in Fig. 2, the process repeats the fourth and fifth generation steps for each entity type defined in the NoSQLSchema model. At the end of the process each handler is closed and resources are released.

6   Conclusions and Future Work

This work proposes Deimos, a domain specific language able to define rules for generating synthetic data. Deimos has been designed so that it overcomes the main disadvantages of existing approaches, offering, among other things: (i) Complete support of the variability inherent to NoSQL data: structural variations, aggregations, and references with referential integrity, (ii) a declarative language with expressiveness to specify restrictions to the data, (iii) the possibility of reusing parts of existing, remote datasets, (iv) it maintains the statistical properties of data, leading to reproducibility, etc.

Future work is going to be focused on introducing improvements at several levels: (i) We intend to extend the Deimos language with more modifiers, in order to fully support functionality of any database paradigm, (ii) we plan to implement a reuse mechanism so a configuration block can be reused into several Deimos specifications, (iii) we will work on the outputs section so more databases are supported as well as other kinds of outputs such as *Apache Spark Streaming*, (iv) we will implement an efficiency study to check if any bottlenecks exist and we will implement parallelization mechanisms on the process, (v) finally, we plan to create a validation process of the generation, in which starting from an inferred NoSQLSchema model we plan to generate data to a new database and infer a new schema, comparing this newly inferred schema to the original.

References

1. Bachteler, T., Reiher, J.: TDGen: A Test Data Generator for Evaluating Record Linkage Methods. Technical Report, German Record Linkage Center, NO. WP-GRLC-2012-01 (2012)
2. Binnig, C., Kossmann, D., Lo, E.: Towards automatic test database generation. IEEE Data Eng. Bull. **31**(1), 28–35 (2008)
3. Brocato, M.: Mockaroo Webpage. https://www.mockaroo.com/. Accessed June 2020
4. Bruno, N., Chaudhuri, S.: Flexible database generators. In: 31st International Conference on VLDB, pp. 1097–1107 (2005)
5. del Carmen Rodríguez-Hernández, M., Ilarri, S., Hermoso, R., Trillo-Lado, R.: DataGenCARS: a generator of synthetic data for the evaluation of context-aware recommendation systems. Pervasive Mob. Comput. **3**(8), 516–541 (2017). https://doi.org/10.1016/j.pmcj.2016.09.020
6. Christen, P., Vatsalan, D.: Flexible and extensible generation and corruption of personal data. In: CIKM 2013: Proceedings of the 22nd ACM International Conference on Information and Knowledge Management, pp. 1165–1168, October 2013. https://doi.org/10.1145/2505515.2507815
7. Hernández, A., Feliciano, S., Sevilla, D., García Molina, J.: Exploring the visualization of schemas for aggregate-oriented NoSQL databases. In: 36th International Conference on Conceptual Modelling (ER) ER Forum 2017, pp. 72–85 (2017)
8. Hernández Chillón, A., Sevilla Ruiz, D., García Molina, J., Feliciano Morales, S.: A model-driven approach to generate schemas for object-document mappers. IEEE Access **7**, 59126–59142 (2019)

9. Hildebrandt, K., Panse, F., Wilcke, N., Ritter, N.: Large-Scale Data Pollution with Apache Spark. IEEE Trans. Big Data **6**, 396–411 (2017)
10. Karger, D., Lehman, E., Leighton, T., Panigrahy, R., Levine, M., Lewin, D.: Consistent hashing and random trees: distributed caching protocols for relieving hot spots on the world wide web. In: Proceedings of the Twenty-Ninth Annual ACM Symposium on Theory of Computing, STOC 1997, pp. 654–663. ACM (1997). https://doi.org/10.1145/258533.258660
11. Keen, B.: Generate-data Webpage. http://www.generatedata.com. Accessed July 2020
12. Hasan Mahmud: Towards a Data Generation Tool for NoSQL Data Stores. Master's thesis, Media Informatics, RWTH Aachen University, Aachen, Germany (2018)
13. Sevilla Ruiz, D., Morales, S.F., García Molina, J.: Inferring versioned schemas from NoSQL databases and its applications. In: Johannesson, P., Lee, M.L., Liddle, S.W., Opdahl, A.L., López, Ó.P. (eds.) ER 2015. LNCS, vol. 9381, pp. 467–480. Springer, Cham (2015). https://doi.org/10.1007/978-3-319-25264-3_35
14. Smaragdakis, Y., et al.: Scalable satisfiability checking and test data generation from modeling diagrams. Autom. Softw. Eng. **16**(1), 73 (2009)

Managing Physical Schemas in MongoDB Stores

Pablo D. Muñoz-Sánchez$^{(\boxtimes)}$ ⓘ, Carlos Javier Fernández Candel ⓘ,
Jesús García Molina ⓘ, and Diego Sevilla Ruiz ⓘ

Faculty of Computer Science, University of Murcia, Campus Espinardo, Murcia, Spain
{pablodavid.munoz,cjferna,jmolina,dsevilla}@um.es

Abstract. Being schemaless is a common feature of most NoSQL systems. It accommodates the change and non-uniformity of stored data, and allows fast deployment of databases. However, the lack of database schemas makes it difficult to develop database applications and tools. Therefore, explicit schemas should be produced, either inferred from NoSQL data, code, or both, to facilitate the work of developers and support the functionality of database tools. Strategies published to discover NoSQL schemas focus on the extraction of the entity types but physical schemas have received very little attention. Our group recently presented an approach to infer logical schemas from aggregate-based NoSQL stores. Because the inferred schemas do not capture physical information on the underlying database, they can not help with the implementation of some typical database tasks, like database migrations, optimization, and schema evolution. In this paper we extend our previous approach by proposing a physical metamodel targeted to MongoDB databases, which captures characteristics such as existing indexes, data organization, and statistical features (e.g. cardinality of values.) We also explain the process of retrieving the physical model from an existing database, and the bidirectional transformations between logical and physical models.

Keywords: Physical schema · Logical schema · Schema mappings · NoSQL stores · Schemaless · Reverse engineering · Metamodel · MongoDB

1 Introduction

Data models are formalisms intended to represent the structure of the data managed by an information system. A *schema* is a database representation (i.e. a model) expressed by means of a data model. Schemas can be defined at three levels of abstraction: conceptual, logical, and physical. This paper focuses on issues related to the management of physical schemas in NoSQL stores.

Most NoSQL systems are *schemaless*: Data can be stored without a previous formal definition of its structure (i.e. its schema.) This favors the agile evolution

This work has been funded by the Spanish Ministry of Science, Innovation and Universities (project grant TIN2017-86853-P).

ⓒ Springer Nature Switzerland AG 2020
G. Grossmann and S. Ram (Eds.): ER 2020 Workshops, LNCS 12584, pp. 162–172, 2020.
https://doi.org/10.1007/978-3-030-65847-2_15

but the advantages offered by explicit schemas are lost, such as validating input data. Therefore, several approaches have been proposed to discover schemas from stored data [10,13,15], and some commercial tools provides utilities to visualize inferred schemas [4,5]. None of these proposals addresses the separation between the physical and logical models, unlike similar works in the relational data engineering field [6,9]. In fact, NoSQL physical models have received very little attention in the emerging NoSQL data engineering field: as far as we know, only the works of Michael Mior for columnar and document stores [11,12].

In this paper, we present our initial work on the management of NoSQL physical schemas. In particular, we propose a physical schema metamodel for the document database MongoDB,[1] and we show (i) how physical schemas can be directly extracted from stored data, and (ii) the bidirectional transformation between physical schemas and the logical schemas described in [13]. Schema mappings are useful to obtain database views of interest for different stakeholders. The bidirectional conceptual-logical mapping is out of the scope of this paper. A third contribution of this work is a discussion on some NoSQL database tasks that could be automated by means of physical schemas.

This paper is organized as follows. First, the logical metamodel is presented. Then, the physical metamodel proposed is shown, and the extraction process from document databases is explained. Once the two kinds of schemas are introduced, the bidirectional mapping between them is described. Then, some related works are discussed. Finally, potential scenarios which could benefit from our contribution are highlighted and new ideas are proposed as future work.

2   Logical Model

Of the four categories in which NoSQL stores are usually classified (document, columnar, key-value, and graph), in the former three, aggregation relationships prevail over references to structure data. Previous work of our research group focuses on extracting logical schemas from data stored in aggregate-based systems [13]. Figure 1 shows the *NoSQLSchema* metamodel defined to represent the extracted schemas. This metamodel was created with the Ecore[2] language. Therefore, schemas are represented as models of the EMF technological space [14].

In schemaless systems, an entity can have multiple structural variations, as they lack of a schema imposing a structure for the stored data. Extracting the entity variations and the relationships (references and aggregations) among database objects are characteristics that differentiate the extraction approach exposed in [13] from the rest of proposals. In [15], variations are also inferred for MongoDB stores in [15], but not relationships.

Given two database objects o_1 and o_2 of the same entity E, and let A and B be the sets of attributes of o_1 and o_2, respectively, o_1 and o_2 are said to belong to the same structural variation if and only if:

---

[1] MongoDB Webpage www.mongodb.com.

[2] Ecore Webpage http://wiki.eclipse.org/ecore.

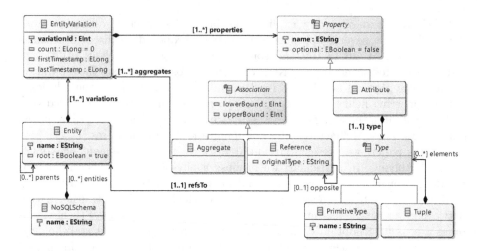

Fig. 1. NoSQLSchema logical metamodel adapted from Fig. 3 in [13].

$$size(A) = size(B) \land \forall a \in A, \exists b \in B | (name(a) = name(b) \land type(a) = type(b)) \quad (1)$$

Type equality is trivial for primitive types. For nested documents, Formula 1 is also valid, and can be recursively applied. For arrays, the equality of types is given by the following formula, being $a \in A$ and $b \in B$ two array attributes:

$$size(types(a)) = size(types(b)) \land \forall ta \in types(a), \exists tb \in types(b) | ta = tb \quad (2)$$

A `NoSQLSchema` logical model is formed by a set of entity types (`Entity` class in Fig. 1). Each `Entity` contains one or more structural variations (`EntityVariation`), characterized by a set of properties (`Property`) that can be either attributes (`Attribute`) or relationships (`Association`). An attribute holds a value of a scalar type (`PrimitiveType`) or an array of scalar types (`Tuple`). Relationships can be either *aggregations* (`Aggregate`) or *references* (`Reference`). Attributes are key-value pairs. In the case of aggregations, the property denotes an embedded (or nested) object of another target entity type, whereas references are links to objects of a target entity type.

3   Physical Model

Extracted NoSQL logical schemas have proved useful for visualizing schemas [7], generating code for object-document mappers [8], and generating test data [2], among other utilities. However, offering other typical functionalities (e.g. database migration, and design pattern discovery) requires to manage information on physical aspects of databases, such as indexes, sharding, or deployment.

Physical models are required then in order to offer an integral set of database tools.

Our first step was to define a metamodel to represent physical schemas for MongoDB stores. It was chosen for being the most widely used NoSQL store.[3] A MongoDB store contains a set of collections that store documents of a given entity. Each collection can contain several entity variations. Documents have a JSON-like structure and they are stored internally using a compact binary representation called *BSON*,[4] with a type system which is a superset of JSON, adding some utility types. Several kinds of indexes can be defined for collections to improve performance of regular and geospatial queries, and text searches. Additionally, it provides high availability through automatic replication of data and scalability through partitioning of collections among the nodes in a cluster.

3.1   Physical Metamodel

An excerpt of the MongoDB *physical metamodel* is shown in Fig. 2. This metamodel represents structural and performance features of the deployed database: existing collections, structural variations in each collection, embedding and reference between variations, indexes for query optimization, and statistics collected for existing data types. For brevity, database topology modeled by `Deployments`, `Hosts`, `ReplicaSets` and `Shards` is not covered in this paper.

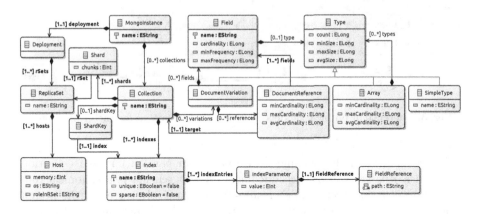

Fig. 2. Physical metamodel.

The root element, `MongoInstance`, models an existing MongoDB database, composed of a set of `Collections`. Each `Collection` contains a number of `DocumentVariations` and `Indexes`. A `DocumentVariation` corresponds to the `StructuralVariation` notion of the logical model. Given a particular collection, it represents a set of documents that have the same `Fields`, and it can contain

---

[3] Fifth position in the DB-Engines ranking, July 2020. db-engines.com/en/ranking.
[4] BSON specification: www.bsonspec.org.

references (`DocumentReference`) to documents in other collections. Each `Field` has a name and a `Type`, and can optionally store the cardinality of their values and their minimum and maximum frequencies. `Types` can be either a nested object (`DocumentVariation`), an `Array` or a `SimpleType` and record their minimum, maximum and average size as well as their number of occurrences. The `Array` type depicts a set of MongoDB arrays whose contained `Types` are the same, regardless of their order, and records the minimum, maximum, and average number of elements it can contain. Other valid BSON Types[5] are modeled as `SimpleTypes`. `Index`es contain the set of fields on which data retrieval is optimized, and unique and sparse constraints are also registered.

3.2   Obtaining Physical Models from MongoDB

The strategy applied to extract physical schemas is based on the one previously defined for logical schemas [13]. Some changes were made due to the different structure of the extracted data, and others due to the new information inferred, such as indexes, deployment, and statistical data. The extraction process now consists of four stages, as shown in Fig. 3: a MapReduce operation, obtaining indexes, building the physical model, and finally statistical information retrieval.

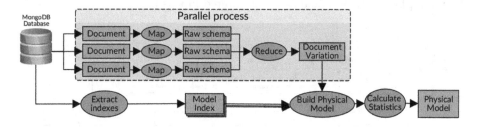

Fig. 3. Inference of physical models. The process is repeated for each collection.

In the map step, the documents are parsed in parallel for each collection to obtain a *raw schema* of each document. A raw schema is a canonical representation of a document, which results from recursively traversing its nested structure replacing each primitive value with their corresponding BSON type, and each array with the set of contained simplified types. Then, a reduce step is performed for each set of documents whose raw schema is the same, and their occurrences, sizes, and cardinality of arrays are aggregated to gather statistics. The set of documents with the same raw schema will then be reduced to a single `DocumentVariation`, that is added to the corresponding `Collection`.

Once the physical structure of a collection is extracted, `Index`es are queried, their values captured as `IndexParameters`, and the fields they refer to as `FieldReferences`. These elements are also added to the current `Collection`.

---

[5] MongoDB BSON types: docs.mongodb.com/manual/reference/bson-types.

The stage of building physical model integrates the variation and index information obtained in the two previous stages.

An optional statistic retrieval step could then be performed to track the number of distinct values and their minimum and maximum frequencies of their fields for each DocumentVariation. A final step is performed on all inferred collections to detect whether a given field is a potential reference (DocumentReference) to an existing collection. As described in [13], it is analyzed if the field name is derived from the collection name by adding certain suffixes or prefixes or by singularization or pluralization, among other heuristics. Figure 4 shows an example of the described extraction process, implemented with Apache Spark.[6]

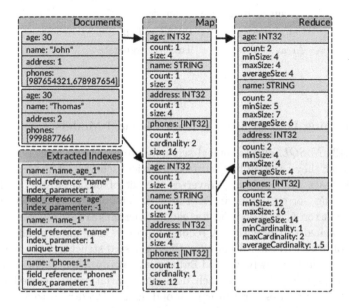

Fig. 4. Inferring a physical model from a given collection (statistics calculation and the detection of the **address DocumentReference** are omitted.)

4   Mapping Between Logical and Physical Models

A bidirectional mapping between physical and logical metamodels has been implemented through two model-to-model transformations: physical→logical, and logical→physical. Table 1 shows the mapping between the elements existing in both metamodels. Note that the logical→physical transformation preserves information recorded in the logical model, but represented at a lower level of abstraction. However, some information is lost in the physical→logical transformation, such as indexes, shards, array cardinality, or field frequency, because

---

[6] Spark Webpage: http://spark.apache.org.

is not present in the logical view. When translating the logical model into the physical one, developers may want to augment the obtained model to include such information. For this, a domain-specific language could be used (e.g. [12]).

Table 1. Physical–Logical models mappings.

Physical Model	Logical Model
Collection	Entity
DocumentVariation	EntityVariation (& Entity)
Field	Attribute—Aggregate
DocumentReference	Reference
SimpleType	PrimitiveType
Array	Tuple—Aggregate

4.1   Obtaining Logical Models from Physical Models

While in [13] *NoSQLSchema* logical schemas are extracted from data, here we will show how they can be obtained from physical schemas. The transformation that implements that mapping traverses the set of Collections in the input model, creating, for each one, an Entity with the root attribute set. Then, an EntityVariation is also created for each DocumentVariation of a collection, which is attached to the entity. A recursive process is applied to all the nested variations of each variation. Dealing with this nested structure, a new Entity is created to attach the newly created EntityVariation when it does not exist.

Next, the set of Fields of each document variation is iterated to generate the set Properties for the corresponding EntityVariation. The generated property depends on the field type: an Attribute if it is a SimpleType or Array of SimpleTypes, an Aggregate for DocumentVariation or Array of DocumentVariations, and a Reference for the DocumentReference type. In the case of attributes, it is also generated a PrimitiveType or Tuple depending on whether the field type is SimpleType or Array. In the case of generating a reference, the refsTo relationship is filled with the target Entity obtained from *target* relationships of the physical model.

Figure 5 shows two examples of exercising the mapping. The Project entity is generated from the Projects collection of the physical model. On the left, the entity variations Manager and Address are generated from the two embedded DocumentVariations with the same name. On the right, an Employee aggregated entity is generated from the array of EmployeeVariation, a reference (to Project) from the hasProjects field, and a tuple from the comments field.

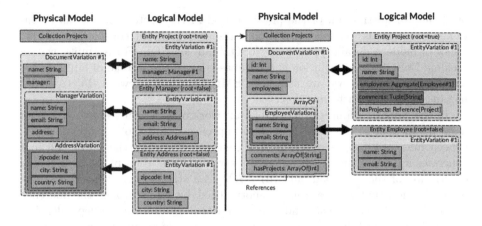

Fig. 5. Two examples of inference between physical and logical models.

4.2   Obtaining Physical Models from Logical Models

The logical→physical transformation generates a partial physical schema from a logical schema. Now, mappings from Table 1 are applied in reverse to recreate the initial physical model. `EntityVariations` are mapped to `DocumentVariations`, and containment relationships between them are rebuilt; Inferred `Tuples`, `References` and `Aggregates` with a `upperBound` greater than one will be mapped back to `Arrays`; `Entities` with `root = true` will be translated into `Collections`.

We implemented this logical→physical transformation to validate that the original physical model is correctly reconstructed, except for the information not mapped in the previous transformation (e.g. indexes, cardinalities, etc.). However, physical models are meant to be obtained directly from the database, if possible.

5   Related Work

We will only consider works that have addressed database schema mappings involving physical schemas or have inferred physical models for any purpose.

A great effort to define transformational approaches for database schemas was carried on at the database group led by Jean Luc Hainaut at Namur University [6]. In [9], J.M. Hick and J.L. Hainaut proposed a CASE tool for database evolution, which is based on the *Generic Entity/Relationship* metamodel. This metamodel is used to represent physical, logical, and conceptual schemas, and allows specifying a list of schema transformations to obtain new representations (e.g. another schema or code). The transformations are recorded in a history and the differential analysis of their stages allows the deployment of changes in the database and related programs. This approach showed the importance of having an abstraction of the physical level in the context of schema evolution. Our group is working on a similar research line, but considering specific issues of modern databases such as NoSQL and NewSQL. For example, we are tackling NoSQL store evolution and database migration. Instead of building our tooling from scratch, we are using the EMF/Eclipse framework [14] to create metamodels and transformations.

In the NoSQL realm, the most relevant work on physical schemas has been done in Michael Mior's PhD [11]. Two approaches and tools involving physical schemas were proposed: (i) Given a conceptual schema, the *NoSE* [12] tool generates a recommended schema and query implementation plans, as well as a description of the workload; and (ii) *ESON* is a strategy for extracting a normalized conceptual schema from a denormalized database through the inference of a *generic physical schema* and a set of functional and inclusion dependencies.

Unlike done in ESON, we currently do not provide an automatic normalization algorithm when performing physical→logical mapping. However, Mior only takes into account columnar and document stores, and our aim is to develop database-paradigm agnostic tools through the definition of generic logical and physical metamodels. Note that no physical metamodel was defined by Mior, but physical structures are directly created.

In [3], a reverse engineering method is applied on relational databases to discover the conceptual schema. For this, *DDL* and *DML* scripts are analyzed, and data mining is performed. Firstly, the physical schema is extracted; then, it is *de-optimized* to facilitate the inference of entities, relationships, and cardinalities; and the conceptual schema is finally obtained. Here, we have discussed the bidirectional logical-physical mapping, but we have not addressed how conceptual schemas can be derived from logical schemas and we also did not perform a *de-optimization* phase when applying the physical→logical mapping. Representing logical schemas as Extended Entity-Relationship models (EER), the logical-conceptual mapping is simple, as both models are at the same level of abstraction, and entity variations do not have to be considered.

A design methodology for aggregation-based stores is introduced in [1], which proposes the definition of both a conceptual and a logical schema prior to the implementation phase. Database designs are mapped to system-independent *NoAM* models. This methodology could take advantage of the definition of a physical schema to facilitate the implementation. The logical→physical transformation could tune the NoAM model taking into account the target database.

6   Final Discussion

The physical model presented in this paper covers specific features of a MongoDB database. It captures data organization, structures for optimizing data access, and statistical information of interest about the stored data. Due to its low-level nature, the proposed solution may prove useful in typical database scenarios such as: (i) modeling the existing source and the desired target as part of a database optimization or a migration, (ii) capture the evolution of a database over time, (iii) wizards and viewers can be implemented on top of this physical model to provide database administrators with an overview of the current state of the database and to give possible maintenance suggestions, and (iv) as a basis for query models to measure their effectiveness and suggest optimizations.

However, further improvements can be made to our metamodel. A more generic document-oriented physical metamodel is in the works, integrating the specifics from other well-known document stores such as CouchBase or OrientDB. This document physical metamodel could be extended even to include details from stores of other database categories (columnar, key-value, and graph), thus defining a *unified physical metamodel*. Additionally, a domain-specific language could be developed to allow the end user to specify structural features that were not inferred from the underlying database (such as field dependencies and references that are not explicit). Finally, it could also be integrated with change notification mechanisms implemented in some NoSQL databases to provide real-time snapshots of the physical model.

Extracting physical schemas from data could be combined with a code analysis of database applications. The application level provides additional information about the data stored in NoSQL databases, and can be used to find reference relationships between stored entities, suggest new indexes for more efficient queries, propose changes to application code to exploit the underlying schema, and suggest changes to the schema, among other operations.

References

1. Atzeni, P., Bugiotti, F., Cabibbo, L., Torlone, R.: Data modeling in the NoSQL world. Comput. Stand. Interfaces **67**, 103149 (2020)
2. Chillon, A.H., Sevilla, D., Garcia-Molina, J.: Deimos: a model-based NoSQL data generation language. In: 1st CoMoNoS Workshop in 39th International Conference on Conceptual Modeling (2020)
3. Comyn-Wattiau, I., Akoka, J.: Reverse engineering of relational database physical schemas. In: Thalheim, B. (ed.) ER 1996. LNCS, vol. 1157, pp. 372–391. Springer, Heidelberg (1996). https://doi.org/10.1007/BFb0019935
4. ER-Studio Webpage. https://www.idera.com/er-studio-enterprise-data-modeling-and-architecture-tools. Accessed April 2019
5. CA ERwin Web Page. http://erwin.com/products/data-modeler. April 2019
6. Hainaut, J.: The transformational approach to database engineering. In: GTTSE, International Summer School, Portugal, pp. 95–143 (2005)
7. Hernández, A., Feliciano, S., Sevilla, D., García Molina, J.: Exploring the visualization of schemas for aggregate-oriented NoSQL databases. In: 36th International Conference on Conceptual Modeling on ER Forum, pp. 72–85 (2017)
8. Hernández, A., Sevilla, D., García Molina, J., Feliciano, S.: A model-driven approach to generate schemas for object-document mappers. IEEE Access **7**, 59126–59142 (2019)
9. Hick, J.M., Hainaut, J.L.: Strategy for database application evolution: the DB-main approach. In: 22nd International Conference on Conceptual Modeling, pp. 291–306 (2003)

10. Klettke, M., Störl, U., Scherzinger, S.: Schema extraction and structural outlier detection for JSON-based NoSQL data stores. In: Conference on Database Systems for Business, Technology, and Web, pp. 425–444 (2015)
11. Mior, M.J.: Physical Design for Non-relational Data Systems. Ph.D. thesis, University of Waterloo, Ontario, Canada (2018)
12. Mior, M.J., Salem, K., Aboulnaga, A., Liu, R.: Nose: schema design for NoSQL applications. In: Proceedings of 32nd IEEE International Conference on Data Engineering, pp. 181–192 (2016)
13. Sevilla Ruiz, D., Morales, S.F., García Molina, J.: Inferring versioned schemas from NoSQL databases and its applications. In: Johannesson, P., Lee, M.L., Liddle, S.W., Opdahl, A.L., López, Ó.P. (eds.) ER 2015. LNCS, vol. 9381, pp. 467–480. Springer, Cham (2015). https://doi.org/10.1007/978-3-319-25264-3_35
14. Steinberg, D., Budinsky, F., Paternostro, M., Merks, E.: EMF: Eclipse Modeling Framework 2.0. Addison-Wesley Professional (2009)
15. Wang, L., Zhang, S., Shi, J., Jiao, L., Hassanzadeh, O., Zou, J., Wangz, C.: Schema management for document stores. In: VLDB Endowment, vol. 8 (2015)

JSON Schema Inference Approaches

Pavel Čontoš[ID] and Martin Svoboda[(✉)][ID]

Faculty of Mathematics and Physics, Charles University, Prague, Czech Republic
{contos,svoboda}@ksi.mff.cuni.cz

Abstract. Since the traditional relational database systems are not capable of following the contemporary requirements on Big Data processing, a family of NoSQL databases emerged. It is not an exception for such systems not to require an explicit schema for the data they store. Nevertheless, application developers must maintain at least the so-called implicit schema. In certain situations, however, the presence of an explicit schema is still necessary, and so it makes sense to propose methods capable of schema inference just from the structure of the available data. In the context of document NoSQL databases, namely those assuming the JSON data format, we focus on several representatives of the existing inference approaches and provide their thorough comparison. Although they are often based on similar principles, their features, support for the detection of references, union types, or required and optional properties differ greatly. We believe that without adequately tackling their disadvantages we identified, uniform schema inference and modeling of the multi-model data simply cannot be pursued straightforwardly.

Keywords: NoSQL databases · Schema inference · JSON

1 Introduction

An interesting feature of the majority of *NoSQL databases*, a newly emerged family of database systems, is the absence of an explicit schema for the stored data, which allows for greater flexibility and simplicity. Nevertheless, various situations still require the knowledge of the schema when performing operations such as data querying, migration, or evolution, and so there is a growing interest in *schema inference* approaches that allow us to create a schema when the explicit one simply does not exist.

In particular, there already exist several schema inference approaches for the *aggregate-oriented* group of NoSQL databases, i.e., databases based on the *key-value*, *wide-column* or *document* models. However, the inference process itself is nontrivial, and the resulting schemas often suffer from various issues. For example, derived entities may contain a large number of properties, including properties of the same name having different data types, as well as various kinds

This work was supported by Czech Science Foundation project 20-22276S and Charles University SVV project 260451.

ⓒ Springer Nature Switzerland AG 2020
G. Grossmann and S. Ram (Eds.): ER 2020 Workshops, LNCS 12584, pp. 173–183, 2020.
https://doi.org/10.1007/978-3-030-65847-2_16

of references between the documents (aggregates). The inferred schemas may be complicated even from the point of view of data modeling when commonly available tools and modeling languages would most likely be used (e.g., UML [18] is not capable of dealing with the mentioned properties of the same name but different types). Another obstacle also arises when querying the data. When a property data type or property content interpretation changes over time, it is difficult to properly construct an evolved query expression that returns the originally intended result.

In this paper, we focus on several existing representatives of the schema inference approaches dealing with collections of JSON [13] documents, namely the following ones: 1) approach proposed by Sevilla et al. [19] working with a concept of distinct versions of entities, 2) approach by Klettke et al. [15] utilizing a graph structure for the schema representation, capable of the detection of outliers, 3) approach by Baazizi et al. [2] that introduces compact yet complex and massively parallelizable schema inference method, 4) approach by Cánovas et al. [6] capable of inferring a schema from multiple collections of documents, and, finally, 5) recent approach by Frozza et al. [10] that is able to infer schemas including data types as they are introduced in BSON (*Binary JSON*) [5].

Our main goal is to provide a static analysis of these approaches to find and identify their strengths and weaknesses, compare them with each other, and verify how each individual approach copes with specific characteristics of JSON documents and non-uniform semi-structured data in general. We compare these approaches based on their capabilities to i) handle properties of the same name but different types, ii) distinguish required and optional properties based on their frequency of occurrences, iii) distinguish reference relationships between documents and nested documents, iv) work with arrays, v) represent the resulting schemas using proprietary or widely used means, respectively, and vi) scale.

The paper is organized as follows. In Sect. 2, we briefly summarize the JSON data format and show the constructs we are dealing with. Section 3 describes the actual schema inference process for the selected existing approaches and illustrates their differences on a simple running example and the corresponding inferred schemas. We then mutually compare these approaches in Sect. 4, present the related work in Sect. 5, and conclude in Sect. 6.

2   JSON Data Format and JSON Schema

JavaScript Object Notation (JSON) [13] is a widely used human-readable textual data format suitable for representing semi-structured, schema-less, often non-uniform data. From the logical point of view, it is based on trees.

The unit of data stored in a JSON document database is a *document* and corresponds to a single JSON *object*. An object consists of an unordered set of *name-value* pairs called *properties*. Property *name* is a string, while *value* can be atomic of any primitive type *string, number,* and *boolean,* or structured in a form of an embedded object or *array*. If no value is to be assigned, a property may be present and bound to the `null` meta-value. Although property names *should* be unique, we actually expect they *must* be (in accordance to the existing systems such as MongoDB[1]). Finally, an array is an ordered collection of items, which can be either atomic values or nested objects or arrays, possibly with duplicates.

```
{ "name": "Smíchovské Nádraží",
  "location": { "latitude": "50.0608367N", "longitude": "14.4093753E" },
  "timetable": [
    { "line": "B",
      "departure": [ "10:10", "10:20", "10:30", "10:40", "10:50" ]
    } ] }
```

```
{ "_id": "SMN_E",
  "name": "Smíchovské Nádraží",
  "location": { "latitude": "50.0597611N", "longitude": "14.4092244E" },
  "timetable": [
    { "line": 190,
      "stop_id": "NBE_0",
      "departure": [ "10:00", "10:15", "10:30" ] },
    { "line": 125,
      "stop_id": "SKA_A",
      "departure": [ "10:05" ] } ] }
```

Fig. 1. Collection of two sample JSON documents

In order to illustrate the mutual differences of the selected schema inference approaches, we will use a collection of two sample JSON documents, each describing a public transport stop in Prague. They are depicted in Fig. 1.

We believe we can omit a detailed description of the involved properties (as their meaning is self-explanatory) and only focus on parts that will become important in relation to the schema inference: i) data type of property `line` is a string in case of the first document while in the second one it is a number, ii) properties such as `_id` and `stop_id` appear only in the second document, iii) property `_id` may be treated as a document identifier while property `stop_id` as a reference, iv) property `departure` has a different number of elements across the documents, and v) some document databases allow us to use extended data types defined in BSON, thus we could easily assume that `_id` would be a property of type `ObjectID` instead of an ordinary string.

To validate the structure of JSON documents, JSON Schema [14] was proposed as a human and machine-readable format. It takes into account the evolution of JSON documents and features of schema-free databases. E.g., JSON Schema introduces i) union types, ii) distinguishes between required and optional properties, and iii) allows us to use extended data types, i.e. `ObjectID`.

3 JSON Schema Inference Approaches

In this section, we describe basic principles of the selected approaches. For each one of them, we also present the resulting inferred schemas for our sample input JSON collection so that these techniques can easily be compared together.

---

[1] https://www.mongodb.com/.

Let us start with an approach proposed by Sevilla et al. [19]. Within three steps and using *MapReduce* [7], their algorithm i) reduces an input collection of JSON documents into a set of structurally different documents, ii) discovers various versions of entities and their properties, and iii) identifies relationships between these entities, including references.

Versioned schema inferred by this approach is illustrated using JSON format in Fig. 2. The algorithm detects all the entities and properties while entities are further divided into versions that differ by the existence of such a property, its data type, or reference. The approach is able to detect references between the documents (property stop_id refers to entity Stop). The existence of versioned entities avoids the necessity of having union types, and the approach also distinguishes between the required and optional properties (intersection or union of properties across versions of the same entity need to be calculated). The only inferred data types are standard types defined by JSON.

```
{ "entities":
  { "Location":
      { "Location_1": { "latitude": "String", "longitude": "String" } },
    "Stop":
      { "Stop_1":
          { "name": "String", "location": "Location_1",
            "timetable": [ "Timetable_1" ] },
        "Stop_2":
          { "_id": "String", "name": "String", "location": "Location_1",
            "timetable": [ "Timetable_2" ] } },
    "Timetable": {
      "Timetable_1": { "line": "String", "departure": [ "String" ] },
      "Timetable_2": { "line": "String", "stop_id": "ref(Stop)",
        "departure": [ "String" ] } } } }
```

Fig. 2. Sample inferred schema for the Sevilla et al. algorithm [19]

Klettke et al. [15] proposed a schema inference algorithm for JSON document collections in MongoDB. The approach works with a so-called *Structure Identification Graph* (SIG) containing everything needed for the inference.

Nodes in this graph represent JSON properties (one node for each distinct property name), while edges model the hierarchical structure of the documents for which the schema is being constructed. Besides other metadata, each node is associated with a so-called *nodeList* describing the detected occurrences of a given property in the input documents. Similarly, each edge is associated with a so-called *edgeList* describing where these occurrences are structurally located.

The sample inferred schema, provided in Fig. 3, is described using JSON Schema. The algorithm is able to detect all the entities, including properties that may be assigned by multiple data types. This *union* type is used, e.g., in case of a property line. The approach does not detect references and uses only data types known by JSON, i.e., it does not use any extended data type. The approach also detects required properties (e.g., properties latitude and longitude in location).

```
{ "type": "object", "properties":
  { "_id": { "type": "string" }, "name": { "type": "string" },
    "location":
    { "type": "object", "properties":
      { "latitude": { "type": "string" }, "longitude": { "type": "string" } },
        "required": [ "latitude", "longitude" ] },
    "timetable":
    { "type": "array", "items":
      { "type": "object", "properties":
        { "line": { "oneOf": [ { "type": "string" }, { "type": "integer" } ] },
          "stop_id": { "type": "string" },
          "departure": { "type": "array", "items": { "type": "string" } } },
          "required": [ "line", "departure" ] } } },
    "required": [ "name", "location", "timetable" ] }
```

Fig. 3. Sample inferred schema for the Klettke et al. algorithm [15]

Baazizi et al. [2] proposed yet another inference algorithm, in this case consisting of two phases only. Based on *Apache Spark*[2], the input collection of JSON documents is first processed by the *Map* function, so that during the *Reduce* phase the union types, as well as required, optional, and repeated elements are identified.

Schema inferred by this approach, as illustrated in Fig. 4, is represented using a compact proprietary language. The optional properties are marked by a question mark symbol ? (e.g. properties _id and stop_id), union types by + (property line may be either *Str* or *Num*), and *repeated* items of arrays by an asterisk * (array departure contains elements of type Str). Extended data types nor references between the documents are discovered by this approach.

```
{ _id: Str?,
  name: Str,
  location: { latitude: Str, longitude: Str },
  timetable: [ { line: (Str+Num), stop_id: Str?, departure: [ (Str)* ] } ] }
```

Fig. 4. Sample inferred schema for the Baazizi et al. algorithm [2]

Another approach, proposed by Cánovas et al. [6], is deployed in the environment of web services providing collections of JSON documents, where each collection is expected to contain documents with similar but not necessarily the same structure. The approach is based on an iterative process in which each JSON document contributes to the extension of an already generated schema. This process consists of three parts: i) extraction of a schema for every document, ii) creation of a schema for each collection, and iii) merging of the schemas of individual collections together into a single resulting schema.

Schema inferred by this approach, illustrated in Fig. 5, is visualized by UML. The approach does not detect references between documents, so the relationships

---

[2] http://spark.apache.org/.

are only modeled through nested documents. The algorithm does not recognize union types nor optional properties. In order to simplify the visualization, it uses the most generic data types (e.g., property `line` is of a type *EString*). The approach also does not detect arrays (property `departure` is of a simple type *EString* instead of an array of strings). No extended data types are discovered.

Fig. 5. Sample inferred schema for the Cánovas et al. algorithm [6]

The last representative approach we covered in this paper is the one proposed by Frozza et al. [10], allowing for the inference of a schema for just one collection of JSON documents. Since it also supports the extraction of particular data types from a broader set of atomic types as they are introduced in BSON, it is therefore suitable especially when working with MongoDB database system. The inference process consists of the following four steps: i) creation of a raw schema for individual input documents, ii) grouping of the same raw schemas together, iii) unification of these schemas, and iv) construction of the final global JSON schema.

Schema inferred by this approach, materialized in Fig. 6, is described by JSON Schema. The approach is able to detect union types (e.g., property `line` may be either string or number). It also distinguishes between the required and optional properties (as every discovered entity may always contain a list of required properties), yet no references are discovered by this approach. In our sample data, we could easily derive the property `_id` to be an instance of the `ObjectID` type if that property was originally set to, e.g., `ObjectID("SMN_E")` instead of an ordinary string.

4   Comparison

Having described all the selected schema inference approaches, we can now mutually compare their main characteristics, as well as advantages and disadvantages. In particular, we focus on i) basic principles and scalability of the involved algorithms, i.e., ways how schemas are inferred and proprietary data structures utilized, ii) output formats, i.e., means how the inferred schemas are represented, iii) eventual support for data types beyond the JSON format itself, iv) distinction of required and optional properties in the inferred schemas, v) dealing with properties of the same name but different data types, i.e., distinguishing between simple and union types, and vi) discovering references between documents. Table 1 summarizes the identified differences and observations.

```
{ "$schema": "http://json-schema.org/draft-06/schema",
  "type": "object", "properties":
  { "_id": { "type": "string" }, "name": { "type": "string" },
    "location": {
      "type": "object", "properties":
        { "latitude": { "type": "string" }, "longitude": { "type": "string" } },
        "required": [ "latitude", "longitude" ], "additionalProperties": false },
    "timetable":
      { "type": "array", "items":
        { "type": "object", "properties":
          { "line": { "anyOf": [ "string", "number" ] },
            "stop_id": { "type": "string" },
            "departure":
              { "type": "array", "items": { "type": "string" }, "minItems": 1,
                "additionalItems": true } },
            "required": [ "line", "departure" ], "additionalProperties": false },
          "minItems": 1, "additionalItems": true } },
      "required": [ "name", "location", "timetable" ], "additionalProperties": false }
```

Fig. 6. Sample inferred schema for the Frozza et al. algorithm [10]

Basic Principles and Scalability. The majority of approaches extract schema information from all the documents stored in the input collection without initially reducing its size, i.e., the number of documents. Exceptions include the approaches by Sevilla et al. and Frozza et al., which initially select just sort of a minimal collection of mutually distinct documents such that it can still be correctly used to derive the schema for all the input documents. A common feature of all the approaches is the replacement of values of properties by names of the primitive types encountered. In addition, this step is usually parallelized using distributed solutions such as MapReduce or Apache Spark, which greatly improves the scalability. Up to our knowledge, the only approach that is not parallelized, so scalability is limited, is Frozza et al.

Output Format. The textual JSON Schema format is used for the inferred schema description by the majority of the approaches, yet they differ in the details. Baazizi et al. use their own and minimalistic proprietary language based on the JSON Schema. Baazizi et al. support the repeating type to describe repeated types in arrays, too. Sevilla et al. represent schema as a model that conforms to a schema metamodel [19], which can be textually described by JSON. Finally, Cánovas et al. represent schemas visually as class diagrams.

Table 1. Comparison of the selected approaches

	Sevilla et al.	Klettke et al.	Baazizi et al.	Cánovas et al.	Frozza et al.
Scalability	Yes	Yes	Yes	Yes	No
Output	Model	JSON Schema	Proprietary	Class diagram	JSON Schema
Data Types	JSON	JSON	JSON	JSON	BSON
Optional	Yes	Yes	Yes	No	Yes
Union Type	No	Yes	Yes	No	Yes
References	Yes	No	No	No	No

Additional Data Types. All the approaches support the basic set of primitive types (string, number, and boolean), as well as complex types, i.e., nested objects and arrays, as they are defined by JSON itself. In addition, and as the only approach, Frozza et al. support extended data types introduced by BSON.

Optional Properties. All properties that are contained in all the input documents in a collection are marked as *required*. Otherwise, when a property does not appear in at least one of them, it is marked as *optional*. Apparently, a set of required properties forms the skeleton of all the documents. Therefore, the visualization of a schema containing only these required properties can be significantly more comfortable for the users to grasp, especially when these documents contain a large number of different optional features that would occur only rarely. Furthermore, this visualization gives the users a very good idea of the structure of the documents. The majority of approaches we covered can distinguish between these two kinds of properties. They only differ in the way of their detection. In particular, approaches by Klettke et al. and Frozza et al. calculate the differences in occurrences of individual properties versus occurrences of their parental properties. When a parental property occurs more frequently, the property is marked as optional. Sevilla et al. is able to detect optional properties by the set operations over versions of entities. Baazizi et al. detect the optional properties during the fuse of types. Finally, the approache by Cánovas et al. is not capable of distinguishing the required and optional properties at all. Thus, all the properties in these cases must then be considered as required.

Union Type. The JSON format natively allows for the data evolution, e.g., a situation when properties of newly added objects may have different types compared to the older ones. Schema inference approaches must, therefore, deal with different types occurring within just one property. Most of the examined approaches work with the concept of the *union* type, where a property may contain several different types at once. In contrast, the approaches by Sevilla et al. and Cánovas et al. use just the most generic of the detected types in such cases. The advantage of the union type is accuracy, simply because we do not lose information about the involved data types. On the other hand, the principle of the most generic type is better visualizable and programmable, because we are able to perform (de)serialization through just a single data type, the generic one. For the purpose of the schema visualization, the widely used models, namely UML and ER, cannot associate properties with more than one type at a time, and, thus, it is better to use the most generic type in this case, but at the expense of the loss of the information accuracy, as outlined.

References. The only approach that detects relationships between the documents, i.e., references, is Sevilla et al. When a JSON property is named following the `entityName_id` suffix convention, then the entity named `entityName` is referenced (if it exists). It means that a reference relationship is created between the referring and referenced entities in the inferred schema.

5   Related Work

To a certain extent, several existing JSON schema inference approaches were experimentally compared in works by Frozza et al. [10] and Feliciano [9]. However, they considered different aspects, worked with not that many approaches, and, most importantly, did not assume the multi-model context. Moreover, schema inference is desirable not only for collections of JSON documents but for semi-structured and non-uniform data in general.

In case of mature XML [21], there are a number of heuristic-based [16] and grammar-inferred approaches [3]. Although both JSON and XML are semi-structured hierarchical formats, inference approaches for XML documents are not directly applicable to JSON because of the significant differences between the two formats. While elements in XML are ordered, names of these elements can appear repeatedly, and elements may contain attributes, properties in JSON objects are unordered and without duplicates as for their names.

Although not that many, there are also approaches dealing with other logical models and formats used within the family of NoSQL databases. Wang et al. [20] suggested a schema management approach for document databases, where frequently occurring structures are grouped using hierarchical structures. The approach proposed by DiScala and Abadi [8] solves the problem of transforming JSON documents from key-value repositories into flat relational structures. The inference of schemas for RDF documents is discussed by Gallinucci et al. [11], where aggregate hierarchies are identified. Bouhamoun et al. [4] then focus on the scalable processing of large amounts of RDF data by extracting patterns for existing combinations of individual properties.

JSON Schema is often used to describe an inferred schema from JSON document collections. The formal model of this language is dealt with by Pezoa et al. [17]. Description of the type system of JSON is designed by Baazizi et al. [1].

6   Conclusion

In this paper, we provided a mutual comparison of five selected representative JSON schema inference approaches, each of which solves a different subset of issues arising from the usage of the document NoSQL databases. As observed, especially the detection of references between the individual documents seems to be a challenging issue, not just since only one of the examined approaches actually recognizes such references, however, only to a very limited and questionable extent. Another open area lies in the visualization and modeling of the inferred schemas because the existing tools do not allow us to visualize all the derived constructs, namely, the union type.

We believe that in order to be able to infer schemas even for the non-uniform data maintained within the family of multi-model databases, the identified drawbacks of the existing approaches first need to be sufficiently tackled. Only then the acquired knowledge can be exploited, and the individual existing solutions extended to the unified inference of truly multi-model schemas. This step is apparently not straightforward, as it is envisioned by Holubová et al. [12], where several open and challenging areas of multi-model data processing are outlined.

References

1. Baazizi, M.A., Colazzo, D., Ghelli, G., Sartiani, C.: A type system for interactive JSON schema inference. In: ICALP 2019. LIPIcs, vol. 132, pp. 101:1–101:13 (2019). https://doi.org/10.4230/LIPIcs.ICALP.2019.101
2. Baazizi, M.-A., Colazzo, D., Ghelli, G., Sartiani, C.: Parametric schema inference for massive JSON datasets. VLDB J. **28**(4), 497–521 (2019). https://doi.org/10.1007/s00778-018-0532-7
3. Bex, G.J., Neven, F., Schwentick, T., Vansummeren, S.: Inference of concise regular expressions and DTDs. ACM Trans. Database Syst. **35**(2), 1–47 (2010). https://doi.org/10.1145/1735886.1735890
4. Bouhamoum, R., Kellou-Menouer, K., Lopes, S., Kedad, Z.: Scaling up schema discovery for RDF datasets. In: ICDEW 2018, pp. 84–89. IEEE (2018). https://doi.org/10.1109/ICDEW.2018.00021
5. BSON: Binary JSON (2012). http://bsonspec.org/spec.html
6. Cánovas Izquierdo, J.L., Cabot, J.: Discovering implicit schemas in JSON data. In: Daniel, F., Dolog, P., Li, Q. (eds.) ICWE 2013. LNCS, vol. 7977, pp. 68–83. Springer, Heidelberg (2013). https://doi.org/10.1007/978-3-642-39200-9_8
7. Dean, J., Ghemawat, S.: MapReduce: simplified data processing on large clusters. Commun. ACM **51**(1), 107–113 (2008). https://doi.org/10.1145/1327452.1327492
8. DiScala, M., Abadi, D.J.: Automatic generation of normalized relational schemas from nested key-value data. In: SIGMOD 2016, pp. 295–310. ACM (2016). https://doi.org/10.1145/2882903.2882924
9. Feliciano Morales, S.: Inferring NoSQL data schemas with model-driven engineering techniques. Ph.D. thesis, Universidad de Murcia (2017)
10. Frozza, A.A., dos Santos Mello, R., da Costa, F.d.S.: An approach for schema extraction of JSON and extended JSON document collections. In: IRI 2018, pp. 356–363 (2018). https://doi.org/10.1109/IRI.2018.00060
11. Gallinucci, E., Golfarelli, M., Rizzi, S., Abelló, A., Romero, O.: Interactive multidimensional modeling of linked data for exploratory OLAP. Inf. Syst. **77**, 86–104 (2018). https://doi.org/10.1016/j.is.2018.06.004
12. Holubová, I., Svoboda, M., Lu, J.: Unified management of multi-model data. In: Laender, A.H.F., Pernici, B., Lim, E.-P., de Oliveira, J.P.M. (eds.) ER 2019. LNCS, vol. 11788, pp. 439–447. Springer, Cham (2019). https://doi.org/10.1007/978-3-030-33223-5_36
13. JavaScript Object Notation (JSON) (2013). http://www.json.org/
14. JSON Schema (2019). https://json-schema.org/
15. Klettke, M., Störl, U., Scherzinger, S.: Schema extraction and structural outlier detection for JSON-based NoSQL data stores. In: Datenbanksysteme für Business, Technologie und Web (BTW 2015), pp. 425–444 (2015)
16. Mlýnková, I., Nečaský, M.: Heuristic methods for inference of XML schemas: lessons learned and open issues. Informatica **24**(4), 577–602 (2013)
17. Pezoa, F., Reutter, J.L., Suarez, F., Ugarte, M., Vrgoč, D.: Foundations of JSON schema. In: Proceedings of the 25th International Conference on World Wide Web, pp. 263–273 (2016). https://doi.org/10.1145/2872427.2883029

18. Rumbaugh, J., Jacobson, I., Booch, G.: The Unified Modeling Language Reference Manual. Pearson Higher Education (2004)
19. Sevilla Ruiz, D., Morales, S.F., García Molina, J.: Inferring versioned schemas from NoSQL databases and its applications. In: Johannesson, P., Lee, M.L., Liddle, S.W., Opdahl, A.L., López, Ó.P. (eds.) ER 2015. LNCS, vol. 9381, pp. 467–480. Springer, Cham (2015). https://doi.org/10.1007/978-3-319-25264-3_35
20. Wang, L.: Schema management for document stores. Proc. VLDB Endow. 8(9), 922–933 (2015). https://doi.org/10.14778/2777598.2777601
21. Extensible Markup Language (XML) 1.0 (Fifth Edition) (2013). https://www.w3.org/TR/REC-xml/

Empirical Methods in Conceptual Modeling (EmpER) 2020

Preface

Dominik Bork[1] and Miguel Goulão[2]

[1] TU Wien, Business Informatics Group, Vienna, Austria
dominik.bork@tuwien.ac.at
[2] Faculdade de Ciências e Tecnologia, Universidade Nova de Lisboa, Portugal
mgoul@fct.unl.pt

Conceptual modeling has enjoyed substantial growth over the past decades in diverse fields such as Information Systems Analysis, Software Engineering, Enterprise Architecture, Business Analysis, and Business Process Engineering. A plethora of conceptual modeling languages, frameworks, and systems have been proposed promising to facilitate activities such as communication, design, documentation or decision-making. Success in designing a conceptual modeling system is, however, predicated on demonstrably attaining such goals through observing their use in practical scenarios. At the same time, the way individuals and groups produce and consume models gives raise to cognitive, behavioral, organizational or other phenomena, whose systematic observation may help us better understand how models are used in practice and how we can make them more effective.

The EmpER workshop series is dedicated to bringing together researchers and practitioners with an interest in the empirical investigation of conceptual modeling systems and practices. Following successful workshops in Xi'an, China (2018) and Salvador, Brazil (2019), this year, the 3rd International Workshop on Empirical Methods in Conceptual Modeling was virtually held from Vienna, Austria. As with previous editions, the objective of the workshop was to provide a unique opportunity for researchers in the area to exchange ideas, compare notes, and forge new collaborations. This year, the workshop was in conjunction with the 39th International Conference on Conceptual Modeling (ER 2020), benefiting from our common themes and interests shared by the two events.

The Program Committee (PC) members reviewed a total of nine submissions, both original ones and fast-tracked ER main conference papers, in this edition. Each submission was reviewed by at least three PC members. Of the submitted papers, we accepted five for presentation on the workshop and inclusion in the ER companion proceedings. The following papers were selected:

- "Replicability and Reproducibility of a Schema Evolution Study in Embedded Databases"
  by Dimitri Braininger, Wolfgang Mauerer, and Stefanie Scherzinger
- "Acquiring and sharing the monopoly of legitimate naming in organizations, an application in conceptual modeling"
  by Samuel Desguin and Wim Laurier
- "Challenges in Checking JSON Schema Containment over Evolving Real-World Schemas"

by Michael Fruth, Mohamed-Amine Baazizi, Dario Colazzo, Giorgio Ghelli, Carlo Sartiani, and Stefanie Scherzinger

- "Empirical evaluation of a new DEMO modelling tool that facilitates model transformations"
  by Thomas Gray and Marne De Vries
- "Experimental practices for measuring the intuitive comprehensibility of modeling constructs: an example design"
  by Sotirios Liaskos, Mehrnaz Zhian, and Ibrahim Jaouhar

We would like to thank all the members of the Program Committee for providing their expertise and suggesting constructive advice to improve the quality of the submissions. Last but not least, we thank the ER conference Steering Committee, conference chairs, and workshop chairs for accepting the EmpER 2020 workshop.

Empirical Evaluation of a New DEMO Modelling Tool that Facilitates Model Transformations

Thomas Gray and Marné De Vries(✉) ⓘD

Department of Industrial and Systems Engineering, University of Pretoria, Pretoria, South Africa
{Thomas.Gray,Marne.DeVries}@up.ac.za

Abstract. The *engineering methodology for organizations* (DEMO) incorporates an *organization construction diagram* (OCD) and *transaction product table* (TPT) to depict a consolidated representation of the enterprise in terms of *actor roles* that coordinate in consistent patterns on different *transaction kinds*. Although managers find the OCD useful due to its high level of abstraction, enterprise implementers and operators prefer detailed flow-chart-like models to guide their operations, such as *business process model and notation* (BPMN) models. BPMN models are prevalent in industry and offer modeling flexibility, but the models are often incomplete, since they are not derived from theoretically-based, consistent coordination patterns. This study addresses the need to develop a DEMO modeling tool that incorporates the novel feature of transforming user-selected parts of a validated OCD, consistently and in a semi-automated way, into BPMN collaboration diagrams. The contribution of this article is two-fold: (1) to demonstrate the *utility* of the new DEMO-ADOxx modelling tool, including its model transformation ability; and (2) to empirically evaluate the *usability* of the tool.

Keywords: DEMO · BPMN · ADOxx · Model transformation · Software modelling · Multi-view modelling

1 Introduction

Domain-specific languages are created to provide insight and understanding within a particular domain context and stakeholder group. As an example, the *design and engineering methodology for organizations* (DEMO) provides models that represent the organization domain of an enterprise [1]. DEMO offers a unique design perspective, since its *four aspect models* represent *organization design domain* knowledge in a concise and consistent way, removing technological realization and implementation details [1]. One of DEMO's aspect models, the construction model, incorporates an *organization construction diagram* (OCD) that provides a concise representation of *enterprise operation*. Managers find the OCD useful due to its high level of abstraction. Yet, enterprise implementers and operators prefer detailed flow-chart-like models to guide their operations, such as *business process model and notation* (BPMN) models. BPMN models are prevalent in industry and offer modeling flexibility, but the models are often incomplete,

© Springer Nature Switzerland AG 2020
G. Grossmann and S. Ram (Eds.): ER 2020 Workshops, LNCS 12584, pp. 189–199, 2020.
https://doi.org/10.1007/978-3-030-65847-2_17

since they are not derived from theoretically-based, consistent coordination patterns [2]. Others [3] identified the need to generate BPMN models from DEMO models, based on transformation specifications. Yet, the specifications did not consider the complexity of hierarchical structures in DEMO models. In addition, their transformation specifications were not supported by tooling to automate DEMO-BPMN transformations [4].

A new DEMO-ADOxx tool, called DMT, addresses the need to compile a DEMO construction model, in accordance with the specifications stated in [5] and [6]. In addition, the tool incorporates the novel feature of transforming user-selected parts of a validated OCD, consistently and in a semi-automated way, into BPMN collaboration diagrams [4].

This article has two main objectives: (1) demonstrating a main feature of the new DEMO-ADOxx tool, i.e. transforming OCD parts into BPMN collaboration diagrams for a complex scenario; and (2) empirically evaluating the usability of the tool.

The article is structured as follows. Section 2 provides background on DEMO models and the development of the DMT. Section 3 suggests a research method to evaluate the DMT, whereas Sect. 4 presents the evaluation results, concluding in Sect. 5 with future research directions.

2 Background

In this section we provide background theory on DEMO, present a demonstration case with sufficient complexity to validate the DMT against specifications for DMT in the form of: (1) a meta-model for the OCD and TPT, and (2) OCD-BPMN transformation specifications.

DEMO uses four linguistically based *aspect models* to represent the ontological model of the *organisation domain* of the enterprise, namely the *construction model* (CM), *process model* (PM), *action model* (AM), and *fact model* (FM) that exclude technology implementation details [5]. A qualitative analysis on DEMO aspect models, indicate that the CM, detailed by the PM, is useful for assigning responsibilities and duties to individuals [7]. According to a study by Decosse et al. [7], the AM and FM *"are necessary if you are going to develop or select applications"*. The conceptual knowledge embedded in the PM is similar to the BPMN collaboration diagram [3]. Yet, BPMN is widely adopted by industry [8] and facilitates simulation and workflow automation, as demonstrated by BPMN-based industrial tools, such as ADONIS, Camunda and Bizagi. Our initial DEMO-ADOxx tool thus focused on representing the CM. Rather than using a PM as the next step of modelling, our tool incorporates a user-interface to capture parent-part structures from the modeler that would normally be indicated on a PM, bridging the gap from the CM to detailed and consistent BPMN diagrams.

The CM is expressed using three diagrams: (1) the *organisation construction diagram* (OCD); (2) the *transaction product table* (TPT) and (3) the *bank contents table* (BCT). We incorporated specifications regarding the OCD and TPT, as stated in [5] and [6], as well as BPMN 2.0 [9] for the first version of the DMT. The *way of modelling* in [10], indicates that a modeller has to validate the definition of each transaction kind (TK) by defining an associated product kind (PK). Due to their tight coupling, the OCD and TPT were incorporated in the first version of our tool. We excluded the BCT, since the "BCT can only be completed when the FM is produced" [1, p 272].

2.1   The Demonstration Case

The demonstration case had to be of such complexity that a modeler would be able to construct a TPT (a list of TKs and PKs - not shown here due to space restrictions) and an OCD (illustrated in Fig. 1). The case represents the *universe of discourse and some operations at a fictitious college*. In accordance with the guidelines presented in [10], our demonstrating OCD, portrayed in Fig. 1, only includes TKs that are of the *original transaction sort*. **Bold** style indicates the type of construct whereas *italics* refers to an instance of the construct (see Fig. 1).

Scope of Interest (SoI) indicates that the modeler analyses a particular scope of operations, namely *some operations at a college*. Given the SoI, Fig. 1 indicates that three **environmental actor roles** are defined, see the grey-shaded constructs *student*, *project sponsor* and *HR of project sponsor* that form part of the environment. Within the SoI, multiple **transaction kinds (TKs)** are linked to different types of **actor roles** via **initiation links** or **executor links**. As an example, *supervisor allocation (T01)* is a **TK** that is initiated (via an **initiation link**) by the **environmental actor role** *student (CA01)*. In accordance with [10], the *student (CA01)* is by default also regarded to be a **composite actor role** "of which one does not know (or want to know) the details". Since *T01* is linked to an **environmental actor role**, it is also called a **border transaction kind**. *T01* is executed (via the **executor link**) by the **elementary actor role** named *supervisor allocator (A01)*.

All the other actor roles in Fig. 1 within the **SoI** are **elementary actor roles**, since each of them is only responsible for executing one **transaction kind**. A special case is where an **elementary actor role** is both the **initiator** and **executor** of a **transaction kind**, also called a **self-activating actor role**. Figure 1 exemplifies the **self-activating actor role** with *module reviser (A04)* and *project controller (A05)*. Since **actor roles** need to use facts created and stored in transaction banks, an **information link** is used to indicate access to facts. As an example, Fig. 1 indicates that *project controller (A05)* has an **information link** to **transaction kind** *module revision (T04)*, indicating that the *project controller (A05)* uses facts in the transaction bank of *module revision (T04)*. It is also possible that **actor roles** within the **SoI** need to use facts that are created via **transaction kinds** that are outside the **SoI**. As an example, Fig. 1 indicates that **actor**

roles within the **SoI** (called, *some operations at a college*) need to use facts that are created outside the SoI and stored in the transaction banks of **aggregate transaction kinds**, namely *person facts* of *AT01*, *college facts* of *AT02*, *accreditation facts* of *AT03*, *timetable facts* of *AT04* and *student enrollment facts* of *AT05*. According to Fig. 1, the *student enrollment facts* of **aggregate transaction kind** *AT05* are not accessed by any **actor roles**, which should be possible (according to the meta-model depicted in [5]).

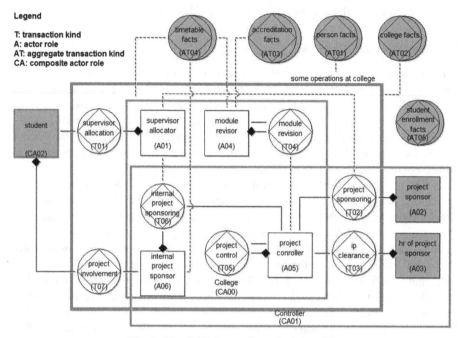

Fig. 1. The OCD for a college, based on [5]

Even though Fig. 1 only includes **elementary actor roles** within the **SoI**, it is possible to consolidate **elementary actor roles** within a **composite actor role**, where a composite actor role "is a network of transaction kinds and (elementary) actor roles" [10]. Figure 1 illustrates two **composite actor roles** within the **SoI,** namely *College (CA0)* and *Controller (CA01)*. Both *CA00* and *CA01* encapsulate a number of transaction kinds and elementary actor roles.

2.2   General DEMO Tool Requirements, Specifications and the New DMT

Previous work [4] highlighted five *minimum requirements* from a tertiary educational perspective for a DEMO modelling tool and compared existing tools against these requirements. The requirements indicated that a DEMO modelling tool should be *comprehensive*, supporting all four DEMO aspect models (R1). The tool should support the most *recent language specification* and facilitate future upgrades of the DEMO language (R2). The tool should facilitate *model transformations* to other modelling languages, such as

BPMN (R3). The tool should be available at *low cost* for educational purposes (R4), and it should be *usable* (R5).

A comparison of existing tools indicated that existing tools do not fulfil the minimum requirements. None of the tools, except the new DMT, facilitated model transformations [4]. The main objective of the new DMT was to demonstrate the *transformation feature*, but also allow for future development of the tool. Even though the DMT addressed the minimum requirements and initial usability tests on DMT were positive [4], additional evaluation was needed, especially in terms of its *utility* (R2 and R3) and *usability* (R5). In terms of R2, the DMT had to address the existence rules encapsulated in the meta-model of the OCD and TPT (see [4]). For R3, the DMT had to address all *four transformation scenarios*, depicted in [11]. This article demonstrates the most complex scenario of the four, where one **TK** has multiple parts, i.e. the **actor role** that **executes** the user-selected **TK**, is also **initiating** one or more other **TKs**. Referring to Fig. 1 the TK labelled *T05* (*project control*) is executed by **actor role** *A05* (*project controller*). The same **actor role** *A05* (*project controller*) also **initiates** multiple other **TKs**, namely *T02* (*project sponsoring*), *T03* (*IP clearance*), and *T06* (*internal project sponsoring*). The DMT was realized as an OMiLAB project which enables free download: https://austria.omilab.org/psm/content/demo [4].

3   Research Method

According to Bagozzi [12] the *unified theory of acceptance and use of technology* (UTAUT) exemplifies the complexity of technology assessment with UTAUT including multiple variables for predicting intentions and predicting behaviour. For this article, our aim was not to perform a comprehensive assessment of DMT, but to prioritise two key variables to guide our decision-making in pursuing further development of the DMT. Empirical evaluation of two critical variables were needed: *utility* and *usability*.

The *utility tests* were performed internally, categorized as *existence rules* tests and *transformation* tests. The *existence rules* tests had to ensure that the DMT facilitated creation of a sound OCD and TPT in accordance with the meta-model. We used the demonstration case presented in Sect. 2.1 to compile valid tests. As an example, one of the existence rules state: *1..* TK is contained in CAR 0..**, meaning that *a transaction kind is contained in zero-to-many composite actor roles*, and *a composite actor role contains one-to-many transaction kinds*. Using the case study presented in Fig. 1, two test cases were compiled: (1) It should be possible to create T01 that is not contained within the CAR CA00 (College) and (2) It should also be possible to create T06 as a part within CAR CA00 (College). The *transformation tests* tested the tool's ability to semi-automate four main OCD-BPMN transformations, associated with the demonstration case presented in Sect. 2.1.

The DMT was empirically validated from a user perspective for *usability*, i.e. using a survey-based approach to measure the DMT's ease of *modelling and validating the OCD and TPT*; and *generating a BPMN diagram*, based on a user-selected TK on the OCD. Survey modelling methods are often used to gather opinions, impressions and beliefs of human subjects via questionnaires [13]. Organisations and individuals will only adopt a new tool if the perceived usefulness is high. We have used a standardized questionnaire due to several advantages stated by [14]: objectivity, replicability, quantification, economy, communication and scientific generalization. The SUMI (Software Usability Measurement Inventory) questionnaire, developed by the Human Factors Research Group (HFRG) at the University College Cork, is widely used and cited in national an international standards with a global reliability of 92% [14]. The 50-item questionnaire has five subscales for efficiency, affect, helpfulness, control, and learnability, with a three-point Likert scale to rate each item as *disagree, undecided* and *agree*. The results of the five subscales are consolidated into a global scale that provides an indication of the software's general usability [14]. The questionnaire would be useful to evaluate the *overall usability* of the DMT for its current scope.

A laboratory experiment (in accordance with [15]) was conducted with 34 post graduate students as participants. The participants all attended a post-graduate module on enterprise design. One of the module components incorporated training on DEMO. Participants also received training on the demonstration case depicted in Sect. 2.1 before they modelled the OCD and TPT, using the DMT, also experimenting with the OCD-BPMN transformation feature. Afterwards, participants had to complete the SUMI questionnaire, availed via the SUMI online form [16]. We also documented all comments or questions posed by the participants during the experiment.

4   Evaluation Results

For the *first utility evaluation* objective we tested whether the DMT-created models comply with the *existence rules* that are specified for the OCD and TPT between the following concepts: (1) aggregate transaction kind (ATK); (2) composite actor role (CAR); (3) elementary actor role (EAR); (4) fact kind (FK); (5) independent P-fact kind (IFK); and (6) transaction kind (TK) (see [4]). Table 1 presents the *existence rule* (grey shaded), *test cases* and *test results*. We only elaborate on the *test results* if additional explanation is needed. The results indicate that the DMT addressed all the existence rules that apply to the OCD and TPT.

For the *second utility evaluation* objective we tested whether a DMT model, generated via DMT's transformation feature, could address the complexity of a TK that has multiple parts. When a modeler selects the TK labelled *T05* (*project control*) on the OCD presented in Fig. 1, a BPMN collaboration diagram is generated, presented in Fig. 2. Addressing threats to validity on the transformation-abilities of DMT, we have also used a second demonstration case, i.e. the Rent-a-car case from [10] to validate the transformation abilities in terms of all *four transformation scenarios*. Due to space limitations, we could only include one demonstration case (in Sect. 2.1) in this paper. The second demonstration case highlighted shortcomings in the transformation specifications of [11], indicating that the four transformation scenarios had to be extended further.

Table 1. Existence rules, test cases and results

From TK: 1..1 the product kind of TK is IFK 1..1
Forward: When T01 is defined, it should be linked to one product kind. When viewing the TPT, the single product kind should be displayed for the TK. **Reverse:** When defining the product kind P02, it should be for one TK. **Forward Results:** The Model Analysis/Validation feature highlights production kinds with no product kind defined. Thus mandatory 1..1 is not enforced. **Reverse Results:** The product kind ID is automatically generated and not editable. The system also blocks any attempt to duplicate product kind names.
From TK: 1..* TK is contained in ATK 0..*
Forward: *Outside SoI:* For DEMOSL 3.7 it should not be possible to indicate the parent-part relationship. *Inside SoI:* It should be possible to create T01 in accordance with Fig. 1 where T01 is not contained in an ATK. It should be possible to create T02, where T02 is contained in the ATK T05. T05 is an ATK with multiple parts (i.e. T02, T03, T06, T07). **Reverse:** *Outside SoI:* For DEMOSL 3.7 it should not be possible to indicate the parent-part relationship. *Inside SoI:* It should not be possible to initially model T05 as an ATK, grey-shading T05, without indicating the parts, i.e. without modelling the parts T02, T03, T06, T07). The software should only allow T05 as a composite (without parts) if created outside the SoI. **Reverse Results:** An ATK placed within the SOI is colored red to indicate non-validity. The Model Analysis/Validation feature also highlights it as an error.
From TK: 1..* TK is contained in CAR 0..*
Forward: It should be possible to create T01 that is not contained within the CAR CA00 (College). It should also be possible to create T06 as a part within CAR CA00 (College). **Reverse Results:** It should be possible to create CAR CA00 (College) with multiple TKs, namely T04, T05 and T06.
From EAR: 1..* EAR is an initiator role of TK 0..*
Forward: It should be possible to create A01 as per Fig. 1 where A01 is not initiating other TKs. It should be possible to create A05, initiating T02, T03 and T06. **Reverse:** It should be possible to create T06, initiated by A05 as per Fig. 1. In addition, it should also be possible to create T06, also initiated by A01 (i.e. A01 is also initiating T06), even though this scenario is not evident on Fig. 1.
From EAR: 1..1 EAR is the executor role of TK 1..1
Forward: When A01 is modelled as an elementary actor role without any execution link attached, a validation message should be shown when validating the model. When A01 is modelled as an elementary actor role, it should not be possible to connect both A1 as the executor for T01 and A01 as the executor for another TK, say T08 (supervision). Note that T08 is not displayed on Fig. 1, but has to be created temporarily to do this test. **Reverse:** When T01 is modelled as a TK without any execution link attached, a validation message should be shown when validating the model. When T01 is linked via an execution link to A01 and T01 is linked to another EAR, say A08 (supervisor), an error message should appear to indicate that a TK may only have one executor. **Reverse Results:** A warning message is displayed and the second connection is not possible.
From EAR: 0..* EAR may inspect the contents of bank TK 0..*
Forward: When A01 is created without any inspection links, no validation rules should appear when saving the model. It should also be possible to link A01 to T02 via an inspection link, as well as A01 to T06, with no validation errors appearing when the model is saved. **Reverse:** It should be possible to create the TK T03 with no inspection links attached. It should also be possible to create an inspection link between T02 and A01, as well as an inspection link from T02 to A06.

(continued)

Table 1. (*continued*)

From EAR: 0..* EAR is contained in CAR 0..*
Forward: It should be possible to create an actor role, say A08 (supervisor) within the SoI, but outside the CAR CA00 (College), without displaying validation errors when saving the model. It should be possible to create A06 as an EAR embedded in the CAR CA00 (College), also embedded in the CAR CA01 (Controller).
Reverse: It should be possible to create the CAR CA00 (College) without embedding any TKs, linking it via an execution link to T01. It should be possible to create the CAR CA00 (College) with multiple embedded EARs, i.e. A01, A04, A05 and A06.
From EAR: 0..* EAR has access to the bank of ATK 0..*
Forward: It should be possible to create the EAR A1 with no inspection links to AT01 and AT02, i.e. no validation errors on saving. It should also be possible to create EAR A4 with inspection links to AT03 and AT04 without validation errors on saving.
Reverse: It should be possible to create AT05 without any inspection links attached, with no validation errors on saving. It should be possible to create both an inspection link from AT04 to A04, as well as an inspection link from AT04 to A06, without validation errors on saving.
From CAR: CAR is a specialization of EAR
The relations of the EAR should also be available for the CAR [6]. Hence, when creating CAR CA00 (College) without any embedded detail, it should be possible to link the CA00 via an execution link to T01, link CA0 via an initiation link to T07, link CA00 via an initiation link to T02, link CA00 via an initiation link to T03, and link CA00 via an inspection link to AT04.
From CAR: CAR is a part of CAR
As explained by [6], the SoI is a special case of a CAR. It should be possible to create a CAR, i.e. CA00 (College) within the SoI without any validation errors when saving the model.

The *usability results* are summarised in Table 2. The results draw a very positive picture, especially considering the prototypical nature of the DMT. The tool is evaluated positive in all five sub-categories and in the global scale. The highest value was found in the category *affect* which measures the participants emotional feeling mentally stimulated and pleasant, or the opposite: stressed and frustrated as a result of interacting with the tool. The results indicate that 31 out of 34 participants perceived the DMT as being *important* or *extremely important* for supporting their task. Most noted things to improve: *Link Usage (7), Menu (3), General Usage (5), Error Handling (4)*. Nine participants did not mention any necessary improvements. Most noted positive things: Ease of use (15), Intuitivity (7), Model Transformation (7), Interface (6), and Drag & Drop (4).

Based on the qualitative feedback on their questionnaire and interactive feedback during the experiment, we have already incorporated the suggestions within the DMT.

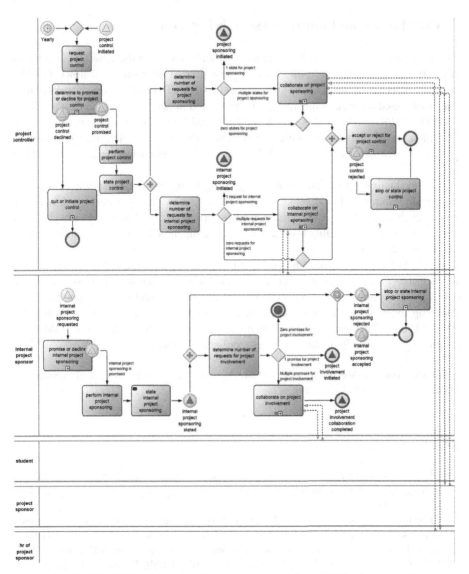

Fig. 2. A BPMN collaboration diagram, generated from T05 (project control)

Table 2. Results of the SUMI questionnaire

	Global	Efficiency	Affect	Helpfulness	Controllability	Learnability
Mean	56.5	54.0	60.8	54.9	55.4	54.6
Std. Dev.	10.8	13.5	10.6	10.9	10.3	11.4
Median	56.5	54.5	64.5	55.0	54.5	57.0

5   Conclusions and Future Research Directions

The main objective of this paper was to empirically evaluate the new DMT in terms of utility and usability. The *utility tests* were performed internally as follows: (1) The *existence rules* associated with the meta-model for the OCD and TPT, were translated into test cases, based on the demonstration case presented in Sect. 2.1; and (2) *Conformance to OCD-BPMN transformation specifications*, tested the tool's ability to semi-automate four main transformations, of which be presented the most complex transformation in Fig. 2. For *usability*, we used the SUMI questionnaire to evaluate the ease-of-use of the DMT.

Our evaluation results are positive regarding both *utility* and *usability*. Since we empirically evaluated the DEMO tool within a laboratory setting, future work is envisaged to evaluate the tool within a real-world enterprise setting. Sauro & Lewis [14] also suggest comparative usability tests, e.g. comparing the new DMT with another existing DEMO modelling tool.

The DMT was developed and evaluated, based on DEMOSL 3.7 (see [5]) as well as extensions (see [6]). Yet, a newer version, DEMOSL 4.5 has been published recently (see [1]). Modelling languages evolve and enforce the evolution of associated models. Realizing the tool as an open source project, using the ADOxx platform within the OMiLAB digital ecosystem, ensures that not only the authors, but also the OMiLAB community, can contribute towards future tool enhancements [17].

Acknowledgements. We would like to thank Dominik Bork for his continued support and collaboration on the DMT project.

References

1. Dietz, J.L.G., Mulder, H.B.F.: Enterprise Ontology: A Human-Centric Approach to Understanding the Essence of Organisation. Springer, Heidelberg (2020). https://doi.org/10.1007/978-3-030-38854-6
2. Caetano, A., Assis, A., Tribolet, J.: Using DEMO to analyse the consistency of business process models. In: Moller, C., Chaudhry, S. (eds.) Advances in Enterprise Information Systems II, pp. 133–146. Taylor & Francis Group, London (2012). https://doi.org/10.1201/b12295-17
3. Mráz, O., Náplava, P., Pergl, R., Skotnica, M.: Converting DEMO PSI transaction pattern into BPMN: a complete method. In: Aveiro, D., Pergl, R., Guizzardi, G., Almeida, J.P., Magalhães, R., Lekkerkerk, H. (eds.) EEWC 2017. LNBIP, vol. 284, pp. 85–98. Springer, Cham (2017). https://doi.org/10.1007/978-3-319-57955-9_7
4. Gray, T., Bork, D., De Vries, M.: A new DEMO modelling tool that facilitates model transformations. In: Nurcan, S., Reinhartz-Berger, I., Soffer, P., Zdravkovic, J. (eds.) BPMDS/EMMSAD -2020. LNBIP, vol. 387, pp. 359–374. Springer, Cham (2020). https://doi.org/10.1007/978-3-030-49418-6_25
5. Dietz, J.L.G., Mulder, M.A.T.: DEMOSL-3: DEMO specification language version 3.7. SAPIO (2017)
6. Mulder, M.A.T.: Towards a complete metamodel for DEMO CM. In: Debruyne, C., Panetto, H., Guédria, W., Bollen, P., Ciuciu, I., Meersman, R. (eds.) OTM 2018. LNCS, vol. 11231, pp. 97–106. Springer, Cham (2019). https://doi.org/10.1007/978-3-030-11683-5_10

7. Décosse, C., Molnar, Wolfgang A., Proper, Henderik A.: What does DEMO do? A qualitative analysis about DEMO in practice: founders, modellers and beneficiaries. In: Aveiro, D., Tribolet, J., Gouveia, D. (eds.) EEWC 2014. LNBIP, vol. 174, pp. 16–30. Springer, Cham (2014). https://doi.org/10.1007/978-3-319-06505-2_2
8. Grigorova, K., Mironov, K.: Comparison of business process modeling standards. Int. J. Eng. Sci. Manag. Res. 1(3), 1–8 (2014)
9. Object Management Group: Business process model & notation. https://www.omg.org/bpmn/. Accessed 30 May 2019
10. Perinforma, A.P.C.: The Essence of Organisation, 3rd ed. Sapio (2017). www.sapio.nl
11. De Vries, M., Bork, D.: Bridging organization design knowledge and executable business processes: a model transformation approach based on DEMO and BPMN (in review)
12. Bagozzi, R.: The legacy of the technology acceptance model and a proposal for a paradigm shift. J. Assoc. Inf. Syst. 8(4), (2007). https://doi.org/10.17705/1jais.00122
13. Siau, K., Rossi, M.: Evaluation techniques for systems analysis and design modelling methods – a review and comparative analysis. Inf. Syst. J. 21(3), 249–268 (2011). https://doi.org/10.1111/j.1365-2575.2007.00255.x
14. Sauro, J., Lewis, J.R.: Quantifying the User Experience: Practical Statistics for User Research. Elsevier Inc., Waltham (2012)
15. Wohlin, C., Runeson, P., Höst, M., Ohlsson, M.C., Regnell, B., Wesslén, A.: Experimentation in Software Engineering. Springer, Heidelberg (2012). https://doi.org/10.1007/978-3-642-29044-2
16. HFRG: Software Usability Measurement Inventory. http://sumi.uxp.ie/en/index.php. Accessed 17 Jan 2020
17. Bork, D., Buchmann, R.A., Karagiannis, D., Lee, M., Miron, E.-T.: An open platform for modeling method conceptualisation: the OMiLAB digital ecosystem. Commun. AIS 44(32), 673–697 (2019). https://doi.org/10.17705/1CAIS.04432

Acquiring and Sharing the Monopoly of Legitimate Naming in Organizations, an Application in Conceptual Modeling

Samuel Desguin[(✉)] and Wim Laurier

Université Saint-Louis Bruxelles (USL-B), Brussels, Belgium
samuel.desguin@usaintlouis.be

Abstract. In 2018, one of the biggest cooperatives of autonomous workers (CAW) in Europe, strong of more than 30.000 members, started the development of a unified lexicon as an informal conceptual model of the organization. Researchers participated in this ambitious project, following an action-design-research method. Democratic and egalitarian values are essential at CAW, but the literature on how to account for these values when developing a conceptual model is scarce. This paper argues that defining a common vocabulary, which can be a first step to building a conceptual model for an organization, is not a politically neutral activity and should be executed transparently and fairly, especially in democratic organizations such as CAW. Based on the classic literature on language and power, this contribution presents five postulates to help modelers to account for power and influence when developing conceptual models in organizations, either when trying to acquire the monopoly of legitimate naming in a field, or when sharing the power he or she possesses, having acquired such a monopoly.

Keywords: Conceptual modeling · Ontological politics · Power in organizations

1 Introduction

In organizations, conceptual models and ontologies play a major role in knowledge transfer, developing domain understanding, or simulating the subject matter they represent, thereby supporting both humans and computer in their tasks [1]. In most use cases of conceptual modelling, the resulting ontology is considered a neutral tool built by experts to help a well-defined group of people; however, as Sect. 3 shows, modelling an ontology in an organization gives the modeler significant power over language and communication in that organization, which translates into power and influence.

In this contribution, we describe the case of one of the biggest cooperative of autonomous workers (CAW) in Europe, strong of more than 30.000 members in 9 European countries. A CAW is an organization that enables its members to work autonomously on their entrepreneurial activity while benefiting from services of the cooperative. CAW feature two main services: (1) the access to an employee status (instead of freelancer or independent statuses), which gives workers an extended access

G. Grossmann and S. Ram (Eds.): ER 2020 Workshops, LNCS 12584, pp. 200–209, 2020.
https://doi.org/10.1007/978-3-030-65847-2_18

to social rights such as unemployment, illness or retirement benefits and (2) the ability to invoice clients and recover expenses from suppliers, using the cooperative's VAT number. CAW can also offer miscellaneous services such as an access to rooms, training, counselling or machines. Through those services, the CAW increases autonomous workers' security while safeguarding their autonomy [2] – thereby, CAW had a particularly crucial role in helping autonomous workers deal with the fallout of the Covid-19 lockdown, as they were twice as likely to lose some income and six times more likely to lose all of their income, in comparison with salaried workers [3]. CAW have a long tradition of democracy and transparency: members are co-operators, which means that they own a share of the organization and have formal voting and representation rights in all decision-making bodies. In addition, there is a social and psychological contract that leads members to expect that they will be informed of and involved in any major decision [4].

In the CAW featured in this contribution, misunderstanding had long been an issue hindering effective coordination and communication, especially when it started expanding internationally [2]. Clarifying the conceptual model – and in particular the **lexicon**, which is the least formal type of conceptual model – has therefore been recognized as a major strategic objective at the general assembly of 2018. At the time of the encounter with the authors of this paper, several attempts had been made to develop such a unified lexicon, but none of them had been successfully rolled out, mainly due to the lack of popularity that the lexicon had gained from end-users when it was delivered. In short, the issue was political, rather than technical. When looking for guidelines on how to address political issues in developing a conceptual model, the researchers found little insights in existing literature (see Sect. 2), and therefore decided to tackle this issue in this piece. The study of this case led to the following **research question**: *what is the impact of power in the development of a lexicon in organizations?*

This research question points to two important considerations. First, the power and influence by the modeler needs for members of the organization to accept the lexicon and use words and concepts in compliance with it, leading to the **first sub-question**: *what should the modeler do to acquire the monopoly of legitimate naming in an organization?* The notion of *monopoly of legitimate naming* is inspired by Bourdieu, as described in Sect. 2. The second consideration is the caution that organizations and modelers should pay to the subtle, invisible power that modelers can acquire by gaining control over the language in an organization. The modeler should be conscious of the power that modelers obtain by developing lexicons, in order to avoid hidden conflicts of interest or abuses of power. This consideration lead to the **second sub-question**: *what should the modeler do to distribute the power given by the monopoly of legitimate naming in an organization?*

Section 2 describes the method that the researchers used to support this organization in its project. Section 3 reviews the literature on conceptual modelling, language and power in organizations. Section 4 discusses early findings in light of the literature and presents postulates to help modelers address power issues in organizations.

2   Method

The researchers applied the *Action-design-research* (ADR) method [5], which aims at solving a real-life issue identified within a domain by developing an artifact. The artifact is the result of iterations between the modeling team and the field, each iteration leading to incremental improvements, until the artifact is sufficiently developed. Each iteration encompasses three steps: **Building** an artifact using modelling techniques, **Intervention**, rolling out the artifact in the field and **Evaluation** of the usefulness of the artifact with regards to the identified issues. This contribution was a case of an *organization-dominant* process, since the primary source of innovation is organizational intervention. As is suited for organization-dominant ADR, the main source of information to build the artifact was the field.

In this paper, the researchers focus on the "build" step of the process, showing how the first version of the artifact was developed. The specific artifact that was built was a lexicon, i.e. a *"list of words in a language (i.e. a vocabulary) along with some knowledge of how each word is used"* [7, p. 1] (see Sect. 3.1). To build it, the researchers collected information via a dozen of focus groups and interviews with two types of respondents: the upper management and the front-office workers who manage members activity and services directly. Interviews were used to collected on how individual users describe key concepts of the business model of CAW, and focus groups were organized to resolve the discrepancies on the understanding of specific definitions. When needed, the upper management settled on disagreements, on basis of arguments from the research team and the end-users. At this stage, members were not yet involved because researchers were seeking to get a broad, transversal view, but member are expected to play a critical role in the upcoming roll-out and evaluation phases.

3   Literature Review

This section discusses two bodies of literature that could help investigate the issue of developing a lexicon within a CAW – conceptual modelling, and language & power – as well as the application of those two bodies to an organization. Below is a representation of those bodies of literature in interaction with each other (Fig. 1).

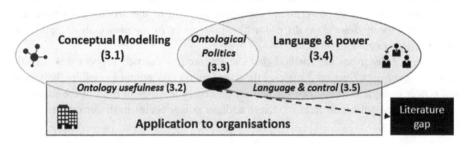

Fig. 1. Literature overview and gaps

3.1 Conceptual Modelling

Roa et al. [1] define an ontology as *"conceptualizations of reality, as agreed to by a group of experts, defined specifically and with varying levels of generality, varying representations and varying levels of formality"* (p. 214). Conceptual modeling entails an instantiation of an ontology within a non-software specific representation [6]. This piece focuses on an informal type of human-readable ontology called a lexicon. Lexicons are important for human uses since they serve as the basis for natural language, thereby facilitating human interaction [1]. Further, lexicon can also constitute a first step towards building a formal ontology that will ultimately serve human-to-computer or computer-to-computer interaction (see for instance [8]).

3.2 Ontology Usefulness

In organizations, the usefulness of conceptual models and ontologies has been largely documented and demonstrated. They play a major role in knowledge transfer, developing domain understanding, or simulating the subject matter they represent, thereby supporting both humans and computer in their tasks and reducing variance in the understanding of a domain [1]; they help improve the interoperability, specification, reliability and reusability of information systems [9]; they facilitate conceptual modeling by providing a more rigorous framework to capture and represent knowledge [10]; they improve the requirements engineering process by facilitating the user validation of conceptual schemas produced by analysts [11].

3.3 Ontological Politics

The notion of "ontological politics" has been coined by Annemarie Mol [12] to describe the impact that the shaping of knowledge – or "ontologies" – has on reality and the decisions that are taken. Her first application was in health care, but her contribution also sparked the debate in organizational studies [13], social sciences [14], educational sciences [15] and even geography [16]. What scientists present as facts are often tainted with the author's subjectivity, which can undermine the trust of the public in scientific expertise – these events are referred to as "knowledge controversies" [16]. In the aforementioned publications, the authors invite researchers to be mindful of the consequences of their actions.

3.4 Language and Power

The importance of language has been largely underestimated *"in the production, maintenance, and change of social relations of power"* [17, p. 1], especially outside of the field of linguistics [17]. This section presents briefly the work of some influential philosophers and sociologists on language and power. A full literature review of this topic would fall outside the scope of this paper, as our purpose is limited to highlighting major principles and insights that link power and language, and to applying them to the field of conceptual modelling. In this paper, the discussion is limited to three authors which we found to be the most prolific, influential and broad on the topic of language and power: Wittgenstein, Bourdieu and Foucault. We selected authors from the 20th century, because their work often builds on and encompass earlier works on the topic.

Wittgenstein and Language. In the *Philosophical Investigations* [18], Austrian philosopher Wittgenstein states that unresolved debates and disputes are often the consequence of language issues as people argue about the true meaning of words. Yet, arguing about the meaning of words is a pointless endeavor as there is not a single true meaning of a word. Rather than a reflection of reality, the meaning of words is the result of an agreed upon way of talking and carrying out activities. In *Tractatus logico-philosophicus* Wittgenstein [19] makes the point that language only covers a part of reality, and that something that cannot be expressed through language also cannot be expressed in the consciousness of the speaker. Because of this, there can be "unspoken truths" in areas, which elude debate and discourse because of the lack of words to speak about them.

Bourdieu and Language. In *Ce que parler veut dire (translated as "What Speaking Means")* [20] and *Language et pouvoir symbolique (translated as "Language and symbolic power")* [21], French sociologist Bourdieu describes how the social world can be perceived differently depending on the observer's mental construct, and how language plays a major role in forming this mental construct as it bridges the gap between the mental consciousness and the reality of the world. The intrinsically political nature of language is explicit in Bourdieu [22]: *"the knowledge of the social world and, more precisely, the categories that make it possible, are the ideal stakes of political struggle, both practically and theoretically, as one struggles to maintain or transform the social world by maintaining or transforming the categories of perception of the world"* (translated from [22, p. 6]). Thereby, *"one of the elementary forms of political power consists of the almost-magical power of naming things and thereby, making them real ... going from implicit to explicit"* (translated from [22, p. 6]). In *Raisons Pratiques (translated as "Practical Reasons")*, Bourdieu [23] synthesizes previous works arguing that the *monopoly of legitimate naming* is the result of a struggle, and the winners of this struggle are those with the most *symbolic capital* – i.e. prestige, reputation or fame, that gives them the capacity to define and legitimize cultural values. This capital can be explicit (written in law, for instance) or not, but has to be earned and recognized within the field in order to impose a certain language.

Foucault and Language. In *Les Mots et les Choses (translated as "The Order of Things")*, French philosopher Foucault [25] describes how institutions that are seemingly neutral – such as medicine or justice – are in fact places where power struggles occur, more or less overtly. Since language is the tool of formalization of knowledge in those fields, it can be broken down and analyzed to logically demonstrate its inconsistencies and manipulations of reality. In *Surveiller et Punir (translated as "Discipline and Punish")*, Foucault [24] discusses his observations in French and reflects upon the ways of exercising coercion. In his discussion of the relationship between knowledge and power, he states that to the observer, it is not the experience of a subject that creates knowledge and its possible forms and domain, but rather the processes and struggles with the subject. Further, the author distinguishes between directly coercive power –

such as threats and physical punishment – and more subtle ways of exerting power – such as the control of the recipient's vision of himself and the world through the influence of the language. According to Foucault, exercising control indirectly through language is more effective when there is no visible conflict.

3.5   Language and Organizational Control

The study of power and language has long been the focus of linguists, in a research body called critical language study [17] and has also been an important topic for philosophers and sociologists, but it has been underwhelmingly adopted in other fields such as conceptual modelling, or in the context of organizations. The role of language as a tool for control in organization has been shown by [26], where the authors show that control can be exercised directly and coercively, but also more subtly *"through language and the construction and use of knowledge ... [to] encourage managers and employees to conform to organizational expectations"* [26, p. 2]. Similarly, in [27, p. 192], *"Objects for management control are decreasingly labor power and behavior and increasingly the mindpower and subjectivities of employees."* – objects for management control are thus more and more often symbolic items, such as language.

3.6   Literature Gap

This section establishes how language has a strong impact on the field it seeks to describe, and that it is both an object of power struggle and a tool for domination. The case described in this paper seeks to apply these insights to the development of a lexicon within an organization, but we were not able to find publications that binds all those issues together.

4   Early Findings and Discussion

This section formulates five postulates based on the literature over language and power adapted to the context of developing a lexicon in an organization. It further discusses the relevance of these postulates in the context of our case. For each postulate, we describe how it was taken into account by the modelling team.

4.1   Postulate 1: Modelers Should Focus on the Pragmatic Convenience of the Concepts They Define, Rather Than Debating the "Truth" of Concepts

This postulate is based on Wittgenstein's Philosophical Investigations [18]. In our case, we noticed that in defining the most important concepts in the organization's domain, respondents' main focus point was to avoid complications and future problems, rather than seek the true meaning of a word. For instance, there is an ongoing discussion about a new name to define an `activity`, which is a unit of production within the cooperative autonomously managed by a member, just like his or her own "quasi-enterprise". Two main candidates are the `unit` (in reference to the business unit) and the enterprise. Both could correctly define what an activity is, but the former conveys the idea that an activity is part of a whole (in this case the CAW) and could not exist without it, while the latter implies that the activity could exist by itself. We discovered that the second understanding could induce severe complications when members wish to withdraw their activity from the CAW, for instance in terms of ownership of the assets of the activity.

The team took this postulate into account by explicitly identifying the potential issues that could arise from choosing each concept. In the aforementioned case, for the sake of pragmatism, the team preferred the term unit over enterprise.

4.2   Postulates 2: Modelers Should Spot Unspoken Areas and Concepts – Concepts for Which Words Are Lacking and Therefore, Are Not Present in the Consciousness of the Speaker

This postulate is based on Wittgenstein's *Tractatus logico-philosophicus* [19], and is also related to the concept of construct incompleteness [28]. A language is said to be complete *"if every concept in a domain conceptualization is covered by at least one modeling construct of the language"* [28, p. 6].

In the case of the CAW we studied, we found that the adequate vocabulary was unable to express some realities. For instance, the vocabulary mostly assumes that an activity (which we described earlier as an autonomous business unit managed by a member) is managed by a sole member. As a result, there is no adequate vocabulary to distinguish between a member and his activity. This issue has been documented in other CAW in France, where *"the person and the activity are one"*, [29, p. 66] such that *"the 'activity' itself is unthought [un impensé]"* [29, p. 57]. This lack of vocabulary to distinguish between the member and his activity has made it harder to conceive more complex activities, in which multiple members participate. For instance, today, it is possible to assign multiple members to an activity, but all revenues of that activity are necessarily attributed to the activity holder, and there are no words or concepts to name the relationship between the activity holder and the other members.

The team took this postulate into account by explicitly identifying some areas as tacit and proposing words and concepts that fill these gaps. In the example mentioned previously, the researchers imposed a clear separation between members and activities; accordingly, they coined two new concepts: personal services (i.e. service to members, regarding pay or employment status), and economic services (i.e. services to activities, including business advise and leasing assets). This allowed the team to start describe the rights and obligations of members towards their activities, which is a relationship that had not been thought of before per lack of vocabulary.

4.3   Postulate 3: In Order to Gain the Monopoly of Legitimate Naming in a Field, Modelers Must First Earn Sufficient Prestige, Reputation or Fame Within the Field

This postulate is based on Bourdieu's *Raisons pratique* [23]. As we mentioned above, other attempts had been made to develop a lexicon at the CAW before, and all had been stopped as the teams had lost the confidence of the upper management along the way.

The team took this postulate into account by taking the time to earn legitimacy within all influence groups within the CAW. Receiving an official mission order from the upper management was but a first step and did not guarantee that all stakeholders would adopt the new unified lexicon and change their way of speaking about the CAW. Actions taken to acquire legitimacy included frequent interaction and communication, showing expertise by demonstrating, with the help of scientific literature, the usefulness of the project and most of all, hearing and incorporating the vision of each stakeholder in the final artifact.

4.4   Postulates 4: Language Is not a Neutral Object and Is Intimately Tied to Power Struggles

This postulate is based on Bourdieu's *Language and symbolic power* [21]. In CAW just like in any organization, members can have conflicting interests, leading to power struggles, and language is one of the places where such a struggle can be observed. CAW are not immune to this, and we identified two types of power struggles in which language plays a major role. On the one hand, power struggles can oppose CAW to external forces such as worker unions who fear CAW represent an alternative to ordinary salaried work, with globally lower stability and worker protection; and government agencies who suspect CAW to give its members access to more social protection than they would otherwise have access to with a traditional freelancer status. This power struggle appeared very clearly in the discussions on naming members. Alternative terms that are considered included salaried entrepreneur – which is the term coined in law for French CAW but does not depict the reality of most members as they do not have an entrepreneurial activity, but rather work in subordination of an organization. On the other hand, internal power struggles can occur, for instance over the name given to the front-office workers. Calling them employees would be confusing, as the members of CAW also have an employee status from the CAW. The upper management tends to push for a term that would entail more involvement and commitment from the front-office workers, such as mutualized team – which would encourage these employees to become themselves co-operators of the CAW and commit voluntarily to tasks that exceed their boundaries, whereas front-office workers themselves tend to rather see themselves as regular employees with clear boundaries to their tasks, which would be more clearly conveyed in terms such as workers of the mutualized services.

The team took this postulate into account by explicitly formulating the consequences of the choosing of each term for each interest group within the CAW before settling on a specific concept.

4.5   Postulate 5: Control Over Language Can Be a Non-conflictual, Indirect Way to Exert Control Over a Group of People

This postulate is based on Foucault's *Surveiller et punir* [24], as well as authors that described the importance of language in the context of power in organizations, such as [26]. This postulate can effectively be illustrated in the case of the CAW. Hitherto, the front-office workers spend a major part of their time on administrative tasks related to billing, invoicing and fiscal obligations of activities and members. Yet, the upper management has long been pushing for front-office workers to also take up a consulting role and act as economic advisors to members. To support this objective, as well as applying the postulate 2 (see above), we coined the terms `personal services` and `economic services` – the earlier being related to administrative and the second to advisory tasks. Distinguishing these services allowed us to effectively monitor the time spent on each task, but also allowed us to complexify the description of the task sheet of front-office workers and change their vision of their own job.

5   Conclusion

The use of language as a tool for control and influence has long been described and discussed by philosophers, sociologists and linguists. However, it was sparsely considered as such in the field of conceptual modelling – rather, informal models such as a lexicon, which serve as basis for language, are seen as neutral objects, and potential first steps to developing formal ontologies.

Our work in a particularly democratic and egalitarian organization such as a CAW showed us the importance of being mindful of the political nature of language when developing a conceptual model. In doing so, we laid down some insights to answer the questions that we raised in the introduction. To the question: *what should the modeler do to acquire the monopoly of legitimate naming in an organization?*, we suggest to pursue pragmatic convenience rather than the truth of a concept (postulate 1), to unveil unspoken areas and concepts (postulate 2) and transparently make the effort of hearing and incorporating the vision of each stakeholder in the final artifact (postulate 3). To the question: *what should the modeler do to distribute the power given by the monopoly of legitimate naming in an organization?*, we suggest to explicitly and transparently describe the consequences of naming a concept for each interest groups (postulate 4), and being mindful of the strategic orientations that are conveyed by the chosen terms and of the influence those terms can have on the recipients' view of their missions.

With this paper, we hope to share some insights in how modelers can integrate those aspects, not only in democratic organizations, but in any organization for which transparency and fairness is important. Future area for research on the topic could include an empirical evaluation of transparent, fair and democratic methods of conceptual modelling in organization, based on a full roll-out of the artifact in an organization.

References

1. Roa, H.N., Sadiq, S., Indulska, M.: Ontology Usefulness in Human Tasks: Seeking Evidence, p. 11, New Zealand (2014)
2. Desguin, S., Laurier, W.: Modelling services of cooperatives of autonomous workers to create a space for autonomy and security, p. 233, Brussels (2020)
3. Charles, J., Desguin, S.: Aux confins – Travail et foyer à l'heure du (dé)confinement, CESEP, UCLouvain, USL-B (2020)

4. Sadi, N.-E., Moulin, F.: Gouvernance coopérative : un éclairage théorique, Rev. Int. Léconomie Soc. Recma, no 333, p. 43–58 (2014)
5. Sein, M., Henfridsson, O., Purao, S., Rossi, M., Lindgren, R.: Action Design Research, MIS Q. vol. 35, no 1, p. 37 (2011)
6. Robinson, S.: Conceptual modelling for simulation Part I: definition and requirements. J. Oper. Res. Soc. **59**(3), 278–290 (2008)
7. Hirst, G.: Ontology and the Lexicon. Springer (2009)
8. Scheidgen, M., Fischer, J.: Human comprehensible and machine processable specifications of operational semantics. In: Akehurst, D.H., Vogel, R., Paige, R.F. (eds.) ECMDA-FA 2007. LNCS, vol. 4530, pp. 157–171. Springer, Heidelberg (2007). https://doi.org/10.1007/978-3-540-72901-3_12
9. Jasper, R., Uschold, M.: A Framework for understanding and classifying ontology applications. In: Proceeding of the 12th International Workshop on Knowledge Acquisition, Modelling, and Management KAW, p. 20 (1999)
10. Wand, Y., Storey, V.C., Weber, R.: An ontological analysis of the relationship construct in conceptual modeling. ACM Trans. Database Syst. **24**(4), 494–528 (1999)
11. Poels, G., Maes, A., Gailly, F., Paemeleire, R.: The pragmatic quality of resources-events-agents diagrams: an experimental evaluation: the pragmatic quality of REA diagrams. Inf. Syst. J. **21**(1), 63–89 (2011)
12. Mol, A.: Ontological politics a word and some questions. Soc. Rev. **47**, 74–89 (1999)
13. Clegg, S.R., Courpasson, D., Phillips, N.: Power and Organizations. Pine Forge Press (2006)
14. Law, J., Urry, J.: Enacting the social. Econ. Soc. **33**, 390–410 (2004)
15. Sørensen, E.: The Materiality of Learning: Technology and Knowledge in Educational Practice. Cambridge University Press, Cambridge (2009)
16. Whatmore, S.J.: Mapping knowledge controversies: science, democracy and the redistribution of expertise. Prog. Hum. Geogr. **33**, 587–598 (2009)
17. Fairclough, N.: Language and Power. Pearson Education (2001)
18. Wittgenstein, L.: Philosophical Investigations (1953)
19. Wittgenstein, L., Logico-Philosophicus, T.: Annalen der Naturphilosophie (1921)
20. Bourdieu, P.: Ce que parler veut dire: L'économie des échanges linguistiques. Fayard, Paris (1982)
21. Bourdieu, P.: Langage et pouvoir symbolique. Le seuil, Paris (1991)
22. Bourdieu, P.: Espace social et genèse des "classes", in Actes de la recherche en sciences sociales, Le travail politique., Paris (1984)
23. Bourdieu, P.: Raisons pratiques. Le Seuil, Paris (1994)
24. Foucault, M.: Surveiller et punir. Gallimard, Paris (1975)
25. Foucault, M.: Les mots et les choses, vol. 42, Gallimard, Paris (1966)
26. Oakes, L.S., Townley, B., Cooper, D.J.: Business planning as pedagogy: language and control in a changing institutional field. Adm. Sci. Q. **43**(2), 257–292 (1998)
27. Alvesson, M., Deetz, S.: Critical theory and postmodernism approaches to organizational studies. In: Handbook of Organization Studies, pp. 191–217, Sage, Thousand Oaks (1996)
28. Guizzardi, G., Ferreira Pires, L., van Sinderen, M.: An ontology-based approach for evaluating the *domain appropriateness* and *comprehensibility appropriateness* of modeling languages. In: Briand, L., Williams, C. (eds.) MODELS 2005. LNCS, vol. 3713, pp. 691–705. Springer, Heidelberg (2005). https://doi.org/10.1007/11557432_51
29. Veyer, S., Sangiorgio, J.: Les parts congrues de la coopération : penser la question de la propriété dans les Coopératives d'activités et d'emploi. L'exemple de la Scop Coopaname, RECMA, vol. N° 350, no 4, pp. 55–69, October 2018

Replicability and Reproducibility of a Schema Evolution Study in Embedded Databases

Dimitri Braininger[1], Wolfgang Mauerer[1,2], and Stefanie Scherzinger[3(✉)]

[1] Technical University of Applied Sciences Regensburg, Regensburg, Germany
d.braininger@yandex.com
[2] Siemens AG, Corporate Research, Munich, Germany
wolfgang.mauerer@othr.de
[3] University of Passau, Passau, Germany
stefanie.scherzinger@uni-passau.de

Abstract. Ascertaining the feasibility of independent falsification or repetition of published results is vital to the scientific process, and replication or reproduction experiments are routinely performed in many disciplines. Unfortunately, such studies are only scarcely available in database research, with few papers dedicated to re-evaluating published results. In this paper, we conduct a case study on replicating and reproducing a study on schema evolution in embedded databases. We can exactly repeat the outcome for one out of four database applications studied, and come close in two further cases. By reporting results, efforts, and obstacles encountered, we hope to increase appreciation for the substantial efforts required to ensure reproducibility. By discussing minutiae details required to ascertain reproducible work, we argue that such important, but often ignored aspects of scientific work should receive more credit in the evaluation of future research.

Keywords: Schema evolution · Replicability · Reproducibility

1 Introduction

Experiments are at the heart of the scientific process. According to the ACM reproducibility guidelines (see "ACM review and badging", hyperlink available in the PDF), experiments are expected to be *repeatable*: Essentially, the same team with the same experimental setup can reliably achieve identical results in subsequent trials. Moreover, experiments should be *replicable*, so that using the same experimental setup operated by a different team achieves the same results. Ideally, experiments are even *reproducible*, and a different team with a different experimental setup can confirm the results.

Such properties are acknowledged to be fundamental, but reproducibility is far from universally permeating most published research. This discrepancy has become an academic topic of debate, and dedicated research evaluates the

© Springer Nature Switzerland AG 2020
G. Grossmann and S. Ram (Eds.): ER 2020 Workshops, LNCS 12584, pp. 210–219, 2020.
https://doi.org/10.1007/978-3-030-65847-2_19

(oftentimes wanting) state of affairs in computer science research in general (see, e.g., Refs. [1,5,9,12]), but also in data management research[1].

In this paper, we examine the state of replicability, and efforts required to achieve reproducibility, for an empirical case study on schema evolution in embedded databases by S. Wu and I. Neamtiu [16] that predates the aforementioned discussions. There is a long-standing tradition of schema evolution case studies in real-world database applications, e.g., [7,13–15]. It used to be difficult to get access to real-world database applications for study, so earlier studies are generally conducted on closed-source systems, for instance [14]. Yet the proliferation of open source software, and the access to code repositories (e.g., GitHub) enables a whole new line of research on open source application code [4]. Most schema evolution studies focus on applications backed by relational database management systems, typically tracking the growth of the schema (counting the number of tables and their columns), and the distribution of *schema modification operations* (a term coined by Curino et al. in [6]).

The authors in the original case study are the first to focus on an important subfamily of database products, namely that of *embedded* (and therefore serverless) databases, such as SQLite. While there are independent schema evolution studies targeting the same open source projects, such as MediaWiki (the software powering Wikipedia), they consider different time frames (such as 4.5 years in [7] and 10 years in [13]), and implement different methodologies. This even leads to partly contradictory results. However, a dedicated replicability and reproducibility study has not yet been conducted so far.

Contributions. This paper makes the following contributions:

- We conduct a replicability and reproducibility study on a well-received, published paper on schema evolution [16]. While there is a long history of schema evolution case studies, to the best of our knowledge, ours is the first effort to ascertain published results on this class of publications.
- Our study is mainly based on the information provided in the original paper. However, we were also provided (incomplete) code artefacts by the authors of the original study. This blurs the line between conducting a replicability and reproducibility study. For simplification, we restrict ourselves to the term *reproducibility* in the remainder of this paper.
- We carefully re-engineer the authors' experiments and present our results. Overall, we achieve a high degree of accordance, albeit at the expense of substantial manual effort. For one out of four applications studied in [16], we even obtain identical results. We document and discuss where our numbers agree, and where they deviate.
- We lay out which instructions were helpful, and which left too much leeway.
- We discuss the threats to the validity of our results (e.g., where we may have erred), and contrast this with the original threats stated in [16]. Doing so, we re-calibrate the level of risk involved with each originally reported threat.

---

[1] Such as in the VLDB ("pVLDB Reproducibility") and SIGMOD communities ("ACM SIGMOD 2019 Reproducibility", clickable links available in PDF).

```
res = logged_sqlite3_exec(sql, "CREATE TABLE file_deltas\n"
"\t(\n"
"\tid not null,    -- strong hash of file contents\n"
"\tbase not null,  -- joins with files.id or file_deltas.id\n"
"\tdelta not null, -- compressed [...]\n"
"\tunique(id, base)\n"
"\t)", NULL, NULL, errmsg);
```

```
CREATE TABLE file_deltas
(
 id integer not null,
 base integer not null,
 delta integer not null,
 unique(id, base)
);
```

(a) Excerpt from the C++ code in *Monotone*.   (b) Extracted stmt.

Fig. 1. (a) A CREATE TABLE statement, embedded as string constants within *Monotone* C++ code (source can be inspected online, "[...]" denotes a shortened comment). The statement must be automatically parsed and translated to the MySQL dialect (b).

Our experience underlines that achieving full reproducibility remains a challenge even with well-designed, well-documented studies, and requires considerable extra effort. We feel that such efforts are not yet universally appreciated, albeit it is in our joint interest that research become reproducible.

Structure. The remainder of this paper is organized as follows. We next summarize the original study. Section 3 states our methodology. Section 4 describes the main part of the reproduction work, as well as the detailed results. Section 5 discusses the overall results, followed by Sect. 6 with a description of threats to validity. Finally, Sect. 7 focuses on related work. Section 8 concludes.

2   Original Study

We briefly summarize the original study. Neamtiu et al. analyze four database applications, all of which are based on SQLite, and provide public development histories by virtue of being available as open source software (OSS): *BiblioteQ*, *Monotone*, *Mozilla Firefox*, and *Vienna*:

- *BiblioteQ* (C++), analyzed in the time frame 03/15/2008–02/19/2010, is a library management system.
- *Monotone* (C++), analyzed in the time frame 04/06/2003–06/13/2010, is a distributed version control system.
- *Mozilla Firefox* (C, C++), analyzed in the time frame 10/02/2004–11/21/2008, is a popular web browser.
- *Vienna* (Objective-C), analyzed in the time frame 06/29/2005–09/03/2010, is an RSS newsreader for MacOS.

The original study uses a custom data processing pipeline for retrieving the source code history, extracting schema declarations embedded in application code, and computing differences between schema revisions. Extracting schema declarations requires careful engineering: Fig. 1(a) shows a CREATE TABLE statement embedded in the program code as a multi-line string constant.

Table 1. Evolution time frames and schema change details (as absolute numbers and percentages) given in the original study [16].

App	Table changes		Attribute changes				
	CREATE TABLE	DROP TABLE	ADD COLUMN	DROP COLUMN	Type change	Init change	Key change
Firefox	5 (4.2%)	26(21.7%)	57(47.5%)	28(23.3%)	0 (0.0%)	3 (2.5%)	1 (0.7%)
Monotone	11(20.4%)	17(31.5%)	14(25.9%)	10(18.5%)	0 (0.0%)	0 (0.0%)	2 (3.7%)
BiblioteQ	4 (2.6%)	8 (5.2%)	27(17.5%)	28(18.2%)	83(53.9%)	0 (0.0%)	4 (2.6%)
Vienna	1 (7.1%)	0 (0.0%)	13(92.9%)	0 (0.0%)	0 (0.0%)	0 (0.0%)	0 (0.0%)
Total	21 (6.1%)	51(14.9%)	111(32.5%)	66(19.3%)	83(24.3%)	3 (0.9%)	7 (2.0%)

We compare different schema versions with utility to derive `mysqldiff` (version 0.30), a utility to derive schema modification operations (SMOs) that transform a predecessor schema into the successor schema. `mysqldiff` only handles MySQL schema declarations, but SQLite uses a custom SQL dialect[2]. For instance, let us again consider the code example from Fig. 1(a). The extracted CREATE TABLE statement is shown in Fig. 1(b). Note that the original statement does not declare attribute types, which is permissible when using SQLite. Since MySQL requires all attributes to be typed, we add a default attribute type in preparation for processing the schemas with `mysqldiff`.

`mysqldiff` generates SMOs for creating or dropping a table, adding or removing a table column, and changing the type or initial value of a column. It also recognizes changes to the table primary key. With this sequence of SMOs, the predecessor schema can be transformed into its successor schema. Further SMOs, such as renaming a table or an attribute, cannot be reliably derived based on automated analysis alone, and would require sophisticated schema matching and mapping solutions [3].

The statistics in the study by Neamtiu et al. derive from `mysqldiff` results; Table 1 provides the number of SMOs for each project. Studies on schema evolution in server-based (non-embedded) DBMS, especially [13], show that attribute type changes are frequent in many projects. In the study by Neamtiu et al., this holds only for *BiblioteQ*, so no type changes were recorded for the other projects. This is a finding that we will revisit at a later point. The original study finds that the shares of CREATE TABLE and ADD COLUMN SMOs are comparable to the observations of related studies on schema evolution in non-embedded DBMS. The observation that changes to initial values and primary keys are uncommon has also been observed in the later study of Qiu et al. [13].

3 Methodology of This Study

We conducted our reproducibility study as follows. Our code, as well as material made available to us by the original authors, is available on Zenodo

---

[2] The SQL dialects reference at https://en.wikibooks.org/wiki/SQL_Dialects_Reference illustrates the richness of proprietary language constructs.

(doi.org/10.5281/zenodo.4012776) to ascertain long-term availability. In particular, we publish all interim results computed by our analysis scripts (such as the extracted schemas and the results of schema comparison), for transparency.

We started with identifying the source code repositories for the four database applications, based on the information given in the original paper. Like in the original work, we wrote a script to extract the database schema declarations embedded in the source code. For *Vienna*, the authors provided us with a partial script that could not be directly made to work (caused by minor syntactic issues, and some missing components), and was therefore re-implemented by us in Python. For all other projects, we had no such templates.

The original study used `mysqldiff` version 0.30 to compare successive schema declarations. However, we used the newer version 0.60, since the output is more succinct and also more convenient to parse. A further reason for abandoning the legacy version is that it sometimes recognizes redundant schema modification operations (as we also discuss in Sect. 6).

Further, the pairwise comparison of schema versions using `mysqldiff` is not very robust: A table declaration that is missing in one version (e.g., due to a parsing problem), and then re-appears later, is recognized as first dropping and later re-creating this table. This problem was pointed out in the original study, and will also be revisited in Sect. 6.

As a summarizing metric, we compute the difference in percentage across all SMOs observed as

$$\frac{\sum_{SMO\ s} |p(s) - r(s)|}{P},$$

where $p(s)$ is the number of changes for SMO s reported in the original publication and $r(s)$ is the number of changes for SMO s identified in our reproducibility study. Further, P is the total number of changes in the project reported in [16].

4   Results

Vienna. For *Vienna*, the authors made their raw input data available to us, so we could apply our script on the exact same data, with the exact same results.

We further attempted to locate the raw input data ourselves, based only on information provided in the original study. Unfortunately, the original Source-forge repository no longer exists, the project is now hosted on GitHub. From there, we obtained fewer files than expected. Thus, searching for the raw input data based on the information in the paper alone would have led to a different baseline, yet the analysis still yields the same results as listed in Table 1.

Monotone. For *Monotone*, the original paper states that the study was conducted on 48 archives available from the project website. However, we have reason to believe that only 41 versions were chosen (specifically, versions 0.1, 0.2, and also from 0.10 up to and including 0.48), based on the list of available archives, as well as comments within the material that we obtained from the authors.

Moreover, it is not exactly clear from which files to extract schema declarations: In the initial versions of *Monotone*, database schemas are only declared

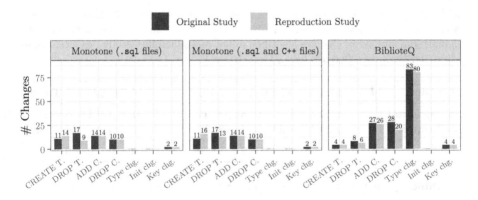

Fig. 2. Comparing the number of schema changes for *Monotone* and *BiblioteQ*.

in files with suffix `.sql`. Later, database schemas are also embedded within C++ files (starting with version 10). We therefore explored two approaches, where we (1) consider *only* schemas declared in `.sql`-suffixed files, and (2) also consider schemas embedded within the program code.

Figure 2 visualizes the results for both approaches. For each type of SMO analyzed, we compare the number of changes reported in the original study with the number of changes determined by us. Overall, our results come close. As pointed out in Sect. 3, problems in parsing SQL statements embedded in program code lead to falsely recognizing tables as dropped and later re-introduced. We suspect that this effect causes the discrepancies observed for CREATE and DROP TABLE statements.

BiblioteQ. At the time when the original study was performed on *BiblioteQ*, all schema declarations were contained in files with suffix `.sql` (this has meanwhile changed). Schema declarations do thus not have to be laboriously parsed from strings embedded in the application source code. MySQL, SQLite, and PostgreSQL were supported as alternative backends. In particular, SQLite was initially not supported, but was introduced with revision 35, while the original study spans the time frame from the very beginning of the project (see Sect. 2). Unfortunately, the original study does not discuss this issue.

We suspect that up to revision 35, the schema declarations of MySQL were analyzed, and only from then on for SQLite.[3] The high number of type changes reported for *BiblioteQ* may thus be overemphasized—the switch causes half the reported type changes. However, this still leaves a significant number of type changes for BiblioteQ, compared to the other projects (see Table 1).

---

[3] Revision 16 only changes the MySQL schema declaration, and the original study reports a schema change in this revision. A peak in schema changes is reported for revision 35 (see Table 2), as switching from MySQL to SQLite schema declarations causes `mysqldiff` to recognize type changes. Since revision 35 only adds support for SQLite, with no schema changes for MySQL or PostgreSQL, we conclude that starting with revision 35, the authors analyzed the SQLite schema.

Table 2. Pairwise comparison of schema versions, and the number of changes w.r.t. the previous version. Stating the number of changes reported in the original paper (#C, original), the number of changes identified in our reproducibility study (#C, repro), as well as the absolute difference (diff), for *BiblioteQ*.

Revision	4	5	11	16	24	35	44	52	80	81	101	102	115	116	154	233	236	285	**Total**
#C,original	1	1	1	1	20	50	5	25	1	8	12	12	1	5	1	3	1	6	154
#C,repro	1	1	1	0	20	42	5	22	1	6	12	12	1	5	1	3	1	6	140
diff	0	0	0	1	0	8	0	3	0	2	0	0	0	0	0	0	0	0	14

Table 3. Comparing of the total number of schema changes across projects.

	Vienna	Monotone (Alt. 1: .sql)	Monotone (Alt. 2: .sql/C++)	BiblioteQ	Mozilla Firefox
Original study	14	54	54	154	120
Repro. study	14	49	55	140	–
Abs. diff	0	11	9	14	–
Rel. diff [%]	0.00	20.37	16.67	9.09	–

The results of our reproducibility study on *BiblioteQ* are visualized in Fig. 2. While we are confident that we have identified the raw input data, due to liberties in the data preparation instructions, our results nevertheless deviate.

In Table 2, we list the changes per revision, comparing the results of the original study against our own. Revision 35, where SQLite was introduced, clearly stands out. In processing the extracted schemas (in particular, revisions 4, 5 and 11), we encountered small syntax errors in SQL statements, that we manually fixed to make the analysis work. Since we can reproduce the exact results of the original study, we may safely assume that Neamtiu et al. have fixed these same errors, even though they do not report this.

Mozilla Firefox. The original paper analyzed 308 revisions of *Mozilla Firefox* in a specific time interval. From the material provided to us by the authors, we further know the table names in database schemas. Unfortunately, this information was not specific enough to identify the exact revisions analyzed. As the original version control system (CVS) has meanwhile been replaced by Mercurial, we inspected the CVS archive, the current GitHub repositories, and the Firefox release website. We searched for the CVS tags mentioned by the authors, and tried to align them with these sources. Despite independent efforts by all three authors, we were not able to reliably identify the analyzed project versions. Consequently, we are not able to report any reproducibility results.

Summary. We summarize our results in Table 3, which reads as follows. For each project, we state the number of schema changes observed in the original study and in our reproducibility study. We state the absolute difference in the results, as well as the relative difference in percent, as introduced in Sect. 3.

While we were able to exactly reproduce the results for *Vienna*, we were not able to conduct the analysis for *Mozilla Firefox*. For *Monotone* and *BiblioteQ*, our results deviate to varying degrees. We next discuss these effects.

5 Discussion

Access to the raw input data, sample code and instructions make project *Vienna* an almost ideal reproduction case. For the other projects, we found the data preparation instructions unspecific. For *Monotone* and *Mozilla Firefox*, we struggled (and in case of *Mozilla Firefox* even failed) to locate the raw input data. Nearly a decade after the original paper has been published in 2011, code repositories have switched hosting platforms. Therefore, *a link is not enough* to unambiguously identify the raw input data, to quote from the title of a recent reproducibility study [12]. Further, the exact revision ranges must be clearly specified, beyond (ambiguous) dates.

The ACM reproducibility badge "Artefacts Available" requires artefacts like the raw input data to be available on an archival repository, identified by a digital object identifier. Considering our own experience, it is vital to ensure long-term access to the raw input data. Various efforts (e.g. [2]) try to ensure long-term availability of OSS repositories. However, without very specific instructions on data preparation, the reproducibility of the results remains at risk.

To quantify how much our results differ, we calculate the difference in percentage across all SMOs. For a more fine grained assessment of the degree of reproducibility, we would require information on the exact SMOs identified in the original study. This motivates us to also provide the output of applying `mysqldiff` in our reproducibility study in our Zenodo repository (see Sect. 3).

6 Threats to Validity

We now turn evaluate threats to the validity of the original study, and comment on additional threats discovered during reproduction.

Threats of the Original Study. Three possible threats to validity are pointed out. Firstly, missing tables in the database schema could arise from using inadequate text matching patterns. We agree that their correctness affects result quality, especially if the pattern is used to extract schemas from code that in some versions or revisions have changed significantly. Inadequate patterns can cause missing tables, missing columns, and other issues.

Secondly, renamings are another possible source of errors. Following usual schema history evolution techniques, the authors consider renaming of tables and columns as a deletion followed by an addition, as implemented by `mysqldiff`. Consequently, renamings cannot be correctly recognized.

Thirdly, the choice of reference systems is considered an external threat to validity. The evolution of database schemas for applications with different characteristics might differ.

Threats of the Reproduction Study. The dominant threat to validity of the reproduction concerns behavior of `mysqldiff`:

- Different versions of `mysqldiff` produce different output, also caused by bugs. Erroneous statements may be mistaken for actual schema changes.
- Syntax errors in table declarations cause `mysqldiff` to ignore any subsequent declarations. This error propagates, since in comparing predecessor and successor schemas, `mysqldiff` will erroneously report additional SMOs, such as DROP TABLE and CREATE TABLE statements.
- Foreign key constraints require table declarations in topological order. CREATE TABLE statements extracted from several input files require careful handling because runtime errors may cause following inputs to be ignored.

`mysqldiff` relies on a MySQL installation, and the handling of table and column identifiers in MySQL can be case-sensitive. The subject projects use lowercase table and column names, so this threat does not materialize.

Finally, incorrectly selected files containing SQL statements are a threat to validity. For instance, one individual file might be used for a specific DBMS when multiple DBMS are supported. If the schemas in different files are not properly synchronized, this leads to deviations. Carefully recording exactly which files were analyzed is necessary.

7 Related Work

The authors of the original study [8,11] analyze on-the-fly relational schema evolution, as well as collateral evolution of applications and databases. Contrariwise to the object of our study [16], the former was carried out *manually*, and risks differ between manual and programmatic analysis.

From the substantial body of work on empirical schema evolution studies, Curino et al. [7] study schema evolution on MediaWiki, and consider schema size growth, lifetime of tables and columns, and per-month revision count. They analyze schema changes at macro and micro levels. Moon et al. [10] and Curino et al. [6] test the PRISM and PRIMA systems using the data set addressed in Ref. [7], as well as SMOs to describe schema evolution. Qiu et al. [13] empirically analyze the co-evolution of relational database schemas and code in ten popular database applications. They also discuss disadvantages of using `mysqldiff`.

Pawlik et al. [12] make a case for reproducibility in the data preparation process, and demonstrate the influence of (undocumented) decisions during data preprocessing on derived results. However, we are not aware of any reproducibility studies on schema evolution.

8 Conclusion and Future Work

In this paper, we perform a reproducibility study on an analysis of the evolution of embedded database schemas. For one out of four real-world database applications, we obtain the exact same results; for two, we come within approx. 20% of the reported changes, and fail to identify the raw input data in one case.

Our study, conducted nearly a decade after the original study, illustrates just how brittle online resources are. Specifically, we realize the importance of archiving the input data analyzed, since repositories can move. This not only changes the URL, but creates further undesirable and previously unforeseeable effects, for instance that timestamps and tags no longer serve as identifiers.

We hope that sharing our insights, we can contribute to a more robust, collective science methodology in the data management research community.

Acknowledgements. We thank the authors of [16] for sharing parts of their analysis code, and their feedback on an earlier version of this report. Stefanie Scherzinger's contribution, within the scope of project *"NoSQL Schema Evolution und Big Data Migration at Scale"*, is funded by the Deutsche Forschungsgemeinschaft (DFG, German Research Foundation)—grant number 385808805.

References

1. Abadi, D., Ailamaki, A., Andersen, D., Bailis, P., et al.: The seattle report on database research. SIGMOD Rec. **48**(4), 44–53 (2020)
2. Abramatic, J.F., Di Cosmo, R., Zacchiroli, S.: Building the universal archive of source code. Commun. ACM **61**(10), 29–31 (2018)
3. Bellahsene, Z., Bonifati, A., Rahm, E.: Schema Matching and Mapping, 1st edn. Springer, Cham (2011)
4. Bird, C., Menzies, T., Zimmermann, T.: The Art and Science of Analyzing Software Data, 1st edn. Morgan Kaufmann Publishers Inc., San Francisco (2015)
5. Collberg, C., Proebsting, T.A.: Repeatability in computer systems research. Commun. ACM **59**(3), 62–69 (2016)
6. Curino, C.A., Moon, H.J., Zaniolo, C.: Graceful database schema evolution: the prism workbench. VLDB Endow. **1**, 761–772 (2008)
7. Curino, C.A., Tanca, L., Moon, H.J., Zaniolo, C.: Schema evolution in Wikipedia: toward a web information system benchmark. In: Proceedings of ICEIS 2008 (2008)
8. Lin, D.Y., Neamtiu, I.: Collateral evolution of applications and databases. In: Proceedings of IWPSE-Evol 2009 (2009)
9. Manolescu, I., Afanasiev, L., Arion, A., Dittrich, J., et al.: The repeatability experiment of SIGMOD 2008. SIGMOD Rec. **37**(1), 39–45 (2008)
10. Moon, H.J., Curino, C.A., Deutsch, A., Hou, C.Y., Zaniolo, C.: Managing and querying transaction-time databases under schema evolution. VLDB Endow. **1**, 882–895 (2008)
11. Neamtiu, I., Lin, D.Y., Uddin, R.: Safe on-the-fly relational schema evolution. Technical report (2009)
12. Pawlik, M., Hütter, T., Kocher, D., Mann, W., Augsten, N.: A link is not enough - reproducibility of data. Datenbank-Spektrum **19**(2), 107–115 (2019)
13. Qiu, D., Li, B., Su, Z.: An empirical analysis of the co-evolution of schema and code in database applications. In: Proceedings of ESEC/FSE 2013 (2013)
14. Sjøberg, D.: Quantifying schema evolution. Inf. Softw. Technol. **35**(1), 35–44 (1993)
15. Vassiliadis, P., Zarras, A.V., Skoulis, I.: How is life for a table in an evolving relational schema? Birth, death and everything in between. In: Johannesson, P., Lee, M.L., Liddle, S.W., Opdahl, A.L., López, Ó.P. (eds.) ER 2015. LNCS, vol. 9381, pp. 453–466. Springer, Cham (2015). https://doi.org/10.1007/978-3-319-25264-3_34
16. Wu, S., Neamtiu, I.: Schema evolution analysis for embedded databases. In: Proceedings of ICDE Workshops 2011 (2011)

Challenges in Checking JSON Schema Containment over Evolving Real-World Schemas

Michael Fruth[1], Mohamed-Amine Baazizi[2], Dario Colazzo[3], Giorgio Ghelli[4], Carlo Sartiani[5], and Stefanie Scherzinger[1(✉)]

[1] University of Passau, Passau, Germany
{michael.fruth,stefanie.scherzinger}@uni-passau.de
[2] Sorbonne Université, LIP6 UMR 7606, Paris, France
baazizi@ia.lip6.fr
[3] Université Paris-Dauphine, PSL Research University, Paris, France
dario.colazzo@dauphine.fr
[4] Dipartimento di Informatica, Università di Pisa, Pisa, Italy
ghelli@di.unipi.it
[5] DIMIE, Università della Basilicata, Potenza, Italy
carlo.sartiani@unibas.it

Abstract. JSON Schema is maturing into the de-facto schema language for JSON documents. When JSON Schema declarations evolve, the question arises how the new schema will deal with JSON documents that still adhere to the legacy schema. This is particularly crucial in the maintenance of software APIs. In this paper, we present the results of our empirical study of the first generation of tools for checking JSON Schema containment which we apply to a diverse collection of over 230 real-world schemas and their altogether 1k historic versions. We assess two such special-purpose tools w.r.t. their applicability to real-world schemas and identify weak spots. Based on this analysis, we enumerate specific open research challenges that are based on real-world problems.

Keywords: JSON Schema containment · Empirical study

1 Introduction

With the proliferation of JSON as a data exchange format, there is a need for a schema language that describes JSON data: By relying on schema languages, software developers can reduce the burden of defensive programming, since they can trust their input to adhere to certain constraints [9]. Among various proposals for a JSON schema language (see [1] for an overview), JSON Schema (link available in the PDF) is on its way to standardization. First results on the theoretical properties of this language have already been published [4,11].

When schemas evolve as part of larger software projects, the question arises how the new schema version compares to the previous version. For instance,

G. Grossmann and S. Ram (Eds.): ER 2020 Workshops, LNCS 12584, pp. 220–230, 2020.
https://doi.org/10.1007/978-3-030-65847-2_20

```
1   { "properties":{        { "properties":{
2       "fruit":{               "fruit":{
3         "enum":[               "enum":[
4           "apple",              "apple",
5   -        "pear"      +         "pear",
6   ] } } }            +         "banana"
7                      ] } } }
```

Fig. 1. JSON Schema document E_1 (left) is a sub-schema of E_2 (right).

developers will want to know whether the new API (described by a schema) will still accept input from legacy clients; if not, developers risk runtime errors. Decisions on *JSON Schema containment*, e.g., whether the language declared by one schema is a subset of the other, require tool support. One such tool is json-schema-diff-validator (link available in PDF). The 1.7k–14k weekly downloads from npmjs since 5-Jan-2020 confirm a strong demand. JSON Schema containment has recently also been explored in academic research [8].

In this paper, we conduct an empirical study on tools for checking JSON Schema containment, which we refer to as *JSC-tools*: We apply JSC-tools on a diverse collection of JSON Schema documents. In particular, we set out to identify weak spots in these tools which are rooted in genuine research challenges.

Contributions. Our paper makes the following contributions:

- We apply state-of-the-art JSC-tools to schemas hosted on SchemaStore (link available in the PDF), where developers share real-world JSON Schema documents for re-use. As of today, SchemaStore is the largest collection of its kind. From the GitHub repository backing this website, we analyze over 230 schemas, with a total of over 1k historical versions.
- We investigate three research questions: (RQ1) We assess the applicability on JSC-tools on real-world schemas, i.e., the share of schemas that can be correctly processed. (RQ2) We ask which real-world language features are difficult to handle. (RQ3) We further determine the degree of consensus among JSC-tools applied to the same input, as an indicator whether classification decisions can be relied upon.
- Based on the insights thus gained, we identify open research challenges.
- We publish our fully automated analysis pipeline, to allow fellow researchers to build upon and reproduce our results.

Structure. In Sect. 2, we motivate that checking JSON Schema containment is not trivial. In Sect. 3, we describe our methodology. We address our research questions and present our results in Sect. 4, with a discussion of research opportunities in Sect. 5. We cover potential threats to validity in Sect. 6, and discuss related work in Sect. 7. Section 8 concludes.

2   Examples of JSON Schema Containment

We motivate that checking JSON Schema containment is not trivial. Our examples are based on instances of JSON Schema evolution that we have observed on SchemaStore. We basic assume familiarity with JSON syntax and otherwise refer to [4] for an introduction to the JSON data model.

```
1    { "properties":{              { "properties":{
2        "address":{                   "address":{
3    -        "type": "string"    +        "properties":{
4    } } }                         +            "street": { "type": "string" },
5                                  +            "number": { "type": "integer" },
6                                  +            "city":   { "type": "string" } }
7                                      } } }
```

Fig. 2. JSON Schema document S_1 (left) is a sub-schema of S_2 (right).

Conditional Semantics. Let us consider schema E_1, shown left in Fig. 1. The JSON Schema language employs a conditional semantics, demanding that *if* a JSON value is an object, and *if* that object has a property named fruit, then its value must be either the string "apple" or "pear". Hence, {"fruit": "banana"} is invalid, yet the raw string value "banana" is valid, since it is not an object. Objects without a property fruit are also valid, such as {"vegetable": "potato"}.

Extending Enumerations. Let us assume that the schema is changed to E_2, as shown in Fig. 1 (right). We employ a diff-based notation, showing the original and the changed schema side-by-side. Removed lines are prefixed with minus, added lines are prefixed with plus. In line 5, a comma is added at the end of the line, and item banana is added in line 6. The document {"fruit": "banana"} is now valid w.r.t. schema E_2. We say schema E_1 is a sub-schema of E_2, since the language it defines is a subset of the language defined by E_2.

Introducing Objects. Schema S_1 in Fig. 2 (left) specifies that if a JSON document is an object with a property named address, then the value of this property is of type string. Thus, document D : {"address": "Burbank California"} is valid w.r.t. S_1. We now refactor the schema to S_2, as shown. Document D is still valid w.r.t. the new schema S_2, as the conditional semantics only imposes restrictions if the type of the address is an object. On the other hand, a JSON document with an address structured as an object is not valid w.r.t. schema S_1, which expects a string. Hence, S_1 is a sub-schema of S_2.

Adding New Properties. We continue with schema S_2 and extend the address properties by "zip": {"type": "integer"} (inserted after line 6 in Fig. 2 on the right), declaring that ZIP codes must be integer values. We refer to this new schema as S_3. Schema S_2 allows any type for the ZIP code (e.g. string: "zip": "1234"), as additional properties are allowed by default. Thus, schema S_3 is more restrictive than S_2 and therefore a sub-schema of S_2.

Summary. Reasoning whether schema containment holds is not trivial, even for toy examples. With real-world schemas, which can be large and complex [10], we absolutely need the support of well-principled tools. Assessing the state-of-the-art in such JSC-tools is the aim of our upcoming empirical study.

3 Methodology

3.1 Context Description

Schema Collection. We target the JSON Schema documents hosted on Schema-Store, a website backed by GitHub, as of 19-Jun-2020 (commit hash c48c727).

JSC-Tools. The JSC-tool json-schema-diff-validator, mentioned in the Introduction, only compares syntactic changes: nodes added, removed, and replaced are considered breaking changes. This can lead to incorrect decisions regarding schema containment, e.g., for the schemas from Fig. 2. We therefore exclude this tool from our analysis.

Instead, we consider two tools that perform a *semantic* analysis, one tool from academia, and another from an open source development project. Since the tools have rather similar names, we refer to them as Tool A and Tool B:

- Tool A is called jsonsubschema (link available in the PDF) and is an academic prototype implemented in Python, based on well-principled theory [8]. Based on the authors' recommendation (in personal communication), we use the GitHub version with commit hash 165f893.
  Tool A supports JSON Schema Draft 4 without recursion, and has only limited support for negation (**not**) and union (**anyOf**).
- Tool B, is-json-schema-subset (link available in the PDF) is also open source and implemented in TypeScript. We use the most recent version available at the time of our analysis (version 1.1.15). Tool B supports JSON Schema Drafts 5 and higher. No further limitations are stated.

3.2 Analysis Process

Our data analysis pipeline is fully automated. The Python 3.7 scripts for our data preparation and analysis pipeline, as well as the raw input data, are available for reproduction analysis.[1] We use the Python modules jsonschema (version 3.2.0) and jsonref (version 0.2) for JSON Schema validation and dereferencing.

Obtaining Schema Versions. We retrieve the historic versions of all JSON Schema documents hosted on SchemaStore from the master branch of its GitHub repository (link available in the PDF), provided that they are reachable by path **src/schemas/json/**. This yields 248 schemas. About half of them have not changed since their initial commit, while some schemas count over 60

---

[1] https://github.com/michaelfruth/jsc-study.

Table 1. Comparing both JSC-tools in two separate experiments: (a) Table 1a shows *reflexivity* of schema equivalence ($\equiv$) for all 1,028 schemas ($\perp$ denotes runtime errors). Table rows show results for Tool A, columns for Tool B. (b) Table 1b states results of checking 796 pairs of *successive schema versions* w.r.t. equivalence, strict containment ($\subset, \supset$), incomparability ($\|$), and runtime errors.

(a) Schema reflexivity.

Tool B

Tool A	$\equiv$	$\perp$	Σ
$\equiv$	36.9%	0.2%	37.1%
$\perp$	48.2%	14.7%	62.9%
Σ	85.1%	14.9%	100.0%

(b) Succeeding schema versions.

Tool B

Tool A	$\equiv$	$\subset$	$\supset$	$\|$	$\perp$
$\equiv$	**9.5%**	0.3%	0.3%	0.4%	0.0%
$\subset$	3.0%	**2.9%**	0.3%	1.6%	0.0%
$\supset$	5.7%	0.0%	**1.0%**	1.1%	0.0%
$\|$	3.4%	0.6%	0.5%	**2.6%**	0.4%
$\perp$	25.9%	3.3%	0.5%	17.1%	**19.7%**

historic versions. In total, we obtain 1,069 historic schema versions which we have validated to ensure they are syntactically correct JSON Schema documents.

Excluding Schema Versions from Analysis. One practical challenge is that the JSC-tools considered support non-overlapping drafts of JSON Schema, while we need to process the same document with both tools. As a workaround, we determine the subset of documents that are both valid w.r.t. Draft 4, Draft 6, and Draft 7, thereby excluding four documents.

Regarding drafts, we need to take further care: JSON Schema is designed as an open standard, which means that a validator will accept/ignore unknown language elements that are introduced in a future draft. Then, running both tools on the same schema document constitutes an unfair comparison, since the tools will have to treat these elements differently. We therefore search for keywords introduced/changed *after* Draft 4 (e.g., `const` or `if-then-else`). In total, we thus exclude 41 documents, a choice that we also discuss in Sect. 6.

Overall, we obtain 1,028 JSON Schema documents, where approx. 10% contain recursive references. We count 232 schemas in their latest version and 796 pairs of documents that are two versions of the same schema, ordered by the time of their commits, where no other commit has changed the schema in between. In the following, we refer to such pairs as *successive schema versions*.

4   Detailed Study Results

4.1   RQ1: What Is the Real-World Applicability of JSC-Tools?

We are interested in the share of real-world schemas that the JSC-tools can reliably process. This is an indicator whether these tools are operational in practice. To this end, we perform a basic check: Given a valid JSON Schema document S, equivalence is reflexive ($S \equiv S$). Given this ground truth, we compare each schema version with itself.

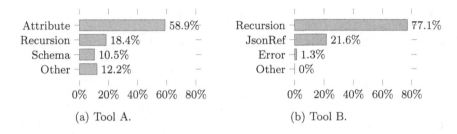

Fig. 3. Error distribution (in %) for the experiment from Table 1a.

The results are shown in Table 1a. The first row states the percentage of documents that Tool A recognizes as equivalent. The second row states the percentage of documents where Tool A fails (denoted "⊥"). "Σ" shows sums over rows/columns. The results for Tool B are shown in columns. The top left entry states that for less than half of the documents, both tools agree they are equivalent to itself. About 15% of documents cannot be checked by either tool.

Results. We observe a high failure rate for Tool A. In the experiments conducted by Habib et al. [8], the authors of Tool A, Tool B performs comparatively worse than Tool A. Further investigations, performing experiments with the exact same version of Tool B as used in [8], have revealed that the applicability of Tool B has meanwhile improved. Moreover the experiments in [8] consider a different schema collection, as we also discuss in Sect. 7.

Since not all real-world language features are supported by Tool A, our first experiment is evidently setting up Tool A for failure. We next look more closely into which language features are problematic.

4.2   RQ2: Which Language Features Are Difficult to Handle?

We are interested in which properties of real-world schemas cause JSC-tools to fail, either because not yet supported or incorrectly handled. As a first step, we inspect the error messages for documents that cannot be processed in the first experiment. Figure 3 visualizes the distribution of the top-3 runtime errors. While the tools use different names in error reporting, it is obvious that recursion and reference errors are frequent.

To further investigate which operators of JSON Schema are problematic, we consider subsets of our document collection, where we exclude schemas with certain language features. In particular, we check pairs of successive schema versions for containment. We register when a tool decides that the schema versions are equivalent; if not, whether the language declared by the predecessor version is a sub-set of the language declared by the successor version, or a super-set. In all remaining non-error cases, we consider the versions incomparable.

In Fig. 4, we show the relative results for (i) the entire collection, (ii) a subset where all references are non-recursive, contain only document-internal references or references to URLs, which can be resolved, (iii) a subset without **not**, and

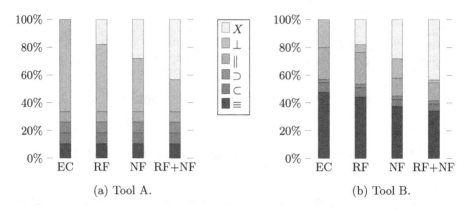

Fig. 4. Checking pairs of successive schemas on (i) the entire collection (EC: 796 pairs), (ii) a subset where all references are non-recursive, document-internal or URLs, and can be resolved (RF: 652 pairs), (iii) without **not** (NF: 572 pairs), and (iv) the combination of (ii) and (iii) (RF+NF: 451 pairs). "X" represents excluded schema documents. Reporting decisions in % of the entire collection.

(iv) the combination of all these restrictions. For Tool A, the classification decisions remain identical throughout, only the error rate decreases. This means we have indeed excluded the problematic schema documents. With Tool B, the classification decisions vary slightly, but we see the error rate decrease to ca. 2%.

Results. Recursion and negation are obvious challenges for JSC-tools. While Tool A explicitly does not support recursion, and negation only to some extent, Tool B (where no limitations are specified) struggles with these language constructs as well. However, recursion and negation do occur in real-world JSON Schema documents, and we refer to Sect. 5 for a discussion of which use cases for JSON Schema are affected when these features are not supported.

4.3 RQ3: What Is the Degree of Consensus Among JSC-Tools?

To assess how well both tools agree, we compare successive schema versions w.r.t. the classification decisions of both tools. Table 1b summarizes the results. Again, results for Tool A are shown in rows, results for Tool B in columns. In an ideal world, the JSC-tools completely agree, so we expect a diagonal matrix (with zeroes in all cells except on the diagonal). However, the tools disagree *considerably*. For instance, for 5.7% of the pairs, Tool A claims that the first schema version declares a super-language of the second, while Tool B regards both versions as equivalent (row $\supset$/column $\equiv$). The tools agree on only approx. 50% of subset of inputs that both tools can process without a runtime error.

Results. Evidently, the degree of consensus is low. Since developers cannot yet rely on JSC-tools, they are forced to visually compare evolving schemas, near-impossible for the complex and large schemas encountered in the real world (some schemas on SchemaStore take up over 10MB stored on disk [10]). In the upcoming discussion, we discuss open research questions in this context.

5 Discussion of Results and Research Opportunities

Summary. Our experiments show that the first generation of JSC-tools is still in an early stage where recursion and negation in schemas are not yet well covered.

In earlier work [10], we have manually categorized all SchemaStore schemas depending on their purpose: *data* schemas use JSON primarily as a data format. *meta* schemas define markup for other schemas. For instance, there are JSON *meta* schemas for every JSON Schema Draft. *conf* schemas describe JSON documents that configure services. *app* schemas are used for data exchange between applications.[2] This categorization provides a general overview how JSON Schema is employed in practice. Aligning the documents excluded in the experiments from Fig. 4 reveals that by ignoring recursive schemas, we primarily exclude *conf* and *meta* schemas. By ignoring schemas with negation, we again mainly exclude *conf* schemas. In summary, the JSC-tools best cover *data* and *app* schemas, while on SchemaStore, *conf* schemas constitute the largest group.

Research Opportunities. Making JSC-tools operable for production is more than just an engineering effort, and we see several opportunities for impactful research:

- Handling *recursion and negation* in checking JSON Schema containment is still unresolved. As recursion combined with negation is a general challenge in database theory, e.g., when specifying sound semantics for Datalog, we may expect some concepts to transfer (as also proposed in [4]).
- Not only do practitioners need robust and complete tools for inclusion checking, they also need to understand why containment holds/does not hold:
  - This could be done by means of *instance generation*, i.e., generating a small example document that captures why the schemas differ. A first proposal for witness generation is sketched in [2].
  - Alternatively, pointing to the positions in the schema declarations that cause containment checks to fail would also provide some degree of *explainability* for developers comparing schemas.
- Having reliable JSC-tools at hand would allow us to build editors that assist with schema refactoring. Then, a JSC-tool can confirm that the refactored schema is still equivalent to its original (while the new version may be easier to comprehend, easier to validate, or simply more succinct).
- We have come to realize that the data management community is in need of a dedicated micro-benchmark for JSC-tools, with small yet realistic documents where we know the ground truth w.r.t. schema containment. Such a benchmark would certainly benefit researchers and practitioners alike.

---

[2] Naturally, such a classification is always subjective, and not necessarily unique, as also remarked in the original work on DTDs [5] that inspired this categorization.

6   Potential Threats to Validity

Supported JSON Schema Drafts. As stated in Sect. 3, the JCS-tools employed in this study support different drafts of JSON Schema: Tool A handles Draft 4, Tool B handles Draft 5+. Due to the open standard policy of JSON Schema, a keyword introduced in Draft 5+ is ignored by Tool A, but will carry meaning for Tool B. As discussed, in order to level the playing field, we exclude affected documents from our analysis: We have diligently checked for keywords, and regard the risk that we may have overlooked problematic documents as minor.

Recursion in Schemas. We noticed minor differences in reporting recursion errors in the Python-based Tool A and the TypeScript-based Tool B, which we trace back to the different programming languages and their libraries. Specifically, we noticed spurious, non-deterministic behavior in the `jsonschema` module for recursive schemas. However, this affects only a handful of JSON Schema documents and is a minor threat to our results at large.

Renaming Schema Files. In our analysis, we consider all historic versions of a schema based on `git` commits. For `git` to recognize that a file is renamed, the content of the file must remain the same. Due to (so far) 13 renamings in the history of SchemaStore, our collection contains 13 duplicate schema versions. Since this is a small number in the context of over 1k schema versions analyzed, this again is a minor threat.

Mining `git` and GitHub. In mining `git` repositories, we face the usual and well understood threats [3]. Our analysis is based on a specific schema collection. One threat to validity is that the historic schema versions in this collection are skewed: Only eight schemas account for almost one third of all historic schema versions. Nevertheless, SchemaStore is to date the largest and also most diverse collection of JSON Schema documents, and thus highly suitable for our purposes.

7   Related Work

There is a mature body of work on schema containment for XML schemas (such as DTDs and XML Schema), e.g. [9], based on automata as the formal vehicle [7]. Other approaches exist that rather relay on a particular class of constraints to check inclusion between XML schemas like Extended DTDs featuring regular expressions with interleaving and counting [6].

First theoretical properties of the JSON Schema language have been studied recently [4,11]. To the best of our knowledge, the tool by Habib et al. [8] ("Tool A" in our study) is the first academic exploration of JSON Schema containment. Their experiments are closest to our work, since they also compare Tools A and B on real-world JSON Schema documents, but they use a different baseline. In particular, the authors choose three sources for JSON Schema documents, while SchemaStore hosts schemas from over 200 different sources.

It seems plausible that the schema collection studied by us is not only larger in terms of the number of distinct schemas (each with its historic versions), but overall also more diverse, while skewed towards schemas for configuring services [10]. This may explain some of the differences in our respective experiments regarding the successful applicability to real-world schemas, plus the fact that Tool B has meanwhile been improved (see our discussion in Sect. 4.1).

In general, checking JSON Schema containment is not a trivial task: As JSON Schema is not an algebraic language, syntactic and semantic interactions between different keywords in the same schema object complicate programmatic handling. In [2], we therefore propose a dedicated algebra for JSON Schema, which has the potential to serve as a formal foundation for new approaches to checking JSON Schema containment.

8 Conclusion

In this paper, we evaluate a first generation of tools for checking JSON Schema containment. Our analysis shows that this is still a *very* young field, with open research opportunities that have immediate practical relevance.

In particular, we recognize the need for a micro-benchmark for JSC-tools. While there is a well-adopted benchmark for JSON Schema validation, the JSON Schema Test Suite (link available in the PDF), no comparable benchmark exists for checking JSON Schema containment, with pairs of documents for which containment was determined manually, for a particular operator or a logical group of operators. Such a micro-benchmark could be inspired by real-world schemas found on SchemaStore. We plan to address this in our future work.

Acknowledgments. This project was partly supported by the *Deutsche Forschungsgemeinschaft* (DFG, German Research Foundation), grant #385808805.

References

1. Baazizi, M.A., Colazzo, D., Ghelli, G., Sartiani, C.: Schemas and types for JSON data: from theory to practice. In: Proceedings of the 2019 International Conference on Management of Data (SIGMOD), pp. 2060–2063 (2019)
2. Baazizi, M.A., Colazzo, D., Ghelli, G., Sartiani, C., Scherzinger, S.: Not elimination and witness generation for JSON schema. In: BDA 2020 (2020)
3. Bird, C., Rigby, P.C., Barr, E.T., Hamilton, D.J., Germán, D.M., Devanbu, P.T.: The promises and perils of mining Git. In: Proceedings of the 6th International Working Conference on Mining Software Repositories (MSR), pp. 1–10 (2009)
4. Bourhis, P., Reutter, J.L., Suárez, F., Vrgoc, D.: JSON: data model, query languages and schema specification. In: Proceedings of the 36th ACM SIGMOD-SIGACT-SIGAI Symposium on Principles of Database Systems (PODS), pp. 123–135 (2017)
5. Choi, B.: What are real DTDs like? In: Proceedings of the Fifth International Workshop on the Web and Databases (WebDB), pp. 43–48 (2002)
6. Colazzo, D., Ghelli, G., Pardini, L., Sartiani, C.: Efficient asymmetric inclusion of regular expressions with interleaving and counting for XML type-checking. Theor. Comput. Sci. **492**, 88–116 (2013)

7. Comon, H., et al.: Tree Automata Techniques and Applications. http://tata.gforge.inria.fr/ (2007). Release October, 12th 2007
8. Habib, A., Shinnar, A., Hirzel, M., Pradel, M.: Type Safety with JSON Subschema. CoRR abs/1911.12651v2 (2020). http://arxiv.org/abs/1911.12651v2
9. Lee, T.Y.T., Cheung, D.W.l.: XML schema computations: schema compatibility testing and subschema extraction. In: Proceedings of the 19th ACM International Conference on Information and Knowledge Management (CIKM), pp. 839–848 (2010)
10. Maiwald, B., Riedle, B., Scherzinger, S.: What are real JSON schemas like? In: Guizzardi, G., Gailly, F., Suzana Pitangueira Maciel, R. (eds.) ER 2019. LNCS, vol. 11787, pp. 95–105. Springer, Cham (2019). https://doi.org/10.1007/978-3-030-34146-6_9
11. Pezoa, F., Reutter, J.L., Suárez, F., Ugarte, M., Vrgoc, D.: Foundations of JSON schema. In: Proceedings of the 25th International Conference on World Wide Web (WWW), pp. 263–273 (2016)

Experimental Practices for Measuring the Intuitive Comprehensibility of Modeling Constructs: An Example Design

Sotirios Liaskos[✉], Mehrnaz Zhian, and Ibrahim Jaouhar

School of Information Technology, York University,
4700 Keele St., Toronto M3J 1P3, Canada
{liaskos,mzhian,jaouhar}@yorku.ca

Abstract. Conceptual model comprehensibility has attracted the interest of many experimental researchers over the past decades. Several studies have employed a variety of definitions and operationalizations of the comprehensibility construct as well as procedures for measuring it on a variety of model types. Intuitive comprehensibility is a specialization of the construct, referring to model or language comprehensibility exhibited by partially trained users. We present an experimental design for measuring the intuitive comprehensibility of a proposed extension to a goal modeling language as a means for reviewing experimental practices we have followed for similar studies in the past. Through such review, we hope to demonstrate the possibility of experimental design and technique reusability and its role as a motivating factor for more experimentation within the conceptual modeling research community.

Keywords: Model comprehensibility/understandability · Empirical conceptual modelling · Goal models

1 Introduction

Experimentally evaluating the quality of conceptual models and conceptual modeling languages has enjoyed substantial attention from researchers over the past decades. Various studies have explored how users interact with diagrammatic representations and how they perceive modeling constructs represented in such ways. Often, the subject of investigation is the *comprehensibility* of models, and various interpretations of the meaning of this construct have been utilized both in theory and in empirical measurement [11].

A specialization of comprehensibility has been put forth that is concerned with the level of understanding of information appearing in a diagrammatically presented conceptual model by viewers with limited training in the corresponding conceptual modeling language. The working term *intuitiveness* has been proposed for this construct and a number of studies have been performed by

© Springer Nature Switzerland AG 2020
G. Grossmann and S. Ram (Eds.): ER 2020 Workshops, LNCS 12584, pp. 231–241, 2020.
https://doi.org/10.1007/978-3-030-65847-2_21

our group for assessing it in requirements goal models [1,14,17,18] and independently elsewhere in process and other diagrams [3,12,22]. Our experiments focussed on the intuitiveness of a specific language construct, namely contribution links within goal models, and the role thereof in making decisions within such models. Through these experiments we adopted and/or developed a set of methodological practices that we found served the purpose of studying the particular construct and may be applicable to a larger class of studies.

In this paper, we describe these practices and discuss their strengths and weaknesses, via presentation of an experimental design for a future study on the intuitiveness of temporal precedence constructs within goal models. We elaborate on the intuitiveness construct (Sect. 2), offer an introduction to our example study (Sect. 3) and describe our proposed design as an opportunity to also reflect on our experimental practices (Sect. 4). We conclude in Sect. 5.

2   Comprehensibility and Intuitiveness

Several efforts to empirically study comprehensibility of conceptual models have emerged in the literature, albeit with no clear consensus of what exactly the construct means and how it is to be measured, as reported by Houy et al. [11]. A possible starting point for understanding the construct may be found in SEQUAL, a semiotic framework for organizing conceptual model qualities [13]. There, the concept of *(manual) model activation* is put forth to describe the ability of models to guide the actions of human actors. Comprehensibility of a model is found within the category of *pragmatic quality* of a conceptual model, measured by the appropriateness of the model's activation. In other words, by being exposed to the model and its information, users (i.e., readers) of the model act (perform inferences, respond to questions, organize their work, make decisions etc.) in ways that satisfy the model, according to the designers of the latter. For example, a business process model is comprehensible by process actors, if, once they read it, said actors, organize their work, communicate with co-workers, answer process questions, troubleshoot etc. in ways that are compliant with the model – according to the model developers.

Model comprehensibility is distinct from *comprehensibility appropriateness of language* [9,24] which refers to the ability of the language to be the basis for the building of comprehensible models. From an empirical standpoint, this would, in principle, be measured by means of evaluating the comprehensibility of samples of several models developed in accordance to a language, controlling for factors that may affect model comprehensibility independent of the language, such as representation medium appropriateness, visual/physical quality [21] or, otherwise, language use. For such controlling and sample identification to be tractable, evaluation may take place at the individual construct level (e.g. individual elements, visualizations and relationship types) and/or a specific language feature or structural pattern (e.g. use of models for a specific task).

Intuitive comprehensibility appropriateness of a language, or part thereof or *language/construct intuitive comprehensibility* or, simply here, *(language/ construct) intuitiveness*, refers to comprehensibility appropriateness exhibited by

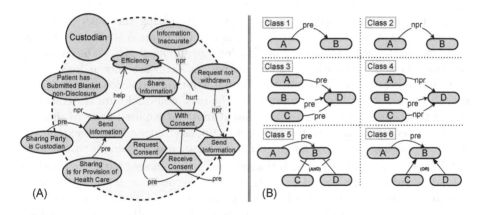

Fig. 1. (A) Goal model with preconditions—(B) Experimental models

users who have had limited previous exposure to the modeling language. The addition of the intuitiveness requirement is motivated by the need to make languages usable by users who would not otherwise dedicate effort to receive training in the language at hand. All else being equal, it is preferable that a language can be effectively used – i.e., allow models that lead to compliant activation – with less required training. Note that the definition of intuitiveness is here distinct from the concept of intuition (versus, e.g., reflection) studied in dual-process cognitive psychology [6,10], in that the former is agnostic to the exact cognitive process employed to interpret and make use of the constructs.

Our work – like much other literature, e.g., [8] – has been focussing on the intuitiveness of the diagrammatic representation choices of the language, i.e., whether shapes and symbols that appear on the diagram allow users to instantly know how to make correct use with the model. In Moody's terms [21] this is *semantic transparency* of the visual constructs, i.e. the ability of notational elements to communicate their meaning. While intuitiveness can be studied at the concept level alone [15] when expressed in natural language and, thus, free from the interference of visualization choices, our discussion here concerns the evaluation of the combination of the concept and its visualization.

3   Example: Preconditions in Diagrammatic Goal Models

To see how a study of intuitiveness appears in the process of language design we consider an example from the goal modeling domain. Goal models have been extensively studied with regards to their ability to represent intentional structures of stakeholders [2,25]. In the latest goal modeling standard, iStar 2.0 [5], elements such as *actors*, their *goals* and ways by which the latter can be decomposed into other goals or *tasks*, through *AND-refinements* and *OR-refinements* are presented. A diagrammatic notation faithful to the tradition of the original i^* language is used to visualize the concepts.

Such goal diagram appears in Fig. 1(A), representing the ways by which, according to a jurisdiction, a custodian of health information is allowed to share such information with another agent. The legal requirement is that the custodian can share health information without the patient's consent only as long as the third party is another custodian, the sharing is for the provision of health care and that the patient has not submitted a blanket non-disclosure statement. If any of these conditions are not met, consent must be acquired prior to sharing.

To model constraints such as the above, suppose that we want to extend the iStar 2.0 language to allow for *precondition* (resp. *negative precondition*) links $\{B \xrightarrow{pre} A\}$ (resp. $\{B \xrightarrow{npr} A\}$). Intuitively, such link shows that a goal/task A cannot be pursued/performed *unless* (resp. *if*) some condition B is met, including that some other goal/task has been achieved/performed or that some state of the world is believed to be true – for representing the latter *beliefs* are added in the diagram. A rigorous semantics of such or similar links is possible [16]. In setting up such semantics, however, designers often have flexibility. For example, what is the rule for combining multiple $\xrightarrow{pre}$ and $\xrightarrow{npr}$ arriving at an element such as *Send Information*; is it a conjunction, a disjunction, or something else? Most designers would probably opt for conjunction, but what if users of the diagram insist to act as if it were a disjunction? Likewise, what does it mean for users that a goal is "pursued"? Given $\{$*Information Inaccurate* $\xrightarrow{npr}$ *Share Information*$\}$ can I allow interpretations in which some *but not all* of the subtasks of goal *Share Information* are performed if *Information Inaccurate* holds, pretending that, e.g., performance of the tasks is for the pursuit of other unmentioned goals? Most designers would probably say no, but what if users act as if that was the correct interpretation? Disagreements between designer intent and user interpretation may imply that either the language features (allowing multiple incoming preconditions and allowing a precondition to a decomposed goal) or their visual representation deserve some reexamination.

In what follows, we use the problem of evaluating this hypothetical language extension to review our past experimental practices and experiences we acquired by applying such practices in similar problems.

4   Experimental Strategy

Our experimental approach consists of: (a) developing models that exemplify the construct or feature that we want evaluated and differ based on factors of interest, (b) identifying a participant sample that can be seen as representative of a user population, (c) partially training participants, (d) exposing participants to the models, observing inferences they perform therewith and comparing them with the ones language designers consider correct. We address these for our example problem.

4.1   Model Sampling

Model Format. When evaluation targets a specific construct or feature, the sampled models are constructed to exactly exemplify use of the construct or feature and abstract away other extraneous elements that may interfere with the measurement. In most of our earlier work [1, 14, 18], for example, we studied the intuitiveness of various representations of contribution links in goal models for the purpose of identifying optimal decisions in such models. Given such narrow focus, sample models were structurally constrained: one OR-decomposition and a soft-goal-only sub-graph connected with contributions in a restricted way. No elements of the language that were extraneous to the research question were included – e.g. actors or AND-decompositions. Elsewhere [17], our samples were even simpler, containing two goals and one contribution link.

The advantage of such focused manufacturing of experimental units are (a) better experimental control and definition of factors (see below), (b) reduced need for training about unrelated modeling constructs. The disadvantages are: (a) the generalizability argument relies on showing that the manufactured models capture the "essence" of the language construct and its use under evaluation, (b) influential (but unknown) factors that exist in real-world models are absent.

An additional variable is how much context should be added to the example models. This can come in the form of: (a) real element descriptions in place of symbolic variables, (b) scenarios that create an even more elaborate context. In our example, we can use uninterpreted literals as in $\{B \xrightarrow{pre} A\}$, refer to specific goals as in Fig. 1(A), or, do the latter and also add introductory material on the health information sharing case. While one can argue that such context information supports external validity by making the model samples more similar to the respective generalization class (real models), they have the potential of disturbing internal validity by switching the focus from the modeling construct to the content. For example, in $\{Request\ Consent \xrightarrow{pre} Receive\ Consent\}$, the precondition relationship is so obvious from the content, that measurement of the influence of $\xrightarrow{pre}$ in conveying such relationship is confounded.

Sample Models and Factors. When manufacturing sample models rather than sampling them in the wild, we have the benefit of introducing model-related factors of interest with more control. Such factors reflect properties, kinds or structural patterns of models, as per the research question. Our experience has shown that such factors are better treated in a *within-subjects* manner: the same participant is sequentially exposed to different classes of model structures, each such class being (part of) a level of the factor. In comparative studies, a *between-subjects* factor often emerges as well. In our past studies the comparison of various ways to represent a construct (e.g. in [14, 17]) was arranged in such between-subjects fashion. The need for different training for each level of the factor in question is one of the main motivators of the between-subjects choice.

Example Design. In our example study, we would devise various examples of precedence links using abstract literals *A, B, C, . . .* for the origin and destination goals, as seen in Fig. 1(B). Several examples of each of the six presented classes can be considered, noticing that: (a) Classes 1 and 3 versus Classes 2 and 4 constitute the two levels of a $\xrightarrow{npr}$ presence/absence factor, (b) Classes 1 and 2 versus Classes 3 and 4 constitute the two levels of a "complexity" factor. These factors are crossed allowing the study of interactions. Classes 5 and 6 can further be compared with each other and with Class 1 as baseline; noting that larger samples will need to be acquired to allow for meaningful statistical analysis. Thus, any or all of three within-subjects factors – negative precondition presence vs. absence, complex vs. simple and AND-decomposed vs. OR-decomposed vs. non-decomposed – can be studied. A between-subjects factor could be considered if we were to compare alternative ways to visualize $\xrightarrow{pre}$ and $\xrightarrow{npr}$, including adding comprehension aids, e.g. an AND arc to signify conjunction of $\xrightarrow{pre}$ links.

4.2 Training

Prior to being exposed to the models, participants are partially trained to the notation just enough so that the language's purpose and function is understood but the solutions to the experimental tasks do not directly follow from the training. We have extensively used short video presentations for such training. The benefits of video presentations over live lectures are manifold. Firstly, the exact training offered to participants is reviewable and reproducible. Secondly, in cases in which different language/construct versions need to be compared in a between-subjects manner, careful scripting and editing of the videos allows uniformity of training between groups. In our past experiments, videos have been fully recorded from script with only components that differ between groups appropriately video-edited. Thirdly, video presentations allow remote participation and consideration of on-line participant pools (more below).

As in any training, the threat in preparing video presentation remains that researcher bias can affect participant training in a way that skews the results towards one or the other direction. A possible way to address this is third-party evaluations or even development of training material. Despite such measures being practically difficult, video instead of in-classroom training removes many obstacles for such validation efforts.

Example Design. A video presentation can be developed to explain relevant goal modeling elements (goals, tasks, decomposition links) and the informal meaning of the $\xrightarrow{pre}$ and $\xrightarrow{npr}$ constructs, but would generally not describe specific uses of the construct for which we want to measure intuitiveness. For example, the video would not discuss how multiple $\xrightarrow{pre}$ links targeting the goal should be interpreted or elaborate on how pursuit of a goal is defined. When comparison with a baseline is desired such details can however be given in a separate control group or, less practically, in a within subjects pre-post manner [23].

4.3 Tasks

Experimental tasks are geared towards triggering and measuring model activation i.e. prompting, observing and recording *inferences* participants make with the displayed models. Parts of the theory of such inferences may need to be explained during training. In our study on assessing the intuitive comprehension of satisfaction propagation rules [17], the notions of partial and full goal satisfaction and denial had to be described in the videos. For the tasks, participants pick an inference that they think valid based on the model and their training. In our decision assessment studies [1,14,18], the task was a choice of goal alternative, while in our propagation rule study [17] it was the specification or choice of the satisfaction level of a recipient of a contribution link.

Example Design. In our example, the notion of a situation (i.e. a state in which goals have been achieved, tasks have been performed, or beliefs are held) satisfying or not the model, needs to be part of the video training. Then, each model is accompanied by descriptions of situations and participants are asked if the model satisfies the situations. For example, a model of Class 1 (Fig. 1(B)) can include the question whether $\{A, \neg B\}$ and $\{\neg A, \neg B\}$ are situations satisfying the link – which test whether participants perceive precondition as also a trigger condition, or whether they think that the presence of a link alone necessitates some satisfaction, as we actually observed with contribution links [17]. Notice how factors of interest can also be thus identified at the task level.

4.4 Operationalizations of Language Intuitiveness

The operationalization of the intuitive comprehension construct follows its theoretical definition (Sect. 2). The main measure we have used in the past is that of the level of agreement between participant responses to the experimental tasks (the model activation) and the normative answers to the questions (the language designer expectations), which agreement we refer to as *accuracy*. The accurate responses are then tallied up into an accuracy score used for the analysis. Calculation of *inter-respondent agreement* is also possible in the absence of a normative response. However, with such measures being aggregates of all participant responses, statistical inference possibilities are limited.

In some of our experiments we also asked the participants to rate their *confidence* to their response, using a Likert-type scale. Confidence can also be offered for the overall task, e.g., through one question in the end [18], which saves from execution time and perhaps allows for a more thoughtful response, but prevents analysis over the within-subjects factors. Whenever applicable, *response time* can also be relevant to understanding intuitive comprehension. However, both response time and confidence *alone* are not indicators of intuitive comprehension, in that participants may quickly and confidently provide inaccurate answers in the tasks. Nevertheless, following Jošt et al. [12], the ratio of accuracy over response time can also be an effective utilization of response time data.

Finally, in some of our experiments we invited participants to type-up a description of the method they used to make inferences and provide a response, as a proxy for a debriefing session. We have found that while some participants' textual descriptions can be usefully coded, they are often difficult to read and comprehend in any useful way. Note that both a debriefing sessions and response time measurements usually necessitate in-person administration.

Example Design. In the example experiment, we could measure accuracy, individual response confidence and, when possible, response time. Soliciting textual descriptions of how participants worked would not be a priority.

4.5   Participant Sampling

The appropriateness of using students as experimental participants is still debated in software engineering [7], where tasks are often specialized and require some technical ability. We believe that in conceptual modeling, user populations are wider and more diverse. Goal models, for instance, are to be used by any person whose intentions and decisions matter, and such persons can be of arbitrary backgrounds and abilities. Furthermore, intuitive comprehension of and distinction between concepts such as intentions, processes, events etc., is something that most senior college/University are expected to be able to perform. Following the same argument, in several instances we have also utilized on-line work platforms and particularly Mechanical Turk (MT). Such platforms have been found to be remarkably reliable for psychological experiments [4]. Assuming a commitment that the prospective users of the language under investigation is not limited to e.g. IT or management backgrounds, for certain simple tasks in conceptual modeling (e.g. discriminating among common concepts, associating notational symbols with concepts, making a decision on a daily-life problem via models) the MT samples appear to be suitable. Future correlation studies similar to the one performed by Crump et al. [4] would shed more light on the strength of this assumption.

Example Design. For our example design a mixture of University students and Mechanical Turk workers can be invited to participate.

4.6   Analysis

A likely approach for analysing data coming from designs such as the above is analysis of variance (ANOVA) [20]. In our most complex past cases such analysis included one between-subjects factor (e.g. a comparison of three visualizations) and one or two repeated-measures factors (e.g. model complexity and type). One problem we have faced with accuracy measures specifically is that, being integer values in the interval $[1..N]$, N the number of participant responses, they often violate normality assumptions – especially for small N, necessitating robust and/or non-parametric testing.

Further, looking at effect sizes is meaningful in our context. We have found that looking at a simple difference between means offers an intuitive picture. For example, that one group scores 1.5 (vs., e.g., 5) out of 20 accuracy points more compared to another is very informative vis-a-vis the practical importance of the effect, irrespective of statistical significance.

Finally, the generalization class needs to be carefully considered when performing inferences. With instruments such as the ones we described, the simplest generalization statement concerns the performance that participants in the entire population would demonstrate. An analytical step, however, needs to be taken to extend this generalization to the population of models, given that the sample models are manufactured specifically to find an effect rather than randomly sampled. Similar non-empirical arguments apply to generalizing to different kinds of activities with the models or in different contexts.

Example Design. In our example, parametric methods for repeated measures would be applied [20], accompanied with an equivalent robust test, if suspicion of violation of assumptions presents itself. Presence of a between-subjects factor entails a split-plot ("mixed") ANOVA whose likely deviation from assumptions, however, requires resorting to a complex range of countermeasures from transformations and bootstrapping to robust tests [19].

5 Concluding Remarks

We presented an experimental design for measuring the intuitiveness of a proposed extension to a conceptual modeling language, as a means to also review experimental practices we have been following to answer similar research questions in the past. Researchers in conceptual modeling often appear to dread the time, effort and risk associated with performing such studies. Our long term goal is to help develop standardized practices, patterns, techniques and tools that allow systematic, quick and efficient design and conduct of comprehensibility studies for use by researchers who otherwise could not afford the effort. Our focus so far has been decisively narrow within the constellation of phenomena that surround the development and use of conceptual models and their languages. However, it has promisingly allowed us to develop re-usable patterns and ideas within the sampling, measuring, training and analysis aspects that have substantially reduced required effort to set-up, run and analyse an experiment. Community-wide sharing, acceptance and continuous improvement of such cost-effective experimental practices, may make conceptual modeling researchers more eager to incorporate empirical investigation in their research.

References

1. Alothman, N., Zhian, M., Liaskos, S.: User perception of numeric contribution semantics for goal models: an exploratory experiment. In: Mayr, H.C., Guizzardi, G., Ma, H., Pastor, O. (eds.) ER 2017. LNCS, vol. 10650, pp. 451–465. Springer, Cham (2017). https://doi.org/10.1007/978-3-319-69904-2_34
2. Amyot, D., Mussbacher, G.: User requirements notation: the first ten years, the next ten years (invited paper). J. Softw. **6**(5), 747–768 (2011)

3. Bork, D., Schrüffer, C., Karagiannis, D.: Intuitive understanding of domain-specific modeling languages: proposition and application of an evaluation technique. In: Laender, A.H.F., Pernici, B., Lim, E.-P., de Oliveira, J.P.M. (eds.) ER 2019. LNCS, vol. 11788, pp. 311–319. Springer, Cham (2019). https://doi.org/10.1007/978-3-030-33223-5_26

4. Crump, M.J.C., McDonnell, J.V., Gureckis, T.M.: Evaluating Amazon's mech. Turk as a tool for experimental behavioral research. PLoS One **8**(3), 1–18 (2013)

5. Dalpiaz, F., Franch, X., Horkoff, J.: iStar 2.0 language guide. The Computing Research Repository (CoRR) abs/1605.0 (2016)

6. Evans, J.S.B.T.: Dual-processing accounts of reasoning, judgment, and social cognition. Annu. Rev. Psychol. **59**(1), 255–278 (2008)

7. Falessi, D., et al.: Empirical software engineering experts on the use of students and professionals in experiments. Empir. Softw. Eng. **23**(1), 452–489 (2017). https://doi.org/10.1007/s10664-017-9523-3

8. Gonçalves, E., Almendra, C., Goulão, M., Araújo, J., Castro, J.: Using empirical studies to mitigate symbol overload in iStar extensions. Softw. Syst. Model. **19**(3), 763–784 (2019). https://doi.org/10.1007/s10270-019-00770-9

9. Guizzardi, G.: Ontological foundations for structural conceptual models. Ph.D. thesis, University of Twente (2005)

10. Hadar, I.: When intuition and logic clash: the case of the object-oriented paradigm. Sci. Comput. Program. **78**(9), 1407–1426 (2013)

11. Houy, C., Fettke, P., Loos, P.: Understanding understandability of conceptual models – what are we actually talking about? In: Atzeni, P., Cheung, D., Ram, S. (eds.) ER 2012. LNCS, vol. 7532, pp. 64–77. Springer, Heidelberg (2012). https://doi.org/10.1007/978-3-642-34002-4_5

12. Jošt, G., Huber, J., Heričko, M., Polančič, G.: An empirical investigation of intuitive understandability of process diagrams. Comput. Stand. Interfaces **48**, 90–111 (2016)

13. Krogstie, J., Sindre, G., Jørgensen, H.: Process models representing knowledge for action: a revised quality framework. Eur. J. Inf. Syst. **15**(1), 91–102 (2006)

14. Liaskos, S., Dundjerovic, T., Gabriel, G.: Comparing alternative goal model visualizations for decision making: an exploratory experiment. In: Proceedings of the 33rd ACM Symposium on Applied Computing (SAC 2018), Pau, France, pp. 1272–1281 (2018)

15. Liaskos, S., Jaouhar, I.: Towards a framework for empirical measurement of conceptualization qualities. In: Dobbie, G., Frank, U., Kappel, G., Liddle, S.W., Mayr, H.C. (eds.) ER 2020. LNCS, vol. 12400, pp. 512–522. Springer, Cham (2020). https://doi.org/10.1007/978-3-030-62522-1_38

16. Liaskos, S., Khan, S.M., Soutchanski, M., Mylopoulos, J.: Modeling and reasoning with decision-theoretic goals. In: Ng, W., Storey, V.C., Trujillo, J.C. (eds.) ER 2013. LNCS, vol. 8217, pp. 19–32. Springer, Heidelberg (2013). https://doi.org/10.1007/978-3-642-41924-9_3

17. Liaskos, S., Ronse, A., Zhian, M.: Assessing the intuitiveness of qualitative contribution relationships in goal models: an exploratory experiment. In: Proceedings of the 11th ACM/IEEE International Symposium on Empirical Software Engineering and Measurement (ESEM 2017), Toronto, Ontario, pp. 466–471 (2017)

18. Liaskos, S., Tambosi, W.: Factors affecting comprehension of contribution links in goal models: an experiment. In: Laender, A.H.F., Pernici, B., Lim, E.-P., de Oliveira, J.P.M. (eds.) ER 2019. LNCS, vol. 11788, pp. 525–539. Springer, Cham (2019). https://doi.org/10.1007/978-3-030-33223-5_43

19. Mair, P., Wilcox, R.: Robust statistical methods in R using the WRS2 package. Behav. Res. Methods **52**(2), 464–488 (2019). https://doi.org/10.3758/s13428-019-01246-w

20. Maxwell, S.E., Delaney, H.D.: Designing Experiments and Analyzing Data, 2nd edn. Taylor and Francis Group, LLC, New York (2004)

21. Moody, D.L.: The "Physics" of notations: toward a scientific basis for constructing visual notations in software engineering. IEEE Trans. Softw. Eng. **35**(6), 756–779 (2009)

22. Roelens, B., Bork, D.: An evaluation of the intuitiveness of the PGA modeling language notation. In: Nurcan, S., Reinhartz-Berger, I., Soffer, P., Zdravkovic, J. (eds.) BPMDS/EMMSAD -2020. LNBIP, vol. 387, pp. 395–410. Springer, Cham (2020). https://doi.org/10.1007/978-3-030-49418-6_27

23. Rosnow, R.L., Rosenthal, R.: Beginning Behavioral Research: A Conceptual Primer, 6th edn. Pearson Prentice Hall, Upper Saddle River (2008)

24. Wand, Y., Weber, R.: On the ontological expressiveness of information systems analysis and design grammars. Inf. Syst. J. **3**(4), 217–237 (1993)

25. Yu, E.S.K.: Towards modelling and reasoning support for early-phase requirements engineering. In: Proceedings of the 3rd IEEE International Symposium on Requirements Engineering (RE 1997), Annapolis, MD, pp. 226–235 (1997)

Author Index

Printed in the United States
By Bookmasters